MICROSOFT®
ACCESS® 2016
PROGRAMMING
Pocket Primer

LICENSE, DISCLAIMER OF LIABILITY, AND LIMITED WARRANTY

MICROSOFT

ACCESS 2016

PROGRAMMING

Pocket Primer

Julitta Korol

MERCURY LEARNING AND INFORMATION
Dulles, Virginia
Boston, Massachusetts
New Delhi

Publisher: David Pallai
MERCURY LEARNING AND INFORMATION
22841 Quicksilver Drive
Dulles, VA 20166
info@merclearning.com
www.merclearning.com
800-232-0223

J.Korol. *Microsoft® Access® 2016 Programming Pocket Primer.*
ISBN: 978-1-942270-81-2

The publisher recognizes and respects all marks used by companies, manufacturers, and developers as a means to distinguish their products. All brand names and product names mentioned in this book are trademarks or service marks of their respective companies. Any omission or misuse (of any kind) of service marks or trademarks, etc. is not an attempt to infringe on the property of others.

Library of Congress Control Number: 2016931652

161718321   Printed in the United States of America
This book is printed on acid-free paper.

Our titles are available for adoption, license, or bulk purchase by institutions, corporations, etc. For additional information, please contact the Customer Service Dept. at 800-232-0223 (toll free).

All of our titles are available in digital format at authorcloudware.com and other digital vendors. Companion files (figures and code listings) for this title are available by contacting info@merclearning.com. The sole obligation of MERCURY LEARNING AND INFORMATION to the purchaser is to replace the disc, based on defective materials or faulty workmanship, but not based on the operation or functionality of the product.

CONTENTS

ACKNOWLEDGMENTS

As years pass and we gain more and more knowledge on a particular subject there is a tendency to publish books for people who want to know it all. But the truth is that we really don't have time to read all the printed pages. I thank my publisher, David Pallai, for suggesting that I consider creating a smaller book that will serve as a starting point for anyone attempting to get into VBA programming in Access. I hope that you as a reader of this primer book will appreciate this short book and find that the knowledge gained from its pages will not only allow you to continue your programming journey, but also take you places you never thought possible.

I'm also thankful to Jennifer Blaney for her expert management of this book project. I owe a heartfelt thanks to my copyeditor at Educator's International Press for the thorough review of the manuscript. I am grateful to the compositor, DataWorks, for all the typesetting efforts that gave this book the easy-to-follow look and feel.

Julitta Korol
Brooklyn, New York
February, 2016

INTRODUCTION

I've been working with Access since the very beginning. Database concepts were completely new to me but Access interface made it a pleasure to work with almost daily. Step by step I acquired the skills of database management and then programming. I learned the latter by trial and error. When the first consulting opportunity came up to use my Access skills I found that I barely knew enough to get started. But challenges do not scare me. I was eager to learn on the job. My first Access programming project was designing a custom quotation system for an automotive manufacturer. Despite my limited prior exposure to the programming concepts I was able to deliver a system that automated a big chunk of work for that company. How was I able to do this? I find reading and doing is the first step towards mastering a skill like programming. This book presents enough programming concepts to get you started tackling your own Access database challenges. This is not a book about using Access. I assume you are already familiar with most tasks that you can achieve using Access built-in commands. But if you are ready to take a look beyond the standard user interface, you have come to the right place and have made a decision that will bring a whole set of new possibilities to Access. So let's forget the menus for now. Do your own thing. Automating Access is something everyone can do. With the right training, that is. This book's purpose is to introduce you to Access built-in language, known as Visual Basic for Applications (VBA). With VBA you can begin delegating repetitive tasks to Access while freeing your time for projects that are more fun to do. Besides, knowing how to program these days is a lucrative skill. It will get you a secure, well-paying job.

This book was designed for someone like you who needs to master Access programming fundamentals without spending too much time. Most of the time all you need is a short book to get you started. It's less overwhelming to deal with a new subject in smaller chunks. The VBA Programming Pocket Primer series will show you only the things you need to know to feel at home with VBA. What you learn in this book on Access programming will apply to, say, Excel programming. Just see my other book, the *Microsoft Excel 2016 Programming Pocket Primer*, to see what I mean. How's that for knowledge transfer? Learn in Access, and use it in Excel or other Microsoft Office applications. I call this sweet learning.

If you are looking for in-depth knowledge of Access programming (and have time to read through a 1,000-page book), then go ahead and try some of my thicker books available from Mercury Learning and Information.

Access is about doing and so is this book. So do not try to read it while not at the computer. You can sit, stand, or lie down; it does not matter. But you do need to work with this book. Do the examples, read the comments. Do this until it becomes easy to do without the step-by-step instructions. Do not skip anything as the concepts in later chapters build on material introduced earlier.

CHAPTER OVERVIEW

Before you get started, allow me to give you a short overview of the things you'll be learning as you progress through this primer book. *Microsoft Access 2016 Programming Pocket Primer* is divided into nine chapters that progressively introduce you to programming Microsoft Access.

Chapter 1 — Getting Started with Access VBA
In this chapter you learn about the types of Access procedures you can write and learn how and where they are written.

Chapter 2 — Getting to Know Visual Basic Editor (VBE)
In this chapter you learn almost everything you need to know about working with the Visual Basic Editor window, commonly referred to as VBE. Some of the programming tools that are not covered here are discussed and put to use in Chapter 9.

Chapter 3 — Access VBA Fundamentals
This chapter introduces basic VBA concepts that allow you to store various pieces of information for later use.

Chapter 4 — Access VBA Built-In and Custom Functions
In this chapter you find out how to provide additional information to your procedures and functions before they are run.

Chapter 5 — Adding Decisions to Your Access VBA Programs
In this chapter you learn how to control your program flow with a number of different decision-making statements.

Chapter 6 — Adding Repeating Actions to Your Access VBA Programs
    In this chapter you learn how to repeat the same actions in your code by using looping structures.

Chapter 7 — Keeping Track of Multiple Values Using Arrays
    In this chapter you learn about static and dynamic arrays and how to use them for holding various values.

Chapter 8 — Keeping Track of Multiple Values Using Object Collections
    This chapter teaches you how you can create and use your own objects and collections of objects.

Chapter 9 — Getting to Know Built-In Tools for Testing and Debugging
    In this chapter you begin using built-in debugging tools to test your programming code. You also learn how to add effective error-handling code to your procedures.
    The above nine chapters will give you the fundamental techniques and concepts you will need in order to continue your Access VBA learning path.

THE COMPANION FILES

The example files for all the hands-on activities in this book are available on the CD-ROM included with this book. Replacement files may be downloaded by contacting the publisher at info@merclearning.com. Digital versions of this title are available at authorcloudware.com and other digital vendors.

CHAPTER 1

GETTING STARTED WITH ACCESS VBA

Visual Basic for Applications (VBA) is the programming language built into all Microsoft® Office® applications, including Microsoft® Access®. In this chapter you acquire the fundamentals of VBA that you will use over and over again in building real-life Microsoft Access database applications.

UNDERSTANDING VBA MODULES AND PROCEDURE TYPES

Your job as a programmer (at least during the course of this book) will boil down to writing various procedures. A *procedure* is a group of instructions that allows you to accomplish specific tasks when your program runs. When you place instructions (programming code) in a procedure, you can call this procedure whenever you need to perform that particular task. Although many tasks can be automated in Access by using macro actions, such as opening forms and reports, finding records, and executing queries, you will need VBA skills to perform advanced customizations in your Access databases.

In VBA *you can write four types of procedures: subroutine procedures, function procedures, event procedures*, and *property procedures*. Procedures are created and stored in modules. A module resembles a blank document in Microsoft Word. Each procedure in the same module must have a unique name; however, procedures in different modules can have the same name. Let's learn a bit about each procedure type so that you can quickly recognize them when you see them in books, magazine articles, or online.

1. Subroutine procedures (also called subroutines or subprocedures)
Subroutine procedures perform useful tasks but never return values. They begin with the keyword Sub and end with the keywords End Sub.

Keywords are words that carry a special meaning in VBA. Let's look at the simple subroutine ShowMessage that displays a message to the user:

```
Sub ShowMessage()
 MsgBox "This is a message box in VBA."
End Sub
```

Notice a pair of empty parentheses after the procedure name. The instruction that the procedure needs to execute is placed on a separate line between the Sub and End Sub keywords. You may place one or more instructions and even complex control structures within a subroutine procedure. Instructions are also called *statements*. The ShowMessage procedure will always display the same message when executed. MsgBox is a built-in VBA function often used for programming user interactions (see Chapter 4, "Access VBA Built-In and Custom Functions," for more information on this function).

If you'd like to write a more universal procedure that can display a different message each time the procedure is executed, you will need to write a subroutine that takes arguments. *Arguments* are values that are needed for a procedure to do something. Arguments are placed within the parentheses after the procedure name. Let's look at the following procedure that also displays a message to the user; however, this time we can pass any text string to display:

```
Sub ShowMessage2(strMessage)
 MsgBox strMessage
End Sub
```

This subprocedure requires one text value before it can be run; strMessage is the arbitrary argument name. It can represent any text you want. Therefore, if you pass it the text "Today is Monday," that is the text the user will see when the procedure is executed. If you don't pass the value to this procedure, VBA will display an error.

If your subprocedure requires more than one argument, list the arguments within the parentheses and separate them with commas. For example, let's improve the preceding procedure by also passing it a text string containing a user name:

```
Sub ShowMessage3(strMessage, strUserName)
 MsgBox strUserName & ", your message is: " & strMessage
End Sub
```

The ampersand (&) operator is used for concatenating text strings inside the VBA procedure. If we pass to the above subroutine the text "Keep on learning." as the strMessage argument and "John" as the strUserName argument, the procedure will display the following text in a message box:

```
John, your message is: Keep on learning.
```

2. Function procedures (functions)

Functions perform specific tasks and can return values. They begin with the keyword `Function` and end with the keywords `End Function`. Let's look at a simple function that adds two numbers:

```
Function addTwoNumbers()
  Dim num1 As Integer
  Dim num2 As Integer
  num1 = 3
  num2 = 2
  addTwoNumbers = num1 + num2
End Function
```

The preceding function procedure always returns the same result, which is the value 5. The `Dim` statements inside this function procedure are used to declare variables that the function will use. A *variable* is a name that is used to refer to an item of data. Because we want the function to perform a calculation, we specify that the variables will hold integer values. Variables and data types are covered in detail in Chapter 3, "Access VBA Fundamentals."

The variable definitions (the lines with the `Dim` statements) are followed by the variable assignment statements in which we assign specific numbers to the variables num1 and num2. Finally, the calculation is performed by adding together the values held in both variables: num1 + num2. To return the result of our calculation, we set the function name to the value or the expression we want to return:

```
addTwoNumbers = num1 + num2
```

Although this function example returns a value, not all functions have to return values. Functions, like subroutines, can perform a number of actions without returning any values.

Similar to procedures, functions can accept arguments. For example, to make our addTwoNumbers function more versatile, we can rewrite it as follows:

```
Function addTwoNumbers2(num1 As Integer, num2 As Integer)
  addTwoNumbers2 = num1 + num2
End Function
```

Now we can pass any two numbers to the preceding function to add them together. For example, we can write the following statement to display the result of the function in a message box:

```
Sub DisplayResult()
    MsgBox("Total=" & addTwoNumbers2(34,80))
End Sub
```

3. Event procedures

Event procedures are automatically executed in response to an event initiated by the user or program code, or triggered by the system. Events, event properties, and event procedures are introduced later in this chapter. They are also covered in Chapter 9, "Getting to Know Built-In Tools for Testing and Debugging."

4. Property procedures

Property procedures are used to get or set the values of custom properties for forms, reports, and class modules. The three types of property procedures (*Property Get*, *Property Let*, and *Property Set*) begin with the `Property` keyword followed by the property type (`Get`, `Let`, or `Set`), the property name, and a pair of empty parentheses, and end with the `End  Property` keywords. Here's an example of a property procedure that retrieves the value of an author's royalty:

```
Property Get Royalty()
 Royalty = (Sales * Percent) - Advance
End Property
```

Property procedures are covered in detail in Chapter 8, "Keeping Track of Multiple Values Using Object Collections."

WRITING PROCEDURES IN A STANDARD MODULE

As mentioned earlier, procedures are created and stored in modules. Access has two types of modules: standard and class. Standard modules are used to hold subprocedures and function procedures that can be run from anywhere in the application because they are not associated with any particular form or report.

Because we already have a couple of procedures to try out, let's do a quick hands-on exercise to learn how to open standard modules, write procedures, and execute them.

Please note files for the hands-on project may be found on the companion CD-ROM.

⦿ Hands-On 1.1. Working in a Standard Module

1. Create a folder on your hard drive named **C:\VBAPrimerAccess_ByExample**.
2. Open Microsoft Access and click **Blank desktop database** (see Figure 1.1). Type **Chap01** in the File Name box, and click the folder button to set the location for the database to the **C:\VBAPrimerAccess_ByExample** folder. Finally, click the **Create** button to create the specified database. Access will create the database in its default .ACCDB format.

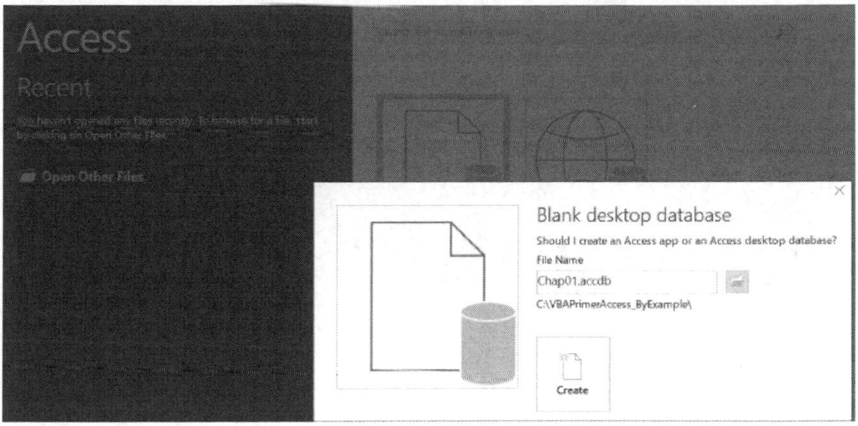

FIGURE 1.1. Creating a blank desktop Access database.

3. To launch the programming environment, select the **Database Tools** tab and click **Visual Basic** (see Figure 1.2). You can also press **Alt+F11** to get to this screen.

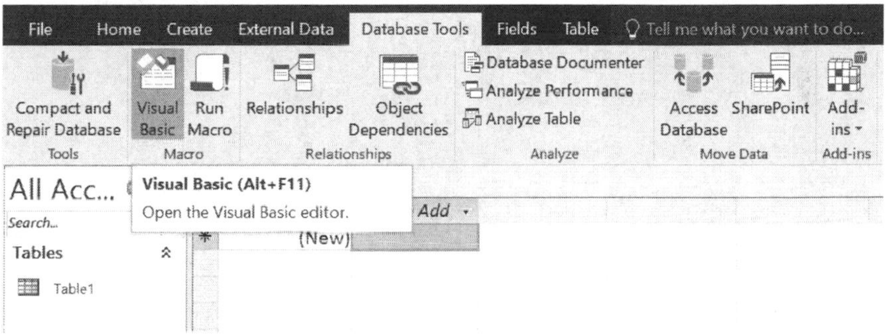

FIGURE 1.2. Activating a Visual Basic development environment.

4. Insert a standard module by choosing **Module** from the **Insert** menu (see Figure 1.3).

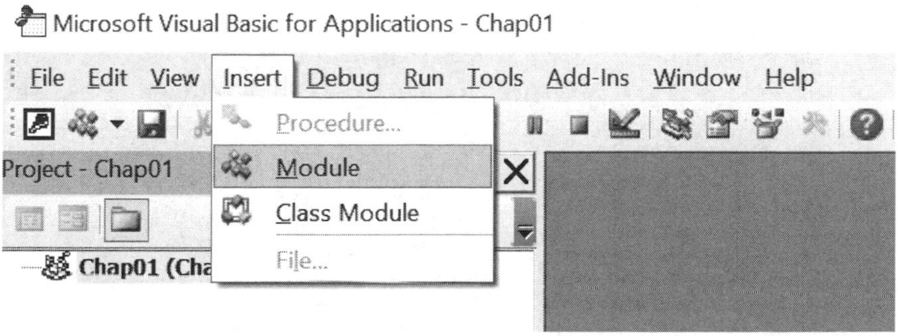

FIGURE 1.3. Inserting a standard module.

Each module begins with a declaration section that lists various settings and declarations that apply to every procedure in the module. Figure 1.4 shows the default declaration. `Option Compare Database` specifies how string comparisons are evaluated in the module—whether the comparison is case-sensitive or insensitive. This is a case-insensitive comparison that respects the sort order of the database. This means that "a" is the same as "A". If you delete the `Option Compare Database` statement, the default string comparison setting for the module is `Option Compare Binary` (used for case-sensitive comparisons where "a" is not the same as "A").

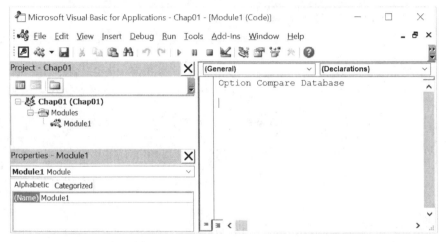

FIGURE 1.4. Standard module.

Another declaration (not shown here) called the `Option Explicit` statement is often used to ensure that all variables used within this module are formally declared. You will learn about this statement and variables in Chapter 4.

Following the declaration section is the procedure section, which holds the module's procedures. You can begin writing your procedures at the cursor position within the Module1 (Code) window.

5. In the Module1 (Code) window, enter the code of subroutines and function procedures as shown in Figure 1.5.

Notice that Access inserts a horizontal line after each `End Sub` or `End Function` keyword to make it easier to identify each procedure. The Procedure drop-down box at the top-right corner of the Module1 (Code) window displays the name of the procedure in which the insertion point is currently located.

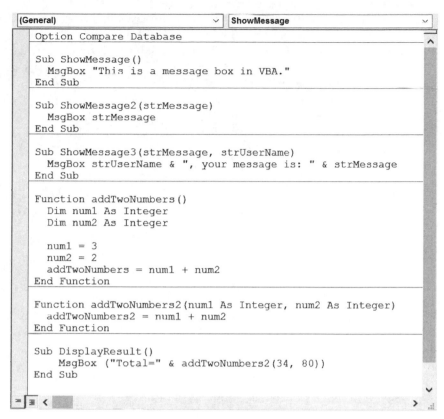

```
(General)                              ▾   ShowMessage                    ▾

    Option Compare Database

    Sub ShowMessage()
      MsgBox "This is a message box in VBA."
    End Sub

    Sub ShowMessage2(strMessage)
      MsgBox strMessage
    End Sub

    Sub ShowMessage3(strMessage, strUserName)
      MsgBox strUserName & ", your message is: " & strMessage
    End Sub

    Function addTwoNumbers()
      Dim num1 As Integer
      Dim num2 As Integer

      num1 = 3
      num2 = 2
      addTwoNumbers = num1 + num2
    End Function

    Function addTwoNumbers2(num1 As Integer, num2 As Integer)
      addTwoNumbers2 = num1 + num2
    End Function

    Sub DisplayResult()
        MsgBox ("Total=" & addTwoNumbers2(34, 80))
    End Sub
```

FIGURE 1.5. Standard module with subprocedures and functions.

EXECUTING YOUR PROCEDURES

Now that you've filled the standard module with some procedures and functions, let's see how you can run them. There are many ways of running your code. In the next hands-on exercise, you will execute your code in four different ways:

- Run menu (Run Sub/UserForm)
- Toolbar button (Run Sub/UserForm)
- Keyboard (F5)
- Immediate window

⊙ Hands-On 1.2. Running Procedures and Functions

1. Place the insertion point anywhere within the ShowMessage procedure. The Procedure box in the top-right corner of the Module1 (Code) window should display ShowMessage. Choose **Run Sub/UserForm** from the **Run** menu.

Access runs the selected procedure and displays the message box with the text "This is a message box in VBA."

2. Click **OK** to close the message box. Try running this procedure again, this time by pressing the **F5** key on the keyboard. Click **OK** to close the message box. If the Access window seems stuck and you can't activate any menu option, this is often an indication that there is a message box open in the background. Access will not permit you to do any operation until you close the pop-up window.

3. Now, run this procedure for the third time by clicking the **Run Sub/UserForm** button (▶) on the toolbar. This button has the same tooltip as the Run Sub/ UserForm (F5) option on the Run menu.

> **NOTE** *Procedures that require arguments cannot be executed directly using the methods you just learned. You need to type some input values for these procedures to run. A perfect place to do this is the Immediate window, which is covered in detail in Chapter 2, "Getting to Know Visual Basic Editor (VBE)." For now, let's open this window and see how you can use it to run VBA procedures.*

4. Select **Immediate Window** from the **View** menu.

Access opens a small window and places it just below the Module1 (Code) window. You can size and reposition this window as needed. Figure 1.6 shows statements that you will run from the Immediate window in steps 5–8.

5. Type the following in the Immediate window and press **Enter** to execute.

```
ShowMessage2 "I'm learning VBA."
```

Access executes the procedure and displays the message in a message box. Click **OK** to close the message box. Notice that to execute the ShowMessage2 procedure, you need to type the procedure name, a space, and the text you want to display. The text string must be surrounded by double quotation marks. In a similar way you can execute the ShowMessage3 procedure by providing two required text strings. For example, on a new line in the Immediate window, type the following statement and press **Enter** to execute:

```
ShowMessage3 "Keep on learning.", "John"
```

When you press the Enter key, Access executes the ShowMessage3 procedure and displays the text "John, your message is: Keep on learning." Click **OK** to close this message box.

> **NOTE** *You can also use the Call statement to run a procedure in the Immediate window. When using this statement, you must place the values of arguments within parentheses, as shown here:*

```
Call ShowMessage3("Keep on learning.", "John")
```

Function procedures are executed using different methods. Step 6 demonstrates how to call the addTwoNumbers function.

6. On a new line in the Immediate window, type a question mark followed by the name of the function procedure and press **Enter**:

```
?addTwoNumbers
```

Access should display the result of this function (the number 5) on the next line in the Immediate window.

7. Now run the addTwoNumbers2 procedure. Type the following instruction in the Immediate window and press **Enter**:

```
?addTwoNumbers2(56, 24)
```

Access displays the result of adding these two numbers on the next line.

8. If you'd rather see the function result in a message box, type the following instruction in the Immediate window and press **Enter**:

```
MsgBox("Total=" & addTwoNumbers2(34,80))
```

Access displays a message box with the text "Total=114".

NOTE *See Chapter 2 for more information on running your procedures and functions from the Immediate window.*

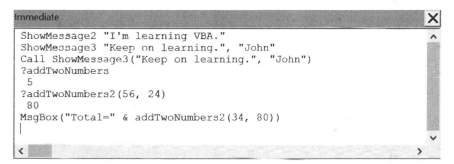

FIGURE 1.6. Running procedures and functions in the Immediate window.

Now that you've familiarized yourself a bit with standard modules, let's move on to another type of module known as the class module.

UNDERSTANDING CLASS MODULES

Class modules come in three varieties: *standalone class modules*, *form modules*, and *report modules*.

1. **Standalone class modules**—These modules are used to create your own custom objects with their own properties and methods. You create a standalone class module by choosing **Insert | Class Module** in the Microsoft Visual Basic for Applications window. Access will create a default class module named *Class1* and will list it in the Class modules folder in the Project Explorer window. You will work with standalone class modules in Chapter 8.

2. and 3. Form modules and report modules—Each Access form can contain a form module, and each report can contain a report module. These modules are special types of class modules that are saved automatically whenever you save the form or report.

All newly created forms and reports are lightweight by design because they don't have modules associated with them when they're first created. Therefore, they load and display faster than forms and reports with modules. These lightweight forms and reports have their Has Module property set to No (see Figure 1.7). When you open a form or report in Design view and click the View Code button in the Tools section of the Design tab, Access creates a form or report module. The Has Module property of a form or report is automatically set to Yes to indicate that the form or report now has a module associated with it. Note that this happens even if you have not written a single line of VBA code. Access opens a module window and assigns a name to the module that consists of three parts: the name of the object (e.g., form or report), an underscore character, and the name of the form or report. For example, a newly created form that has not been saved is named *Form_Form1*, a form module in the Customers form is named *Form_Customers*, and a report module in the Customers report is named *Report_Customers* (see Figure 1.8).

As with report modules, form modules store event procedures for events recognized by the form and its controls, as well as general function procedures and subprocedures. You can also write Property Get, Property Let, and Property Set procedures to create custom properties for the form or report. The procedures stored in their class modules are available only while you are using that particular form or report.

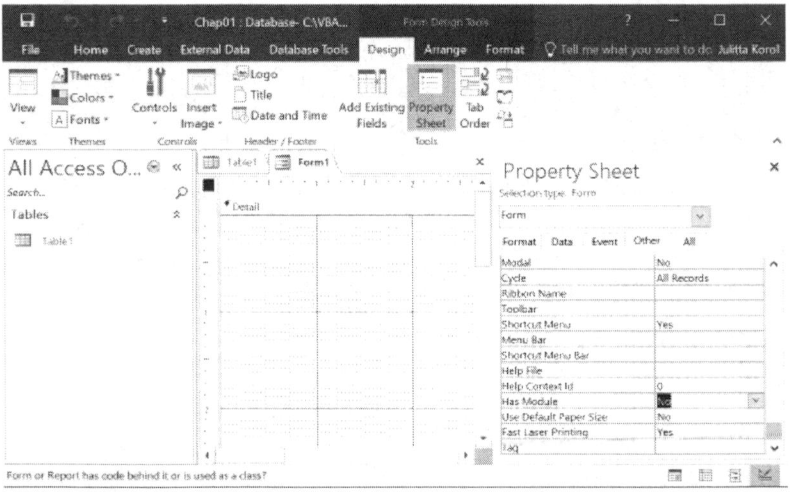

FIGURE 1.7. When you begin designing a new form in the Microsoft Access user interface, the form does not have a module associated with it. Notice that the Has Module property on the form's property sheet is set to No.

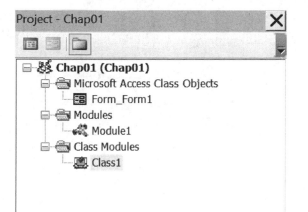

FIGURE 1.8. Database modules are automatically organized in folders. Form and report modules are listed in the Microsoft Access Class Objects folder. Standard modules can be found in the Modules folder. The Class Modules folder organizes standalone class modules.

EVENTS, EVENT PROPERTIES, AND EVENT PROCEDURES

In order to customize your database applications or to deliver products that fit your users' specific needs, you'll be doing quite a bit of event-driven programming. Microsoft Access is an *event-driven* application. This means that whatever happens in an Access application is the result of an event that Access has detected. *Events* are things that happen to objects, and can be triggered by the user or by the system, such as clicking a mouse button, pressing a key, selecting an item from a list, or changing a list of items available in a listbox. As a programmer, you will often want to modify the application's built-in response to a particular event. Before the application processes the user's mouseclicks and keypresses in the usual way, you can tell the application how to react to the activity. For example, if a user clicks a Delete button on your form, you can display a custom delete confirmation message to ensure that the user selected the intended record for deletion.

For each event defined for a form, form control, or report, there is a corresponding *eventproperty*. If you open any Microsoft Access form in Design view and choose Properties in the Tools section of the Design tab, and then click the Event tab of the property sheet, you will see a long list of events your form can respond to (see Figure 1.9).

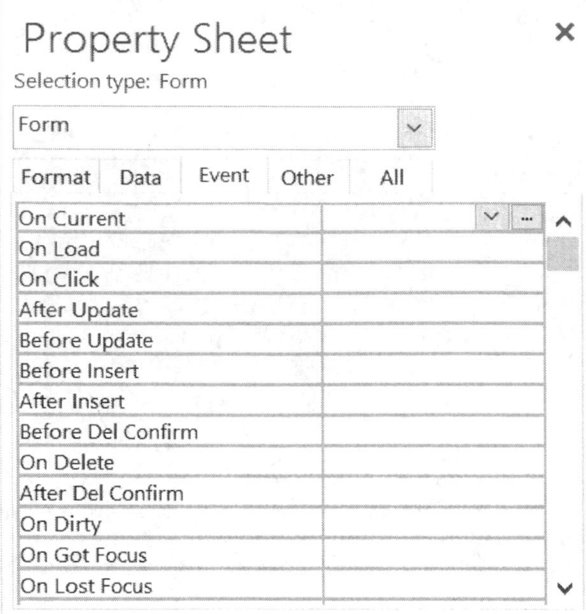

Property Sheet ✕

Selection type: Form

Form	∨

Format	Data	Event	Other	All

On Current	∨ … ∧
On Load	
On Click	
After Update	
Before Update	
Before Insert	
After Insert	
Before Del Confirm	
On Delete	
After Del Confirm	
On Dirty	
On Got Focus	
On Lost Focus	∨

FIGURE 1.9. Event properties for an Access form are listed on the Event tab in the property sheet.

Forms, reports, and the controls that appear on them have various event properties you can use to trigger desired actions. For example, you can open or close a form when a user clicks a command button, or you can enable or disable controls when the form loads.

To specify how a form, report, or control should respond to events, you can write *event procedures*. In your programming code, you may need to describe what should happen if a user clicks on a particular command button or makes a selection from a combo box. For example, when you design a custom form, you should anticipate and program events that can occur at runtime (while the form is being used). The most common event is the Click event. Every time a command button is clicked, it triggers an event procedure to respond to the Click event for that button.

When you assign your event procedure to an event property, you set an *event trap*. Event trapping gives you considerable control in handling events because you basically interrupt the default processing that Access would normally carry out in response to the user's keypress or mouseclick. If a user clicks a command button to save a form, whatever code you've written in the Click event of that command button will run. The event programming code is stored as a part of a form, report, or control and is triggered only when user interaction with a form or report generates a specific event; therefore, it cannot be used as a standalone procedure.

Why Use Events?

Events allow you to make your applications dynamic and interactive. To handle a specific event, you need to select the appropriate event property on the property sheet and then write an event handling procedure. Access will provide its own default response to those events you have not programmed. Events cannot be defined for tables or queries.

Walking Through an Event Procedure

The following hands-on exercise demonstrates how to write event procedures. Your task is to change the background color of a text box control on a form when the text box is selected and then return the default background color when you tab or click out of that text box.

◎ Hands-On 1.3. Writing an Event Procedure

1. Close the **Chap01.accdb** database file used in Hands-On 1.1, and save changes to the file when prompted.
2. Copy the **AssetTracking.accdb** database from the companion CD to your **C:\VBAPrimerAccess_ByExample** folder. This file is a copy of the Asset tracking database provided with Microsoft Access 2016.
3. Open the database **C:\VBAPrimerAccess_ByExample\AssetTracking.accdb**. Upon loading, when you see a Welcome screen, click the **Get Started** button.
4. Access opens the database and displays a security warning message (see Figure 1.10). In order to use the file, click the **Enable Content** button in the message bar. Access will close the database and reopen it. If you see the Welcome screen, click the Get Started button again.

_____ *The last section of this chapter explains how you can use trusted loca-*
NOTE *tions to keep Access from disabling the VBA code upon opening a database.*

5. Open the **Asset Details** form in Design view. To do this, right-click the **Asset Details** form and choose **Design View** from the shortcut menu.

_____ *If the property sheet is not displayed next to the Customers form, click the*
NOTE **Property Sheet** *button in the* **Tools** *group of the* **Form Design Tools** *tab on the Ribbon.*

6. Click the **Manufacturer** text box control on the Asset Details form, and then click the **Event** tab in the property sheet. The property sheet will display **Manufacturer** in the control drop-down box.
   The list of event procedures available for the text box control appears, as shown in Figure 1.11.

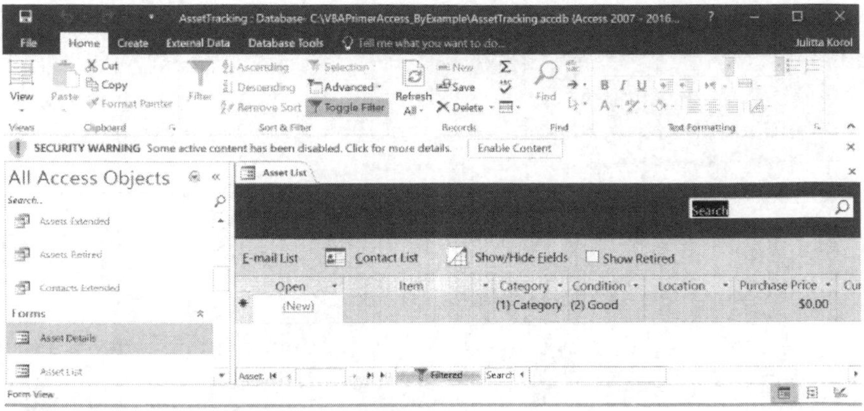

FIGURE 1.10. Active content such as VBA Macros can contain viruses and other security hazards. By default, Access displays a Security Warning message when you first load a database file that contains active content. You should enable content only if you trust the contents of the file.

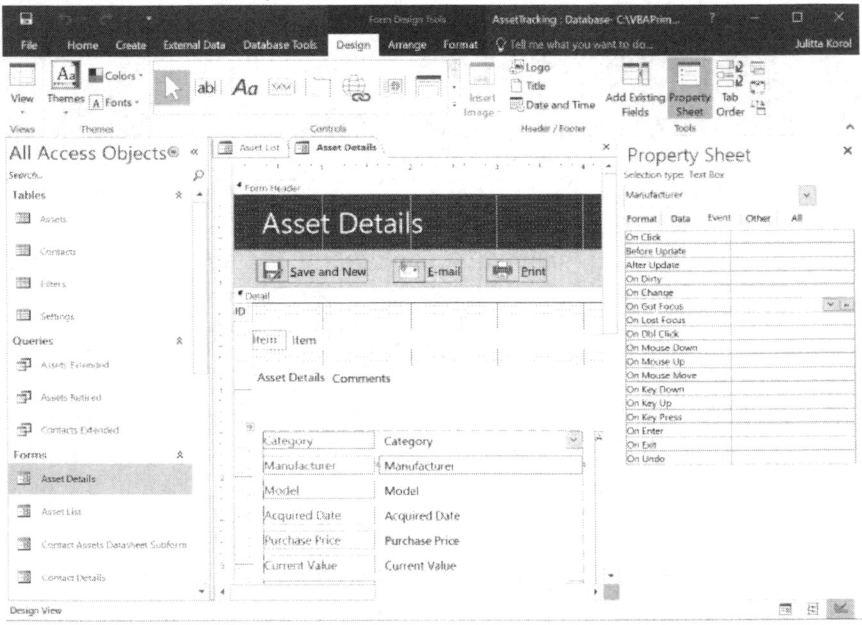

FIGURE 1.11. To create an event procedure for a form control, use the Build button, which is displayed as an ellipsis (...). This button is not available unless an event is selected.

7. Click in the column next to the **On Got Focus** event name, and then click the **Build** button (...), as shown in Figure 1.11 in the previous step. This will bring up the Choose Builder dialog box (see Figure 1.12).

FIGURE 1.12. To write VBA programming code for your event procedure, choose Code Builder in the Choose Builder dialog box.

8. Select **Code Builder** in the Choose Builder dialog box and click **OK**. This will display a VBA code module in the Visual Basic Editor window (see Figure 1.13). This window (often referred to as VBE) is discussed in detail in Chapter 2.

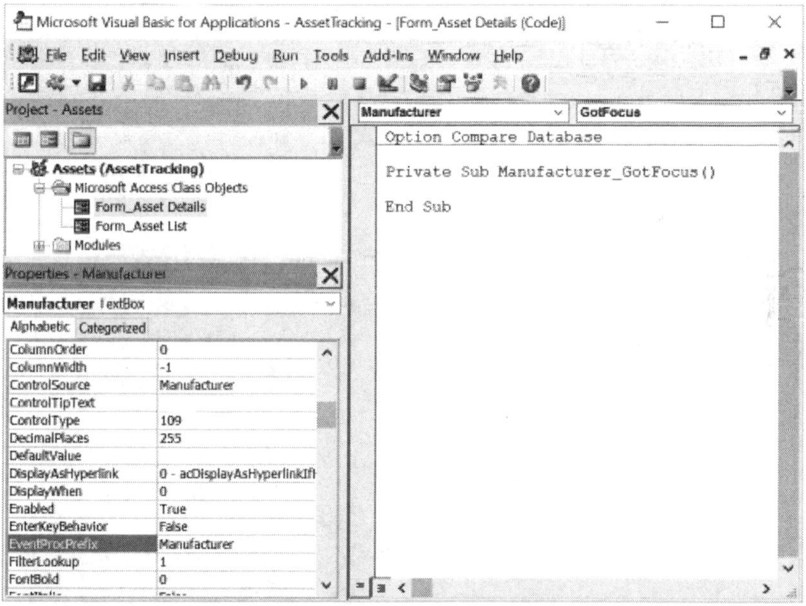

FIGURE 1.13. Code Builder displays the event procedure Code window with a blank event procedure for the selected object. Here you can enter the code for Access to run when the specified GotFocus procedure is triggered.

Take a look at Figure 1.13. Access creates a skeleton of the GotFocus event procedure. The name of the event procedure consists of three parts: the object name (Manufacturer), an underscore character (_), and the name of the event (GotFocus) occurring to that object. The word `Private` indicates that the event procedure cannot be triggered by an event from another form. The word `Sub` in the first line denotes the beginning of the event procedure. The words `End Sub` in the last line denote the end of the event procedure. The statements to be executed when the event occurs are written between these two lines.

Notice that each procedure name ends with a pair of empty parentheses ( ). Words such as `Sub`, `End`, or `Private` have special meaning to Visual Basic and are called *keywords* (reserved words). Visual Basic displays keywords in blue, but you can change the color of your keywords from the Editor Format tab in the Options dialog box (choose Tools | Options in the Visual Basic Editor window). All VBA keywords are automatically capitalized.

At the top of the Code window (see Figure 1.13), there are two drop-down listboxes. The one on the left is called Object. This box displays the currently selected control (Manufacturer). The box on the right is called Procedure. If you position the mouse over one of these boxes, the tooltip indicates the name of the box. Clicking on the down arrow at the right of the Procedure box displays a list of all possible event procedures associated with the object type selected in the Object box. You can close the drop-down listbox by clicking anywhere in the unused portion of the Code window.

9. To change the background color of a text box control to green, enter the following statement between the existing lines:

```
Me.Manufacturer.BackColor = RGB(0, 255, 0)
```

Notice that when you type each period, Visual Basic displays a list containing possible item choices. This feature, called List Properties/ Methods, is a part of Visual Basic's on-the-fly syntax and programming assistance, and is covered in Chapter 2. When finished, your first event procedure should look as follows:

```
Private Sub Manufacturer_GotFocus()
 Me.Manufacturer.BackColor = RGB(0, 255, 0)
End Sub
```

The statement you just entered tells Visual Basic to change the background color of the Manufacturer text box to green when the cursor is moved into that control. The color is specified by using the RGB function.

RGB Colors

Color values are combinations of red, green, and blue components. The RGB function has the following syntax:

RGB(red, green, blue)

The intensity of red, green, and blue can range from 0 to 255. Here are some frequently used colors:

White	255, 255, 255	Dark Green	0, 128, 0
Black	0, 0, 0	Cyan	0, 255, 255
Gray	192, 192, 192	Dark Cyan	0, 128, 128
Red	255, 0, 0	Blue	0, 0, 255
Dark Red	128, 0, 0	Dark Blue	0, 0, 128
Yellow	255, 255, 0	Magenta	255, 0, 255
Dark Yellow	128, 128, 0	Dark Magenta	128, 0, 128
Green	0, 255, 0		

10. In the Visual Basic window, choose **File | Close and Return to Microsoft Access**. Notice that [Event Procedure] now appears next to the On Got Focus event property in the property sheet for the selected Manufacturer text box control (see Figure 1.14).

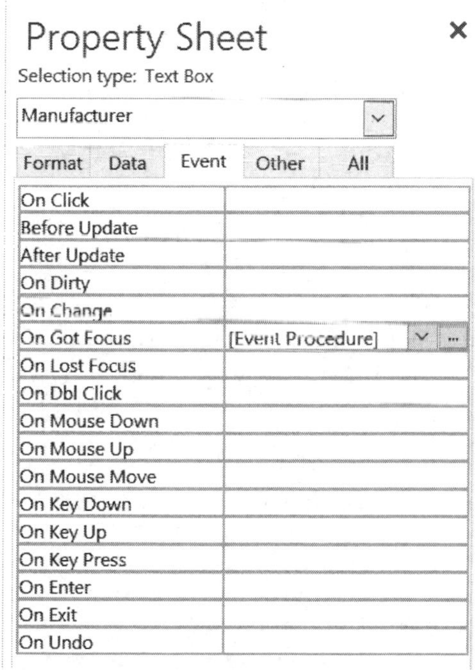

Property Sheet   ✕

Selection type: Text Box

Manufacturer	∨

Format	Data	Event	Other	All

On Click	
Before Update	
After Update	
On Dirty	
On Change	
On Got Focus	[Event Procedure] ∨ ...
On Lost Focus	
On Dbl Click	
On Mouse Down	
On Mouse Up	
On Mouse Move	
On Key Down	
On Key Up	
On Key Press	
On Enter	
On Exit	
On Undo	

FIGURE 1.14. [Event Procedure] in the property sheet denotes that the text box's On Got Focus event has an event procedure associated with it.

11. To test your GotFocus event procedure, switch from the Design view of the Asset Details form to Form view by clicking the **View** button on the Ribbon's Design tab.
12. While in the Form view, click in the **Manufacturer** text box and notice the change in the background color.
13. Now, click on any other text box control on the Asset Details form.

    Notice that the Manufacturer text box does not return to the original color. So far, you've told Visual Basic only what to do when the specified control receives the focus. If you want the background color to change when the focus moves to another control, there is one more event procedure to write—On Lost Focus.
14. To create the LostFocus procedure, return your form to Design view and click the **Manufacturer** control. In the property sheet for this control, select the **Event** tab, and then click the **Build** button to the right of the On Lost Focus event property. In the Choose Builder dialog box, select **Code Builder**.
15. To change the background color of a text box control to white, enter the following statement inside the Manufacturer_LostFocus event procedure:

```
Me.Manufacturer.BackColor = RGB(255,255,255)
```

The completed On Lost Focus procedure is shown in Figure 1.15.

```
Manufacturer                    ▼   LostFocus                              ▼
Option Compare Database                                                    ^

Private Sub Manufacturer_GotFocus()
    Me.Manufacturer.BackColor = RGB(0, 255, 0)
End Sub

Private Sub Manufacturer_LostFocus()
    Me.Manufacturer.BackColor = RGB(255, 255, 255)
End Sub

                                                                           ∨
≡ ≡ <  ▨                                                              >
```

FIGURE 1.15. The GotFocus and LostFocus event procedures will now control the behavior of the Manufacturer control when the control is in focus and out of focus.

16. In the Visual Basic window, choose **File | Close and Return to Microsoft Access**. Notice that [Event Procedure] now appears next to the On Lost Focus event property in the property sheet for the selected Manufacturer text box control.
17. Repeat steps 11–12 to test both of the event procedures you have written.
18. When you are done, close the **Asset Tracking** database and click **OK** when prompted to save the changes.

COMPILING YOUR PROCEDURES

The VBA code you write in the Visual Basic Editor Code window is automatically compiled by Microsoft Access before you run it. The syntax of your VBA statements is first thoroughly checked for errors, and then your procedures are converted into executable format. If an error is discovered during the compilation process, Access stops compiling and displays an error message. It also highlights the line of code that contains the error. The compiling process can take from seconds to minutes or longer, depending on the number of procedures written and the number of modules used.

To ensure that your procedures have been compiled, you can explicitly compile them after you are done programming. You can do this by choosing Debug | Compile in the Visual Basic Editor window.

Microsoft Access saves all the code in your database in its compiled form. Compiled code runs more quickly the next time you open it. You should always save your modules after you compile them. In Chapter 9, "Getting to Know Built-In Tools for Testing and Debugging," you will learn how to test and troubleshoot your VBA procedures.

PLACING A DATABASE IN A TRUSTED LOCATION

By default, the security features built into Access disable the VBA code when you open a database. To make it easy to work with Access databases in this book, you will not want to bother with enabling content each time you open a database. To trust your databases permanently, you can place them in a *trusted location*—a folder on your local or network drive that you mark as trusted. You can get more information about the Enable Content button and access the Trust Center to set up a trusted folder by choosing File | Info (see Figure 1.16). This screen can also be activated by clicking the text message in the Security Warning message bar: "Some active content has been disabled. Click for more details." (See Figure 1.10 earlier.)

FIGURE 1.16. **The Info tab with an explanation of the Security Warning message.**

Hands-On 1.4 will take you through the process of setting up a trusted folder for your Access databases by using the Options button.

Hands-On 1.4. Placing an Access Database in a Trusted Location

1. Open the Chap01.accdb database and click the Enable Content button in the Security Warning message.
2. Choose **File | Options**.
3. In the left pane of the Access Options dialog box, click **Trust Center**, and then click **Trust Center Settings** in the right pane, as shown in Figure 1.17.

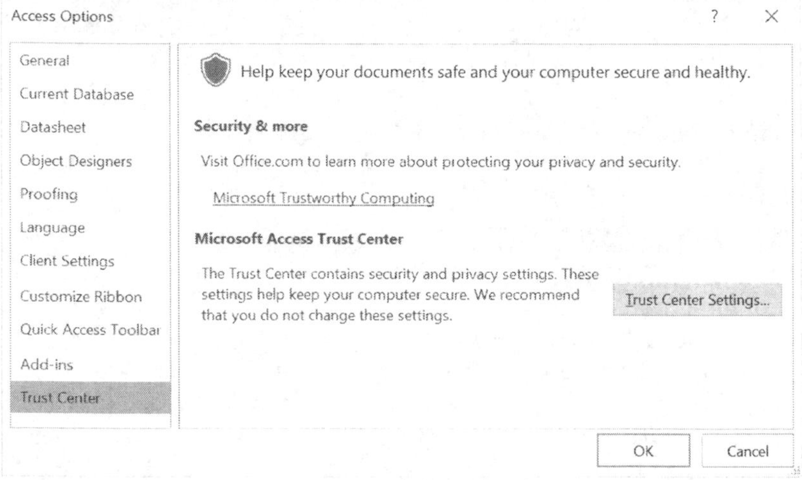

FIGURE 1.17. Working with the Trust Center (Step 1).

4. In the left pane of the Trust Center dialog box, click **Trusted Locations**, as shown in Figure 1.18.

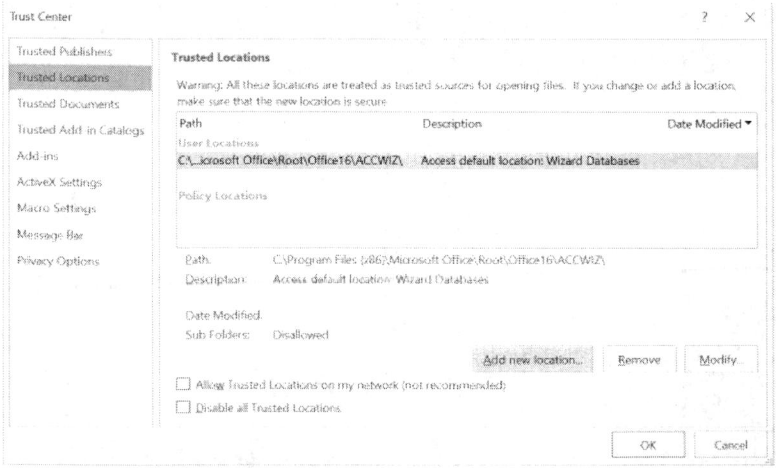

FIGURE 1.18. Working with the Trust Center (Step 2).

5. Click the **Add new location** button, as shown in Figure 1.18.
6. In the Path text box, type the path and folder name of the location on your local drive that you want to set up as a trusted source for opening files. Let's enter **C:\VBAPrimerAccess_ByExample** to designate this folder as a trusted location for this book's database programming exercises (see Figure 1.19).

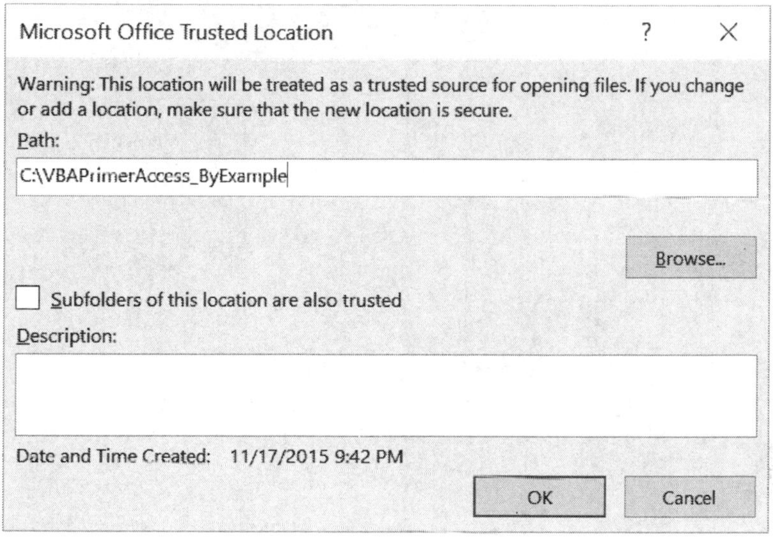

FIGURE 1.19. Working with the Trust Center (Step 3).

7. Click **OK** to close the Microsoft Office Trusted Location dialog box.
8. The Trusted Locations list in the Trust Center dialog box now includes the C:\VBAPrimerAccess_ByExample folder as a trusted source (see Figure 1.20). Files put in a trusted location can be opened without being checked by the Trust Center security feature. Click **OK** to close the Trust Center dialog box.

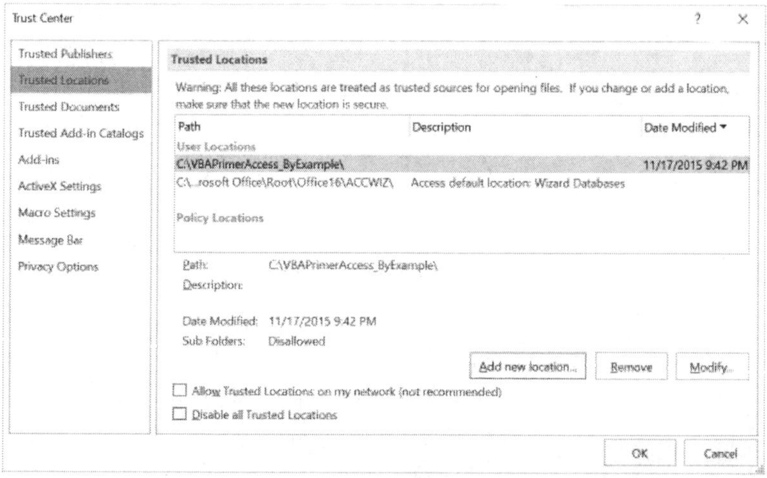

FIGURE 1.20. Working with the Trust Center (Step 4).

9. Click **OK** to close the Access Options dialog box.
10. Close the open Access databases and exit Microsoft Access.
11. Open the **Chap01.accdb** database file from your **C:\VBAPrimerAccess_ ByExample** folder and notice that Access no longer displays the Security Warning message.
12. Close the **Chap01.accdb** database.

SUMMARY

In this chapter, you learned about subroutine procedures, function procedures, property procedures, and event procedures. You also learned different ways of executing subroutines and functions. The main hands-on exercise in this chapter walked you through writing two event procedures in the Asset Details form's class module for a Manufacturer text control placed in the form. You finished this chapter by designating a trusted location folder for your Access databases.

This chapter has given you a glimpse of the Microsoft Visual Basic programming environment built into Access. The next chapter will take you deeper into this interface, showing you various windows and shortcuts that you can use to program faster and with fewer errors.

CHAPTER 2

GETTING TO KNOW
VISUAL BASIC EDITOR (VBE)

N ow that you know how to write procedures and functions in standard modules and event procedures in modules placed behind a form, we'll spend some time in the Visual Basic Editor window to become familiar with the multitude of tools it offers to simplify your programming tasks. With the tools located in the Visual Basic Editor window, you can:

■ Write your own VBA procedures
■ Create custom forms
■ View and modify object properties
■ Test and debug VBA procedures and locate errors

You can enter the VBA programming environment in either of the following ways:

■ By selecting the Database Tools tab, and then Visual Basic in the Macro group
■ From the keyboard, by pressing Alt+F11

UNDERSTANDING THE PROJECT EXPLORER WINDOW

The Project Explorer window, located on the left side of the Visual Basic Editor window, provides access to modules behind forms and reports via the Microsoft Access Class Objects folder (see Figure 2.1). The Modules folder lists only standard modules that are not behind a form or report.

In addition to the Microsoft Access Class Objects and Modules folders, the VBA Project Explorer window can contain a Class Modules folder. Class modules are used for creating your own objects, as demonstrated in Chapter 8. Using the Project Explorer window, you can easily move between modules currently loaded into memory.

You can activate the Project Explorer window in one of three ways:

- From the View menu by selecting Project Explorer
- From the keyboard by pressing Ctrl-R
- From the Standard toolbar by clicking the Project Explorer button ( ) as shown in Figure 2.2

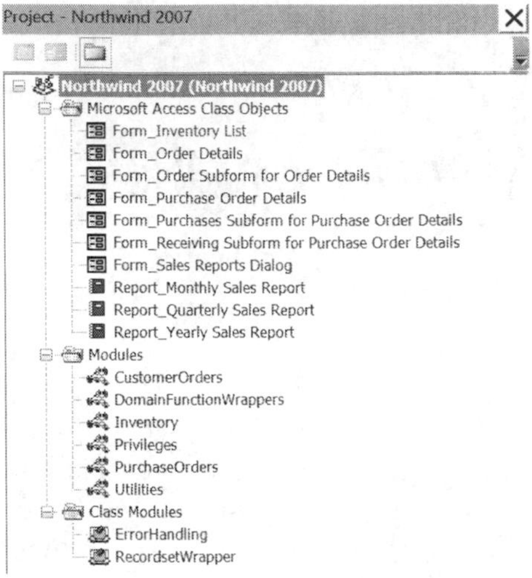

FIGURE 2.1. Provides easy access to your VBA procedure code.

NOTE *If the Project Explorer window is visible but not active, activate it by clicking the Project Explorer titlebar.*

Buttons on the Standard toolbar (Figure 2.2) provide a quick way to access many Visual Basic features.

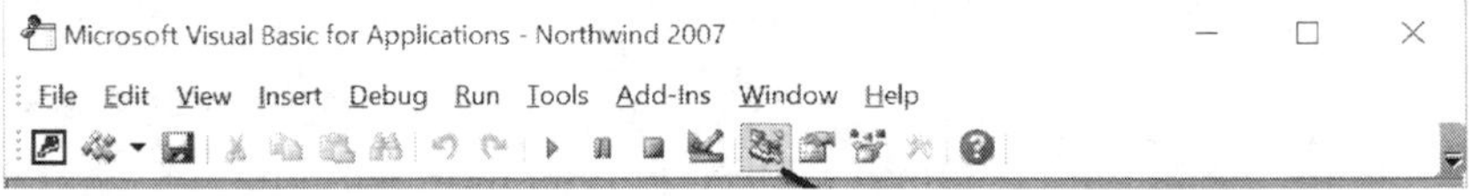

FIGURE 2.2. Use the toolbar buttons to quickly access frequently used features in the VBE window.

The Project Explorer window (see Figure 2.3) contains three buttons:

- **View Code**—Displays the Code window for the selected module.
- **View Object**—Displays the selected form or report in the Microsoft Access Class Objects folder. This button is disabled when an object in the Modules or Class Modules folder is selected.
- **Toggle Folders**—Hides and unhides the display of folders in the Project Explorer window.

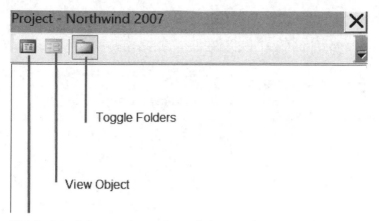

FIGURE 2.3. The VBE Project Explorer window contains three buttons that allow you to view code or objects and toggle folders.

UNDERSTANDING THE PROPERTIES WINDOW

The Properties window allows you to review and set properties for the currently selected Access class or module. The name of the selected object is displayed in the Object box located just below the Properties window titlebar. The Properties window displays the current settings for the selected object. Object properties can be viewed alphabetically or by category by clicking on the appropriate tab.

- **Alphabetic tab**—Lists all properties for the selected object alphabetically. You can change the property setting by selecting the property name, and then typing or selecting the new setting.
- **Categorized tab**—Lists all properties for the selected object by category. You can collapse the list so that you see only the category names or you can expand a category to see the properties. The plus (+) icon to the left of the category name indicates that the category list can be expanded. The minus (–) indicates that the category is currently expanded.

The Properties window can be accessed in the following ways:

- From the View menu by selecting Properties Window
- From the keyboard by pressing F4
- From the Standard toolbar by clicking the Properties Window button (🖼️) located to the right of the Project Explorer button

Figure 2.4 displays the properties of the E-mail Address text box control located in the Form_Order Details form in the Northwind 2007 sample Access database. In order to access properties for a form control, you need to perform the steps outlined in Hands-On 2.1.

Please note files for the hands-on project may be found on the companion CD-ROM.

⊙ **Hands-On 2.1. Using the Properties Window to View Control Properties**

1. Copy the **Northwind 2007** sample database from the companion CD to your **C:\AccessVBAPrimer_ByExample** folder.
2. Open Access 2013 and load the **C:\AccessVBAPrimer_ByExample\ Northwind 2007.accdb** file. Log in to the database as **Andrew Cencini**.
3. When Northwind 2007 opens, press **Alt+F11** to activate the Visual Basic Editor window.
4. In the Project Explorer window, click the **Toggle Folders** button ( ) and select the **Microsoft Access Class Objects** folder. Highlight the **Form_ Order Details** form (Figure 2.4) and click the **View Object** button ( ). This will open the selected form in Design view.

Press **Alt+F11** to return to the Visual Basic Editor. The Properties window will be filled with the properties for the Form_Order Details form. To view the properties of the E-mail Address text box control on this form, as shown in Figure 2.4, select **E-mail Address** from the drop-down list located below the Properties window's titlebar.

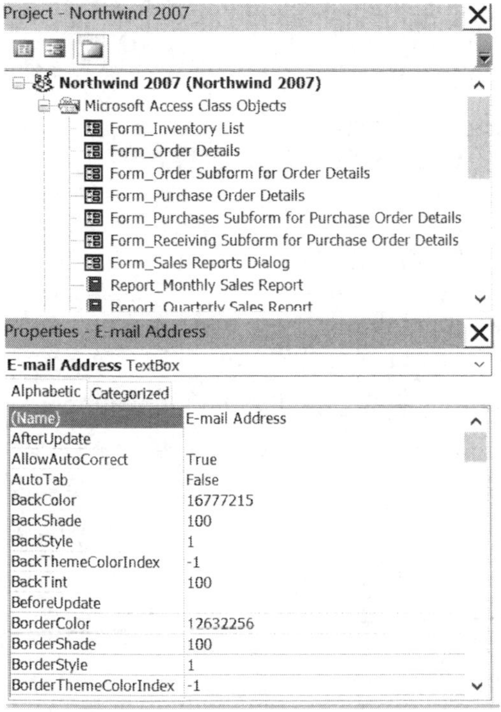

FIGURE 2.4. You can edit object properties in the Properties window, or you can edit them in the property sheet when a form or report is open in Design view.

UNDERSTANDING THE CODE WINDOW

The Code window is used for Visual Basic programming as well as for viewing and modifying the code of existing Visual Basic procedures. Each VBA module can be opened in a separate Code window.

There are several ways to activate the Code window:

- From the Project Explorer window, choose the appropriate module and then click the View Code button (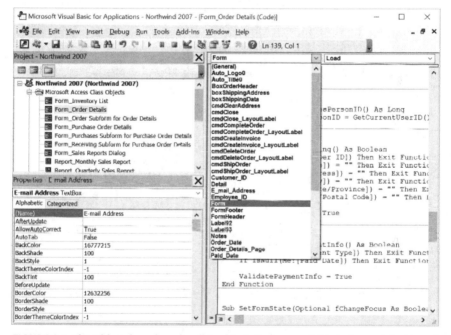)
- From the Microsoft Visual Basic menu bar, choose View | Code
- From the keyboard, press F7

At the top of the Code window there are two drop-down listboxes that allow you to move quickly within the Visual Basic code. In the Object box on the left side of the Code window, you can select the object whose code you want to view, as shown in Figure 2.5.

FIGURE 2.5. **The Object drop-down box lists objects that are available in the module selected in the Project Explorer window.**

The box on the right side of the Code window lets you select a procedure to view. When you click the down arrow at the right of this box, the names of all procedures located in a module are listed alphabetically, as shown in Figure 2.6. When you select a procedure in the Procedure box, the cursor will jump to the first line of that procedure.

Form	⌄	Current	⌄

```
      Private Sub Form_Curren  BeforeRender
          SetFormState           BeforeScreenTip
      End Sub                    BeforeUpdate
                                 Click
                                 Close
                                 CommandBeforeExecute
                                 CommandChecked
      Private Sub Form_Load()    CommandEnabled
          SetFormState           CommandExecute
      End Sub                    Current
                                 DataChange
                                 DataSetChange
                                 DblClick
      Function GetDefaultSales  Deactivate
          GetDefaultSalesPerso  Delete
      End Function               Dirty
                                 Error
                                 Filter
                                 GotFocus
      Function ValidateShippi   KeyDown
          If IsNull(Me![Shipp   KeyPress
          If Nz(Me![Ship Name    KeyUp
          If Nz(Me![Ship Addr    Load
```

FIGURE 2.6. The Procedure drop-down box lists events to which the object selected in the Object drop-down box can respond. If the selected module contains events written for the highlighted object, the names of these events appear in bold type.

By choosing Window | Split or dragging the split bar down to a selected position in the Code window, you can divide the Code window into two panes, as shown in Figure 2.7.

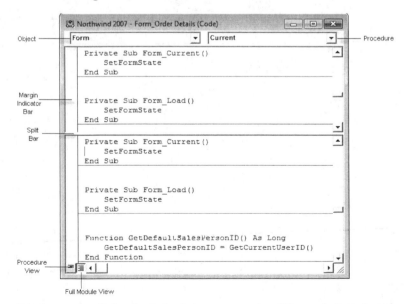

FIGURE 2.7. By splitting the Code window, you can view different sections of a long procedure or a different procedure in each window pane.

Setting up the Code window for the two-pane display is useful for copying, cutting, and pasting sections of code between procedures in the same module. To return to a one-window display, drag the split bar all the way to the top of the Code window or choose Window | Split again.

There are two icons at the bottom of the Code window (see Figure 2.7). The Procedure View icon changes the display to only one procedure at a time in the Code window. To select another procedure, use the Procedure drop-down box. The Full Module View icon changes the display to all the procedures in the selected module. Use the vertical scrollbar in the Code window to scroll through the module's code. The Margin Indicator bar is used by the Visual Basic Editor to display helpful indicators during editing and debugging.

OTHER WINDOWS IN THE VBE

In addition to the Code window, there are several other windows that are frequently used in the Visual Basic environment, such as the Immediate, Locals, Watch, Project Explorer, Properties, and Object Browser windows. The Docking tab in the Options dialog box, shown in Figure 2.8, displays a list of available windows and allows you to choose which windows you want to be dockable. To access this dialog box, select Tools | Options in the Visual Basic Editor window.

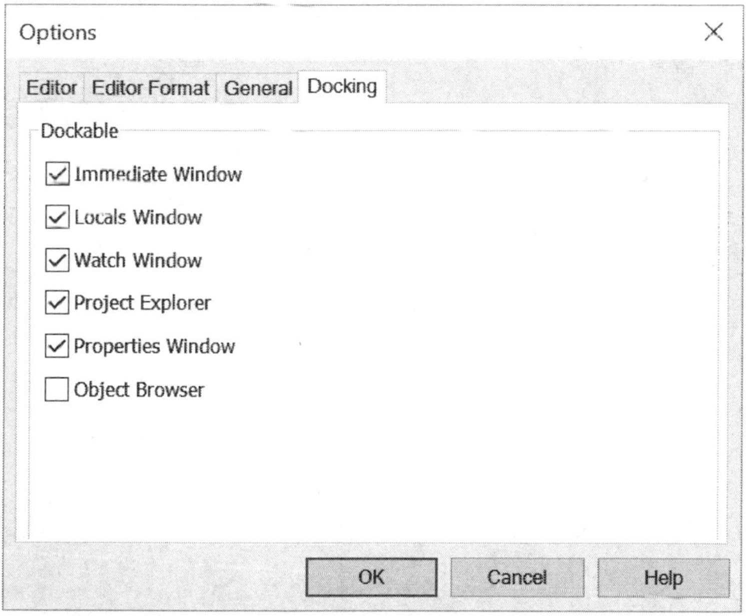

FIGURE 2.8. You can use the Docking tab in the Options dialog box to control which windows are currently displayed in the Visual Basic programming environment.

ASSIGNING A NAME TO THE VBA PROJECT

A VBA Project is a set of Microsoft Access objects, modules, forms, and references.

When you create a Microsoft Access database and later switch to the VBE window, you will see in the Project Explorer window that Access had automatically assigned the database name to the VBA Project. For example, if your database is named Chap01.accdb, the Project Properties window displays Chap01 (Chap01) where the first "Chap01" denotes the VBA Project name and the "Chap01" in the parentheses is the name of the database. You can change the name of the VBA Project in one of the following ways:

- Choose Tools | <database name> Properties, enter a new name in the Project Name box of the Project Properties window (see Figure 2.9), and click OK.
- In the Project Explorer window, right-click the name of the project and select <database name> Properties. Enter a new name in the Project Name box of the Project Properties window (see Figure 2.9) and click OK.

To avoid naming conflicts between projects, make sure that you give your projects unique names.

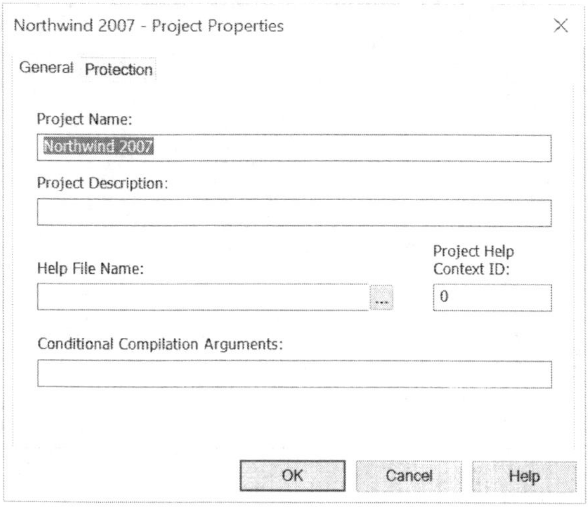

FIGURE 2.9. Use the Project Properties dialog box to rename the VBA Project.

RENAMING THE MODULE

When you insert a new module to your VBA Project, Access generates a default name for the module—Module1, Module2, and so on. You can rename your modules right after you insert them into the VBA project or when your project is being saved for the first time. In the latter case, Access will iterate through all the newly added (not saved) modules and will prompt you with the Save As dialog box to accept or change the module name. You can change the module name at any time via the Properties window. Simply select the module name (e.g., Module1) in the Project Explorer window and double-click the Name property in the Properties window. This action will highlight the default module name next to the Name property. Type the new name for the module and press Enter. The module name in the Project Explorer window should now reflect your change.

SYNTAX AND PROGRAMMING ASSISTANCE

Writing procedures in Visual Basic requires that you use hundreds of built-in instructions and functions. Because most people cannot memorize the correct syntax of all the instructions available in VBA, the IntelliSense® technology provides you with syntax and programming assistance on demand while you are entering instructions. While working in the Code window, you can have special tools pop up and guide you through the process of creating correct VBA code. The Edit toolbar in the VBE window, shown in Figure 2.10, contains several buttons that let you enter correctly formatted VBA instructions with speed and ease. If the Edit toolbar isn't currently docked in the Visual Basic Editor window, you can turn it on by choosing View | Toolbars.

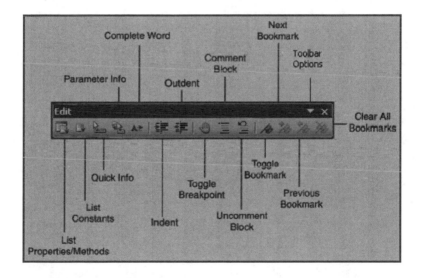

FIGURE 2.10. The Edit toolbar provides timesaving buttons while entering VBA code.

List Properties/Methods

Each object can contain one or more properties and methods. When you enter the name of the object in the Code window followed by a period that separates the name of the object from its property or method, a pop-up menu may appear. This menu lists the properties and methods available for the object that precedes the period. To turn on this automated feature, choose

Tools | Options. In the Options dialog box, click the Editor tab, and make sure the Auto List Members checkbox is selected. As you enter VBA instructions, Visual Basic suggests properties and methods that can be used with the particular object, as demonstrated in Figure 2.11.

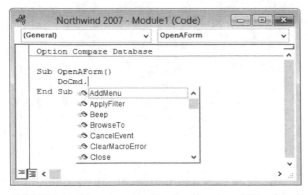

FIGURE 2.11. When Auto List Members is selected, Visual Basic suggests properties and methods that can be used with the object as you are entering the VBA instructions.

To choose an item from the pop-up menu, start typing the name of the property or method you want to use. When the correct item name is highlighted, press Enter to insert the item into your code and start a new line, or press the Tab key to insert the item and continue writing instructions on the same line. You can also double-click the item to insert it in your code. To close the pop-up menu without inserting an item, press Esc. When you press Esc to remove the pop-up menu, Visual Basic will not display the menu for the same object again.

To display the Properties/Methods pop-up menu again, you can:

■ Press Ctrl-J
■ Use the Backspace key to delete the period, and then type the period again
■ Right-click in the Code window, and select List Properties/Methods from the shortcut menu
■ Choose Edit | List Properties/Methods
■ Click the List Properties/Methods button ( ) on the Edit toolbar

Parameter Info

Some VBA functions and methods can take one or more arguments (or parameters). If a Visual Basic function or method requires an argument, you can see the names of required and optional arguments in a tip box that appears just below the cursor as soon as you type the open parenthesis or enter a space. The Parameter Info feature (see Figure 2.12) makes it easy for you to supply correct arguments to a VBA function or method. In addition, it reminds you of two other things that are very important for the function or method to work correctly: the order of the arguments and the required data type of each argument. For example, if you enter in the Code window the instruction DoCmd.OpenForm and type a space after the OpenForm method, a tip box appears just below the cursor. Then as soon as you supply the first argument and enter the comma, Visual Basic displays the next argument in bold. Optional arguments are surrounded by square brackets [ ]. To close the Parameter Info window, all you need to do is press Esc.

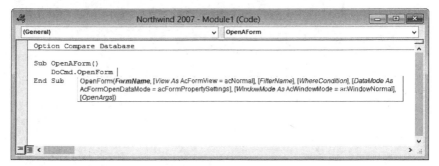

FIGURE 2.12. A tip window displays a list of arguments used by a VBA function or method.

To open the tip box using the keyboard, enter the instruction or function, followed by the open parenthesis, and then press Ctrl-Shift-I. You can also click the Parameter Info button ( ) on the Edit toolbar or choose Edit | Parameter Info from the menu bar.

You can also display the Parameter Info box when entering a VBA function. To try this out quickly, choose View | Immediate Window, and then type the following in the Immediate window:

```
Mkdir(
```

You should see the MkDir(Path As String) tip box just below the cursor. Now, type `"C:\NewFolder"` followed by the ending parenthesis. When you press Enter, Visual Basic will create a folder named NewFolder in the root directory of your computer. Activate Explorer and check it out!

List Constants

If there is a check mark next to the Auto List Members setting in the Options dialog box (Editor tab), Visual Basic displays a pop-up menu listing the constants that are valid for the property or method. A *constant* is a value that indicates a specific state or result. Access and other members of the Microsoft Office suite have a number of predefined, built-in constants.

Suppose you want to open a form in Design view. In Microsoft Access, a form can be viewed in Design view (acDesign), Datasheet view (acFormDS), PivotChart view (acFormPivotChart), PivotTable view (acFormPivotTable), Form view (acNormal), and Print Preview (acPreview). Each of these options is represented by a built-in constant. Microsoft Access constant names begin with the letters "ac." As soon as you enter a comma and a space following your instruction in the Code window (e.g., `DoCmd.OpenForm "Products", `), a pop-up menu will appear with the names of valid constants for the OpenForm method, as shown in Figure 2.13.

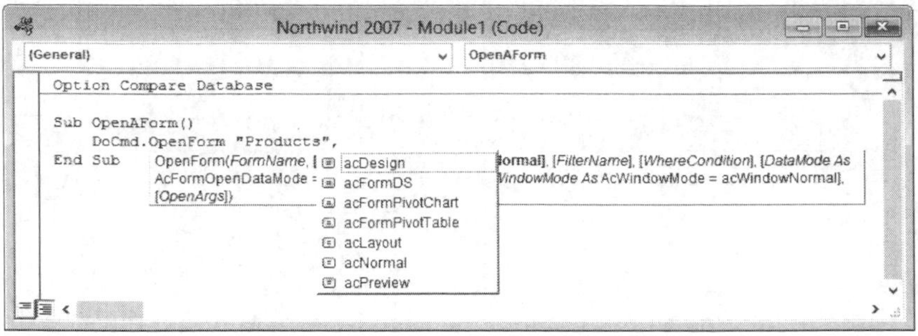

FIGURE 2.13. The List Constants pop-up menu displays a list of constants that are valid for the property or method typed.

The List Constants menu can be activated by pressing Ctrl+Shift+J or by clicking the List Constants button ( ) on the Edit toolbar.

Quick Info

When you select an instruction, function, method, procedure name, or constant in the Code window and then click the Quick Info button ( ) on the Edit toolbar (or press Ctrl+I), Visual Basic will display the syntax of the highlighted item as well as the value of its constant (see Figure 2.14). The Quick Info feature can be turned on or off using the Options dialog box (Tools | Options). To use the feature, click the Editor tab in the Options dialog box, and make sure there is a check mark in the box next to Auto Quick Info.

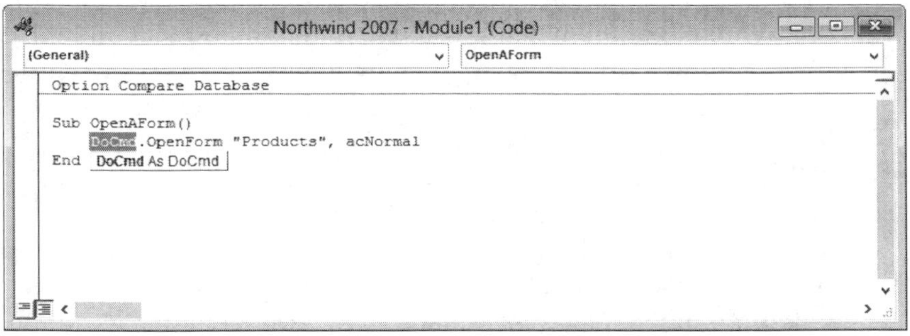

FIGURE 2.14. The Quick Info feature provides a list of function parameters, as well as constant values and VBA statement syntax.

Complete Word

Another way to increase the speed of writing VBA procedures in the Code window is with the Complete Word feature. As you enter the first few letters of a keyword and click the Complete Word button ( ) on the Edit toolbar,

Visual Basic will complete the keyword entry for you. For example, if you enter the first three letters of the keyword DoCmd (DoC) in the Code window, and then click the Complete Word button on the Edit toolbar, Visual Basic will complete the rest of the command. In the place of DoC you will see the entire instruction, DoCmd.

If there are several VBA keywords that begin with the same letters, when you click the Complete Word button on the Edit toolbar Visual Basic will display a pop-up menu listing all of them. To try this, enter only the first three letters of the word Application (App), and then press the Complete Word button on the toolbar. You can then select the appropriate word from the pop-up menu.

Indent/Outdent

The Editor tab in the Options dialog box, shown in Figure 2.15, contains many settings you can enable to make automated features available in the Code window.

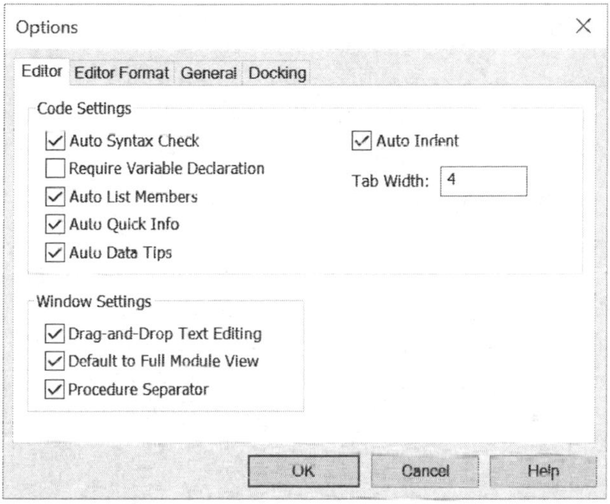

FIGURE 2.15. **The Options dialog box lists features you can turn on and off to fit the VBA programming environment to your needs.**

When the Auto Indent option is turned on, Visual Basic automatically indents the selected lines of code using the Tab Width value. The default entry for Auto Indent is four characters (see Figure 2.15). You can easily change the tab width by typing a new value in the text box. Why would you want to use indentation in your code? Indentation makes your VBA procedures more readable and easier to understand. Indenting is especially recommended for entering lines of code that make decisions or repeat actions.

Let's see how you can indent and outdent lines of code using the Form_ InventoryList form in the Northwind database that you opened in the previous hands-on exercise.

⊙ Hands-On 2.2. Using the Indent/Outdent Feature

1. In the Project Explorer window in the Microsoft Access Class Objects folder, double-click **Form_Inventory List**. The Code window should now show the CmdPurchase_Click event procedure written for this form.
2. In the Code window, select the block of code beginning with the keyword **If** and ending with the keywords **End If**.
3. Click the **Indent** button ( ) on the Edit toolbar or press **Tab** on the keyboard. The selected block of code will move four spaces to the right. You can adjust the number of spaces to indent by choosing **Tools | Options** and entering the appropriate value in the Tab Width box on the Editor tab.
4. Now, click the **Outdent** button ( ) on the Edit toolbar or press **Shift+Tab** to return the selected lines of code to the previous location in the Code window. The Indent and Outdent options are also available from Visual Basic Editor's Edit menu.

Comment Block/Uncomment Block

The apostrophe placed at the beginning of a line of code denotes a comment. Besides the fact that comments make it easier to understand what the procedure does, comments are also very useful in testing and troubleshooting VBA procedures. For example, when you execute a procedure, it may not run as expected. Instead of deleting the lines of code that may be responsible for the problems encountered, you may want to skip the lines for now and return to them later. By placing an apostrophe at the beginning of the line you want to avoid, you can continue checking the other parts of your procedure. While commenting one line of code by typing an apostrophe works fine for most people, when it comes to turning entire blocks of code into comments, you'll find the Comment Block and Uncomment Block buttons on the Edit toolbar very handy and easy to use.

To comment a few lines of code, select the lines and click the Comment Block button ( ). To turn the commented code back into VBA instructions, click the Uncomment Block button ( ). If you click the Comment Block button without selecting a block of text, the apostrophe is added only to the line of code where the cursor is currently located.

USING THE OBJECT BROWSER

If you want to move easily through the myriad of VBA elements and features, examine the capabilities of the Object Browser. This special built-in tool is available in the Visual Basic Editor window.

To access the Object Browser, use any of the following methods:

- Press F2
- Choose View | Object Browser
- Click the Object Browser button ( ) on the toolbar

The Object Browser allows you to browse through the objects available to your VBA procedures, as well as view their properties, methods, and events. With the aid of the Object Browser, you can quickly move between procedures in your database application and search for objects and methods across various type libraries.

The Object Browser window, shown in Figure 2.16, is divided into several sections. The top of the window displays the Project/Library drop-down listbox with the names of all currently available libraries and projects.

A *library* is a special file that contains information about the objects in an application. New libraries can be added via the References dialog box (select Tools | References). The entry for <All Libraries> lists the objects of all libraries installed on your computer. While the Access library contains objects specific to using Microsoft Access, the VBA library provides access to three objects (Debug, Err, and Collection), as well as a number of built-in functions and constants that give you flexibility in programming. You can send output to the Immediate window, get information about runtime errors, work with the Collection object, manage files, deal with text strings, convert data types, set date and time, and perform mathematical operations.

Below the Project/Library drop-down listbox is a search box (Search Text) that allows you to quickly find information in a particular library. This field remembers the last four items you searched for. To find only whole words, right-click anywhere in the Object Browser window, and then choose Find Whole Word Only from the shortcut menu. The Search Results section of the Object Browser displays the Library, Class, and Member elements that meet the criteria entered in the Search Text box. When you type the search text and click the Search button, Visual Basic expands the Object Browser window to show the search results. You can hide or show the Search Results section by clicking the button located to the right of the binoculars. In the lower section of the Object Browser window, the Classes listbox displays the available object classes in the selected library. If you select the name of the open database (e.g., Northwind) in the Project/Library listbox, the Classes list will display the objects as listed in the Explorer window.

In Figure 2.16, the Form_Inventory List object class is selected. When you highlight a class, the list on the right side (Members) shows the properties, methods, and events available for that class. By default, members are listed alphabetically. You can, however, organize the Members list by group type (properties, methods, or events) using the Group Members command from the Object Browser shortcut menu (right-click anywhere in the Object Browser window to display this menu).

When you select the Northwind 2007 project in the Project/Library listbox, the Members listbox will list all the procedures available in this project. To examine a procedure's code, double-click its name. When you select a VBA library in the Project/Library listbox, you will see the Visual Basic built-in functions and constants. If you need more information on the selected class or member, click the question mark button located at the top of the Object Browser window.

The bottom of the Object Browser window displays a code template area with the definition of the selected member. Clicking the green hyperlink text in the code template lets you jump to the selected member's class or library in the Object Browser window. Text displayed in the code template area can be copied and pasted to a Code window. If the Code window is visible while the Object Browser window is open, you can save time by dragging the highlighted code template and dropping it into the Code window. You can easily adjust the size of the various sections of the Object Browser window by dragging the dividing horizontal and vertical lines.

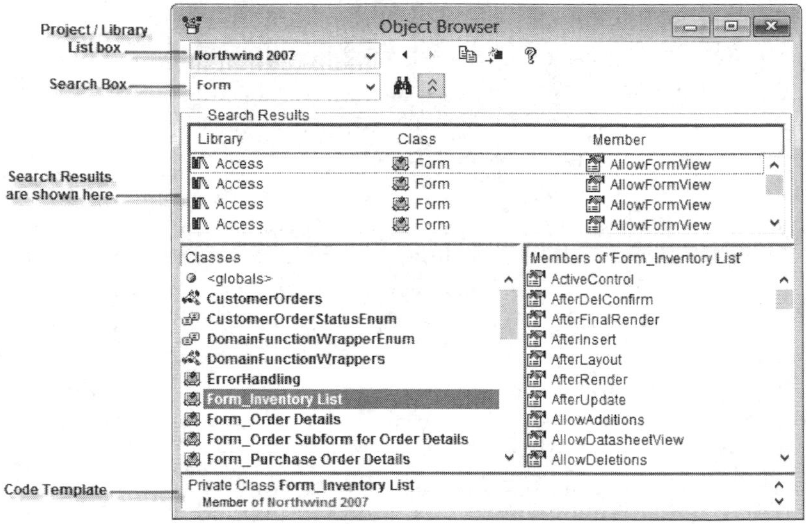

FIGURE 2.16. The Object Browser window allows you to browse through all the objects, properties, and methods available to the current VBA project.

Let's put the Object Browser to use in VBA programming. Assume that you want to write a VBA procedure to control a checkbox placed on a form and would like to see the list of properties and methods that are available for working with checkboxes.

⊙ Hands-On 2.3. Using the Object Browser

1. In the Visual Basic Editor window, press **F2** to display the Object Browser.
2. In the Project/Library listbox (see Figure 2.16), click the drop-down arrow and select the **Access** library.
3. Type **checkbox** in the Search Text box and click the **Search** button (🔍). Make sure you don't enter a space in the search string.
   Visual Basic begins to search the Access library and displays the search results. By analyzing the search results in the Object Browser window, you can find the appropriate VBA instructions for writing your VBA procedures.

For example, looking at the Members list lets you quickly determine that you can enable or disable a checkbox by setting the Enabled property. To get detailed information on any item found in the Object Browser, select the item and press F1 to activate online help.

USING THE VBA OBJECT LIBRARY

While the Access library contains objects specific to using Microsoft Access, the VBA Object Library provides access to many built-in VBA functions grouped by categories. These functions are general in nature. They allow you to manage files, set the date and time, interact with users, convert data types, deal with text strings, or perform mathematical calculations. In the following exercise, you will see how to use one of the built-in VBA functions to create a new subfolder without leaving Access.

(●) Hands-On 2.4. Using Built-In VBA Functions

1. In the Visual Basic Editor window with the Northwind 2007 database open, choose **Insert | Module** to create a new standard module.
2. In the Properties Window, change the Name property of Module1 to **Access-VBAPrimer_Chapter2**.
3. In the Code window, enter **Sub NewFolder()** as the name of the procedure and press **Enter**. Visual Basic will enter the ending keywords: **End Sub**.
4. Press **F2** to display the Object Browser.
5. Click the drop-down arrow in the Project/Library listbox and select **VBA**.
6. Enter **file** in the Search Text box and press **Enter**.
7. Scroll down in the Members listbox and highlight the **MkDir** method.
8. Click the **Copy** button in the Object Browser window to copy the selected method name to the Windows clipboard.
9. Close the Object Browser and return to the Code window. Paste the copied instruction inside the **NewFolder** procedure.
10. Now, enter a space, followed by **"C:\Study"**. Be sure to enter the name of the entire path and the quotation marks. Your NewFolder procedure should look like the following:

```
Sub NewFolder()
   MkDir "C:\Study"
End Sub
```

11. Choose **Run | Run Sub/UserForm** to run the NewFolder procedure.
    After you run the NewFolder procedure, Visual Basic creates a new folder on drive C called Study. To see the folder, activate Windows Explorer. After creating a new folder, you may realize that you don't need it after all. Although you could easily delete the folder while in Windows Explorer, how about getting rid of it programmatically?
    The Object Browser contains many other methods that are useful for working with folders and files. The RmDir method is just as simple to use

as the MkDir method. To remove the Study folder from your hard drive, replace the MkDir method with the RmDir method and rerun the NewFolder procedure. Or create a new procedure called RemoveFolder, as shown here:

```
Sub RemoveFolder()
    RmDir "C:\Study"
End Sub
```

When writing procedures from scratch, it's a good idea to consult the Object Browser for names of the built-in VBA functions.

USING THE IMMEDIATE WINDOW

The Immediate window is a sort of VBA programmer's scratch pad. Here you can test VBA instructions before putting them to work in your VBA procedures. It is a great tool for experimenting with your new language. Use it to try out your statements. If the statement produces the expected result, you can copy the statement from the Immediate window into your procedure (or you can drag it right onto the Code window if the window is visible).

To activate the Immediate window, choose View | Immediate Window in the Visual Basic Editor, or press Ctrl+G while in the Visual Basic Editor window.

The Immediate window can be moved anywhere on the Visual Basic Editor window, or it can be docked so that it always appears in the same area of the screen. The docking setting can be turned on and off from the Docking tab in the Options dialog box (Tools | Options).

To close the Immediate window, click the Close button in the top-right corner of the window.

The following hands-on exercise demonstrates how to use the Immediate window to check instructions and get answers.

Hands-On 2.5. Experiments in the Immediate Window

1. If you are not in the VBE window, press **Alt+F11** to activate it.
2. Press **Ctrl+G** to activate the Immediate window, or choose **View | Immediate Window**.
3. In the Immediate window, type the following instruction and press **Enter**:

```
DoCmd.OpenForm "Inventory List"
```

4. If you entered the preceding VBA statement correctly, Visual Basic opens the Inventory List form, assuming the Northwind database is open.
5. Enter the following instruction in the Immediate window:

```
Debug.Print Forms![Inventory List].RecordSource
```

When you press **Enter**, Visual Basic indicates that Inventory is the RecordSource for the Inventory List form. Every time you type an instruction in the Immediate window and press Enter, Visual Basic executes the statement on the line where the insertion point is located. If you want to execute the same instruction again, click anywhere in the line containing the instruction and press Enter. For more practice, rerun the statements shown in Figure 2.17. Start from the instruction displayed in the first line of the Immediate window. Execute the instructions one by one by clicking in the appropriate line and pressing Enter.

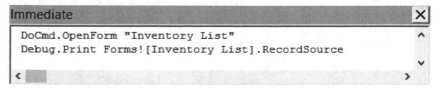

FIGURE 2.17. Use the Immediate window to evaluate and try Visual Basic statements.

So far you have used the Immediate window to perform some actions. The Immediate window also allows you to ask questions. Suppose you want to find out the answers to "How many controls are in the Inventory List form?" or "What's the name of the current application?" When working in the Immediate window, you can easily get answers to these and other questions.

In the preceding exercise, you entered two instructions. Let's return to the Immediate window to ask some questions. Access remembers the instructions entered in the Immediate window even after you close this window. The contents of the Immediate window are automatically deleted when you exit Microsoft Access.

Hands-On 2.6. Asking Questions in the Immediate Window

1. Click in a new line of the Immediate window and enter the following statement to find out the number of controls in the Inventory List form:

```
?Forms![Inventory List].Controls.Count
```

When you press **Enter**, Visual Basic enters the number of controls on a new line in the Immediate window.

2. Click in a new line of the Immediate window, and enter the following statement:

```
?Application.Name
```

When you press **Enter**, Visual Basic enters the name of the active application on a new line in the Immediate window.

3. In a new line in the Immediate window, enter the following instruction:

```
?12/3
```

When you press **Enter**, Visual Basic shows the result of the division on a new line. But what if you want to know the result of 3 + 2 and 12 × 8 right away? Instead of entering these instructions on separate lines, you can enter them on one line as in the following example:

```
?3+2:?12*8
```

Notice the colon separating the two blocks of instructions. When you press the Enter key, Visual Basic displays the results 5 and 96 on separate lines in the Immediate window.

Here are a couple of other statements you may want to try out on your own in the Immediate window:

```
?Application.GetOption("Default Database Directory")
?Application.CodeProject.Name
```

Instead of using the question mark, you may precede the statement typed in the Immediate window with the Print command, like this:

```
Print Application.CodeProject.Name
```

To delete the instructions from the Immediate window, highlight all the lines and press **Delete**.

4. In the Visual Basic Editor window, choose **File | Close and Return to Microsoft Access**.

5. Close the **Northwind 2007.accdb** database.

NOTE *Recall that in Chapter 1 you learned how to run subroutine procedures and functions from the Immediate window. You will find other examples of running procedures and functions from this window in subsequent chapters.*

SUMMARY

Programming in Access requires a working knowledge of objects and collections of objects. In this chapter, you explored features of the Visual Basic Editor window that can assist you in writing VBA code. Here are some important points:

1. When in doubt about objects, properties, or methods in an existing VBA procedure, highlight the instruction in question and fire up the online help by pressing F1.

2. When you need on-the-fly programming assistance while typing your VBA code, use the shortcut keys or buttons available on the Edit toolbar.

3. If you need a quick listing of properties and methods for every available object, or have trouble locating a hard-to-find procedure, go with the Object Browser.

4. If you want to experiment with VBA and see the results of VBA commands immediately, use the Immediate window.

In the next chapter, you will learn how you can remember values in your VBA procedures by using various types of variables and constants.

CHAPTER 3

ACCESS VBA FUNDAMENTALS

I n Chapter 2, you used the question mark to have Visual Basic return some information in the Immediate window. Unfortunately, when you write Visual Basic procedures outside the Immediate window, you can't use the question mark. So how do you obtain answers to your questions in VBA procedures? To find out what a particular VBA instruction (statement) has returned, you must tell Visual Basic to memorize it. This is done by using variables. This chapter introduces you to many types of variables, data types, and constants that you can and should use in your VBA procedures.

INTRODUCTION TO DATA TYPES

When you create Visual Basic procedures you have a purpose in mind: You want to manipulate data. Because your procedures will handle different kinds of information, you should understand how Visual Basic stores data.

The *data type* determines how the data is stored in the computer's memory. For example, data can be stored as a number, text, date, object, etc. If you forget to tell Visual Basic the data type, it is assigned the Variant data type. The *Variant* type has the ability to figure out on its own what kind of data is being manipulated and then take on that type. The Visual Basic data types are shown in Table 3.1. In addition to the built-in data types, you can define your own data types; these are known as user-defined data types. Because data types take up different amounts of space in the computer's memory, some of them are more expensive than others. Therefore, to conserve memory and make your procedure run faster, you should select the data type that uses the fewest bytes but at the same time is capable of handling the data that your procedure has to manipulate.

Table 3.1. VBA data types.

Data Type	Storage Size	Range
Byte	1 byte	A number in the range of 0 to 255.
Boolean	2 bytes	Stores a value of True (0) or False (–1).
Integer	2 bytes	A number in the range of –32,768 to 32,767. The type declaration character for Integer is the percent sign (%).
Long (long integer)	4 bytes	A number in the range of –2,147,483,648 to 2,147,483,647. The type declaration character for Long is the ampersand (&).
LongLong	8 bytes	Stored as a signed 64-bit (8-byte) number ranging in value from –9,223,372,036,854,775,808 to 9,223,372,036,854,775,807. The type declaration character for LongLong is the caret (^). LongLong is a valid declared type only on 64-bit platforms.
LongPtr (Long integer on 32-bit systems; LongLong integer on 64-bit systems)	4 bytes on 32-bit; 8 bytes on 64-bit	Numbers ranging in value from –2,147,483,648 to 2,147,483,647 on 32-bit systems; –9,223,372,036,854,775,808 to 9,223,372,036,854,775,807 on 64-bit systems. Using LongPtr enables writing code that can run in both 32-bit and 64-bit environments.
Single (single-precision floating-point)	4 bytes	Single-precision floating-point real number ranging in value from –3.402823E38 to –1.401298E–45 for negative values and from 1.401298E–45 to 3.402823E38 for positive values. The type declaration character for Single is the exclamation point (!).
Double (double-precision floating-point)	8 bytes	Double-precision floating-point real number in the range of –1.79769313486231E308 to –4.94065645841247E–324 for negative values and 4.94065645841247E–324 to 1.79769313486231E308 for positive values. The type declaration character for Double is the number sign (#).
Currency (scaled integer)	8 bytes	Monetary values used in fixed-point calculations: –922,337,203,685,477.5808 to 922,337,203,685,477.5807. The type declaration character for Currency is the at sign (@).

Data Type	Storage Size	Range
Decimal	14 bytes	96-bit (12-byte) signed integer scaled by a variable power of 10. The power of 10 scaling factor specifies the number of digits to the right of the decimal point, and ranges from 0 to 28. With no decimal point (scale of 0), the largest value is +/–79,228,162,514,264,337,593,543,950,335. With 28 decimal places, the largest value is +/–7.9228162514264337593543950335. The smallest nonzero value is +/–0.0000000000000000000000000001. You cannot declare a variable to be of type Decimal. You must use the Variant data type. Use the CDec function to convert a value to a decimal number: Dim numDecimal As Variant numDecimal = CDec(0.02 × 15.75 × 0.0006)
Date	8 bytes	Date from January 1, 100, to December 31, 9999, and times from 0:00:00 to 23:59:59. Date literals must be enclosed within number signs (#); for example: #January 1, 2011#
Object	4 bytes	Any Object reference. Use the Set statement to declare a variable as an Object.
String (variable-length)	10 bytes + string length	A variable-length string can contain up to approximately 2 billion characters. The type declaration character for String is the dollar sign ($).
String (fixed-length)	Length of string	A fixed-length string can contain 1 to approximately 65,400 characters.
Variant (with numbers)	16 bytes	Any numeric value up to the range of a Double.
Variant (with characters)	22 bytes + string length	Any valid nonnumeric data type in the same range as for a variable-length string.
User-defined (using Type)	One or more elements	A data type you define using the Type statement. User-defined data types can contain one or more elements of a data type, an array, or a previously defined user-defined type. For example: Type custInfo custFullName as String custTitle as String custBusinessName as String custFirstOrderDate as Date End Type

UNDERSTANDING AND USING VARIABLES

A *variable* is a name used to refer to an item of data. Each time you want to remember the result of a VBA instruction, think of a name that will represent it. For example, if you want to keep track of the number of controls on a particular form, you can make up a name such as NumOfControls, TotalControls, or FormsControlCount.

The names of variables can contain characters, numbers, and punctuation marks except for the following:

, # $ % & @ !

The name of a variable cannot begin with a number or contain a space. If you want the name of the variable to include more than one word, use the underscore (_) as a separator. Although a variable name can contain as many as 254 characters, it's best to use short and simple names. Using short names will save you typing time when you need to reuse the variable in your Visual Basic procedure. Visual Basic doesn't care whether you use uppercase or lowercase letters in variable names; however, most programmers use lowercase letters. When the variable name is composed of more than one word, most programmers capitalize the first letter of each word, as in the following: NumOfControls, First_Name.

SIDEBAR *Reserved Words Can't Be Used for Variable Names*

You can use any label you want for a variable name except for the reserved words that VBA uses. Visual Basic function names and words that have a special meaning in VBA cannot be used as variable names. For example, words such as Name, Len, Empty, Local, Currency, or Exit will generate an error message if used as a variable name.

Give your variables names that can help you remember their roles. Some programmers use a prefix to identify the variable's type. A variable name preceded with "str," such as strName, can be quickly recognized within the procedure code as the variable holding the text string.

Declaring Variables

You can create a variable by declaring it with a special command or by just using it in a statement. When you declare your variable, you make Visual Basic aware of the variable's name and data type. This is called *explicit variable declaration*.

SIDEBAR *Advantages of Explicit Variable Declaration*

Explicit variable declaration:

- Speeds up the execution of your procedure. Since Visual Basic knows the data type, it reserves only as much memory as is absolutely necessary to store the data.

■ Makes your code easier to read and understand because all the variables are listed at the very beginning of the procedure.

■ Helps prevent errors caused by misspelling a variable name. Visual Basic automatically corrects the variable name based on the spelling used in the variable declaration.

If you don't let Visual Basic know about the variable prior to using it, you are implicitly telling VBA that you want to create this variable. *Implicit variables* are automatically assigned the Variant data type (see Table 3.1 earlier in the chapter). Although implicit variable declaration is convenient (it allows you to create variables on the fly and assign values to them without knowing in advance the data type of the values being assigned), it can cause several problems.

SIDEBAR   *Disadvantages of Implicit Variable Declaration*

■ If you misspell a variable name in your procedure, Visual Basic may display a runtime error or create a new variable. You are guaranteed to waste some time troubleshooting problems that could easily have been avoided had you declared your variable at the beginning of the procedure.

■ Since Visual Basic does not know what type of data your variable will store, it assigns it a Variant data type. This causes your procedure to run slower because Visual Basic has to check the data type every time it deals with your variable. And because Variant variables can store any type of data, Visual Basic has to reserve more memory to store your data.

You declare a variable with the `Dim` keyword. Dim stands for "dimension." The `Dim` keyword is followed by the variable's name and type.

Suppose you want the procedure to display the age of an employee. Before you can calculate the age, you must feed the procedure the employee's date of birth. To do this, you declare a variable called `dateOfBirth`, as follows:

```
Dim dateOfBirth As Date
```

Notice that the `Dim` keyword is followed by the name of the variable (`dateOfBirth`). If you don't like this name, you are free to replace it with another word, as long as the word you are planning to use is not one of the VBA keywords. You specify the data type the variable will hold by including the `As` keyword followed by one of the data types from Table 3.1. The Date data type tells Visual Basic that the variable `dateOfBirth` will store a date.

To store the employee's age, you declare the variable as follows:

```
Dim intAge As Integer
```

The `intAge` variable will store the number of years between today's date and the employee's date of birth. Because age is displayed as a whole number, the `intAge` variable has been assigned the Integer data type. You may also want your procedure to keep track of the employee's name, so you declare another variable to hold the employee's first and last name:

```
Dim strFullName As String
```

Because the word Name is on the VBA list of reserved words, using it in your VBA procedure would guarantee an error. To hold the employee's full name, we used the variable `strFullName` and declared it as the String data type because the data it will hold is text. Declaring variables is regarded as good programming practice because it makes programs easier to read and helps prevent certain types of errors.

<hr>

SIDEBAR   *Informal (Implicit) Variables*

Variables that are not explicitly declared with `Dim` statements are said to be implicitly declared. These variables are automatically assigned a data type called Variant. They can hold numbers, strings, and other types of information. You can create an informal variable by assigning some value to a variable name anywhere in your *VBA* procedure. For example, you implicitly declare a variable in the following way: `intDaysLeft = 100`.

Now that you know how to declare your variables, let's write a procedure that uses them.

Please note that files for the hands-on project may be found on the companion CD-ROM.

Hands-On 3.1. Using Variables

1. Start Microsoft Access and create a new database named **Chap03.accdb** in your **C:\VBAPrimerAccess_ByExample** folder.
2. Once your new database is opened, press **Alt+F11** to switch to the Visual Basic Editor window.
3. Choose **Insert | Module** to add a new standard module, and notice Module1 under the Modules folder in the Project Explorer window.
4. In the Module1 (Code) window, enter the following **AgeCalc** procedure.

```
Sub AgeCalc()
 ' variable declaration
 Dim strFullName As String
 Dim dateOfBirth As Date
 Dim intAge As Integer

 ' assign values to variables
 strFullName = "John Smith"
 dateOfBirth = #1/3/1967#

 ' calculate age
 IntAge = Year(Now()) - Year(dateOfBirth)

 ' print results to the Immediate window
 Debug.Print strFullName & " is " & intAge & " years old."
End Sub
```

Notice that in the AgeCalc procedure the variables are declared on separate lines at the beginning of the procedure. You can also declare several variables on the same line, separating each variable name with a comma, as shown here (be sure to enter this on one line):

```
Dim strFullName As String, dateOfBirth As Date, intAge As
Integer
```

When you list all your variables on one line, the Dim keyword appears only once at the beginning of the variable declaration line.

5. If the Immediate window is not open, press **Ctrl+G** or choose **View|Immediate Window**. Because the example procedure writes the results to the Immediate window, you should ensure that this window is open prior to executing Step 6.

6. To run the AgeCalc procedure, click any line between the Sub and End Sub keywords and press **F5**.

SIDEBAR *What Is the Variable Type?*

You can find out the type of a variable used in your procedure by right-clicking the variable name and selecting Quick Info from the shortcut menu.

When Visual Basic executes the variable declaration statements, it creates the variables with the specified names and reserves memory space to store their values. Then specific values are assigned to these variables. To assign a value to a variable, you begin with a variable name followed by an equal sign. The value entered to the right of the equal sign is the data you want to store in the variable. The data you enter here must be of the type stated in the variable declaration. Text data should be surrounded by quotation marks and dates by # characters.

Using the data supplied by the dateOfBirth variable, Visual Basic calculates the age of an employee and stores the result of the calculation in the variable called intAge. Then, the full name of the employee and the age are printed to the Immediate window using the instruction Debug.Print.

SIDEBAR *Concatenation*

You can combine two or more strings to form a new string. The joining operation is called concatenation. You saw an example of concatenated strings in the AgeCalc procedure in Hands-On 3.1. Concatenation is represented by an ampersand character (&). For instance, "His name is " & strFirstName will produce a string like: His name is John or His name is Michael. The name of the person is determined by the contents of the strFirstName variable. Notice that there is an extra space between "is" and the ending quotation mark: "His name is ".

Concatenation of strings can also be represented by a plus sign (+); however, many programmers prefer to restrict the plus sign to numerical operations to eliminate ambiguity.

Specifying the Data Type of a Variable

If you don't specify the variable's data type in the Dim statement, you end up with the *untyped* variable. Untyped variables in VBA are always assigned the Variant data type. Variant data types can hold all the other data types (except for user-defined data types). This feature makes Variant a very flexible and popular data type. Despite this flexibility, it is highly recommended that you create typed variables. When you declare a variable of a certain data type, your VBA procedure runs faster because Visual Basic does not have to stop to analyze the variable to determine its type.

Visual Basic can work with many types of numeric variables. Integer variables can hold only whole numbers from –32,768 to 32,767. Other types of numeric variables are Long, Single, Double, and Currency. The Long variables can hold whole numbers in the range –2,147,483,648 to 2,147,483,647. As opposed to Integer and Long variables, Single and Double variables can hold decimals.

String variables are used to refer to text. When you declare a variable of the String data type, you can tell Visual Basic how long the string should be. For instance, Dim strExtension As String * 3 declares the fixed-length String variable named strExtension that is three characters long. If you don't assign a specific length, the String variable will be *dynamic*. This means that Visual Basic will make enough space in computer memory to handle whatever text length is assigned to it.

After a variable is declared, it can store only the type of information that you stated in the declaration statement.

Assigning string values to numeric variables or numeric values to string variables results in the error message "Type Mismatch" or causes Visual Basic to modify the value. For example, if your variable was declared to hold whole numbers and your data uses decimals, Visual Basic will disregard the decimals and use only the whole part of the number.

Let's use the MyNumber procedure in Hands-On 3.2 as an example of how Visual Basic modifies the data according to the assigned data types.

◉ Hands-On 3.2. Understanding the Data Type of a Variable

This hands-on exercise uses the C:\VBAPrimerAccess_ByExample\ Chap03.accdb database that you created in Hands-On 3.1.

1. In the Visual Basic Editor window, choose **Insert | Module** to add a new module.
2. Enter the following procedure code for **MyNumber** in the new module's Code window.

```
Sub MyNumber()
 Dim intNum As Integer
 intNum = 23.11
 MsgBox intNum
End Sub
```

3. To run the procedure, click any line between the Sub and End Sub keywords and press **F5** or choose **Run | Run Sub/UserForm**.

When you run this procedure, Visual Basic displays the contents of the variable intNum as 23, and not 23.11, because the intNum variable was declared as an Integer data type.

Using Type Declaration Characters

If you don't declare a variable with a Dim statement, you can still designate a type for it by using a special character at the end of the variable name. For example, to declare the FirstName variable as String, you append the dollar sign to the variable name:

```
Dim FirstName$
```

This is the same as Dim FirstName As String. Other type declaration characters are shown in Table 3.2. Notice that the type declaration characters can be used only with six data types. To use the type declaration character, append the character to the end of the variable name.

Table 3.2. Type declaration characters.

Data Type	Character
Integer	%
Long	&
Single	!
Double	#
Currency	@
String	$

SIDEBAR *Declaring Typed Variables*

The variable type can be indicated by the As keyword or by attaching a type symbol. If you don't add the type symbol or the As command, VBA will default the variable to the Variant data type.

⊙ Hands-On 3.3. Using Type Declaration Characters in Variable Names

This hands-on exercise uses the Chap03.accdb database that you created in Hands-On 3.1.

1. In the Visual Basic window, choose **Insert | Module** to add a new module.

2. Enter the **AgeCalc2** procedure code in the new module's Code window.

```
Sub AgeCalc2()
 ' variable declaration
 Dim FullName$
 Dim DateOfBirth As Date
 Dim age%
 ' assign values to variables
 FullName$ = "John Smith"
 DateOfBirth = #1/3/1967#
 ' calculate age
 age% = Year(Now()) - Year(DateOfBirth)
 ' print results to the Immediate window
 Debug.Print FullName$ & " is " & age% & " years old."
End Sub
```

3. To run the procedure, click any line between the Sub and End Sub keywords and press **F5** or choose **Run | Run Sub/UserForm**.

Assigning Values to Variables

Now that you know how to correctly name and declare variables, it's time to learn how to initialize them.

(◉) Hands-On 3.4. Assigning Values to Variables

This hands-on exercise uses the C:\VBAPrimerAccess_ByExample\ Chap03.accdb database that you created in Hands-On 3.1.

1. In the Visual Basic window, choose **Insert | Module** to add a new module.
2. Enter the code of the **CalcCost** procedure in the new module's Code window.

```
Sub CalcCost()
    slsPrice = 35
 slsTax = 0.085
 cost = slsPrice + (slsPrice * slsTax)
 strMsg = "The calculator total is " & "$" & cost & "."
 MsgBox strMsg
End Sub
```

3. To run the procedure, click any line between the Sub and End Sub keywords and press **F5** or choose **Run | Run Sub/UserForm**.
4. Change the calculation of the cost variable in the **CalcCost** procedure as follows:

```
cost = Format(slsPrice + (slsPrice * slsTax), "0.00")
```

5. To run the modified procedure, click any line between the Sub and End Sub keywords and press **F5** or choose **Run | Run Sub/UserForm**.

The CalcCost procedure uses four variables: `slsPrice`, `slsTax`, `cost`, and `strMsg`. Because none of these variables have been explicitly declared with the `Dim` keyword and a specific data type, they all have the same data type—Variant. The variables `slsPrice` and `slsTax` were created by assigning some values to the variable names at the beginning of the procedure. The `cost` variable was assigned the value resulting from the calculation `slsPrice + (slsPrice x slsTax)`. The `cost` calculation uses the values supplied by the `slsPrice` and `slsTax` variables. The `strMsg` variable puts together a text message to the user. This message is then displayed with the `MsgBox` function.

When you assign values to variables, you follow the name of the variable with the equal sign. After the equal sign you enter the value of the variable. This can be text surrounded by quotation marks, a number, or an expression. While the values assigned to the variables `slsPrice`, `slsTax`, and `cost` are easily understood, the value stored in the `strMsg` variable is a little more involved.

Let's examine the content of the `strMsg` variable:

```
strMsg = "The calculator total is " & "$" & cost & "."
```

- The string `"The calculator total is "` begins and ends with quotation marks. Notice the extra space before the ending quotation mark.
- The & symbol allows one string to be appended to another string or to the contents of a variable and must be used every time you want to append a new piece of information to the previous string.
- The $ character is used to denote the type of currency. Because it is a character, it is surrounded by quotation marks.
- The & symbol attaches another string.
- The `cost` variable is a placeholder. The actual cost of the calculator will be displayed here when the procedure runs.
- The & symbol attaches yet another string.
- The period (.) is a character and must be surrounded by quotation marks. When you require a period at the end of the sentence, you must attach it separately when it follows the name of a variable.

SIDEBAR *Variable Initialization*

Visual Basic automatically initializes a new variable to its default value when it is created. Numerical variables are set to zero (0), Boolean variables are initialized to False, string variables are set to the empty string (""), and Date variables are set to December 30, 1899.

Notice that the cost displayed in the message box has three decimal places. To display the cost of a calculator with two decimal places, you need to use a function. VBA has special functions that allow you to change the format of data. To change the format of the cost variable you should use the Format function. This function has the following syntax:

```
Format(expression, format)
```

where `expression` is a value or variable you want to format and `format` is the type of format you want to apply.

After having tried the CalcCost procedure, you may wonder why you should bother declaring variables if Visual Basic can handle undeclared variables so well. The CalcCost procedure is very short, so you don't need to worry about how many bytes of memory will be consumed each time Visual Basic uses the Variant variable. In short procedures, however, it is not the memory that matters but the mistakes you are bound to make when typing variable names. What will happen if the second time you use the `cost` variable you omit the "o" and refer to it as `cst`?

```
strMsg = "The calculator total is " & "$" & cst & "."
```

And what will you end up with if, instead of `slsTax`, you use the word `tax` in the formula?

```
cost = Format(slsPrice + (slsPrice * tax), "0.00")
```

When you run the procedure with the preceding errors introduced, Visual Basic will not show the cost of the calculator because it does not find the assignment statement for the `cst` variable. And because Visual Basic does not know the sales tax, it displays the price of the calculator as the total cost. Visual Basic does not guess—it simply does what you tell it to do. This brings us to the next section, which explains how to make sure that errors of this sort don't occur.

NOTE *Before you continue with this chapter, be sure to replace the names of the variables* cst *and* tax *with* cost *and* slsTax.

Forcing Declaration of Variables

Visual Basic has an `Option Explicit` statement that you can use to automatically remind yourself to formally declare all your variables. This statement must be entered at the top of each of your modules. The `Option Explicit` statement will cause Visual Basic to generate an error message when you try to run a procedure that contains undeclared variables.

⦿ Hands-On 3.5. Forcing Declaration of Variables

1. Return to the Code window where you entered the **CalcCost** procedure (see Hands-On 3.4).

2. At the top of the module window (below the Option Compare Database statement), enter

```
Option Explicit
```

   and press **Enter**. Visual Basic will display the statement in blue.

3. Position the insertion point anywhere within the CalcCost procedure and press **F5** to run it. Visual Basic displays this error message: "Compile error: Variable not defined."

4. Click **OK** to exit the message box. Visual Basic selects the name of the variable, slsPrice, and highlights in yellow the name of the procedure, Sub CalcCost(). The titlebar displays "Microsoft Visual Basic for Applications—Chap03 [break]—[Module4 (Code)]." The Visual Basic Break mode allows you to correct the problem before you continue. Now you have to formally declare the slsPrice variable.

5. Enter the declaration statement

```
Dim slsPrice As Currency
```

   on a new line just below Sub CalcCost() and press **F5** to continue. When you declare the slsPrice variable and rerun your procedure, Visual Basic will generate the same compile error as soon as it encounters another variable name that was not declared. To fix the remaining problems with the variable declaration in this procedure, choose **Run | Reset** to exit the Break mode.

6. Enter the following declarations at the beginning of the CalcCost procedure:

```
' declaration of variables
Dim slsPrice As Currency
Dim slsTax As Single
Dim cost As Currency
Dim strMsg As String
```

7. To run the procedure, click any line between the Sub and End Sub keywords and press **F5** or choose **Run | Run Sub/UserForm**. Your revised CalcCost procedure looks like this:

```
' revised CalcCost procedure with variable declarations
Sub CalcCost()
  ' declaration of variables
  Dim slsPrice As Currency
  Dim slsTax As Single
  Dim cost As Currency
  Dim strMsg As String
  slsPrice = 35
  slsTax = 0.085
  cost = Format(slsPrice + (slsPrice * slsTax), "0.00")
  strMsg = "The calculator total is " & "$" & cost & "."
  MsgBox strMsg
End Sub
```

The `Option Explicit` statement you entered at the top of the module Code window (see step 2) forced you to declare variables. Because you must include the `Option Explicit` statement in each module where you want to require variable declaration, you can have Visual Basic enter this statement for you each time you insert a new module.

To automatically include `Option Explicit` in every new module you create, follow these steps:

1. Choose **Tools | Options**.
2. Ensure that the **Require Variable Declaration** checkbox is selected in the Options dialog box (Editor tab).
3. Choose **OK** to close the Options dialog box.

From now on, every new module will be added with the `Option Explicit` statement. If you want to require variables to be explicitly declared in a module you created prior to enabling Require Variable Declaration in the Options dialog box, you must enter the `Option Explicit` statement manually by editing the module yourself.

SIDEBAR   *More about* `Option Explicit`

`Option Explicit` forces formal (explicit) declaration of all variables in a particular module. One big advantage of using `Option Explicit` is that misspellings of variable names will be detected at compile time (when Visual Basic attempts to translate the source code to executable code). The `Option Explicit` statement must appear in a module before any procedures.

Understanding the Scope of Variables

Variables can have different ranges of influence in a VBA procedure. *Scope* defines the availability of a particular variable to the same procedure or other procedures.

Variables can have the following three levels of scope in Visual Basic for Applications:

- Procedure-level scope
- Module-level scope
- Project-level scope

Procedure-Level (Local) Variables

From this chapter you already know how to declare a variable using the `Dim` statement. The position of the `Dim` statement in the module determines the scope of a variable. Variables declared with the `Dim` statement within a VBA procedure have a *procedure-level* scope. Procedure-level variables can also be declared by using the `Static` statement (see "Using Static Variables" later in this chapter).

Procedure-level variables are frequently referred to as *local* variables, which can be used only in the procedure where they were declared. Undeclared variables always have a procedure-level scope.

A variable's name must be unique within its scope. This means that you cannot declare two variables with the same name in the same procedure. However, you can use the same variable name in different procedures. In other words, the CalcCost procedure can have the `slsTax` variable, and the ExpenseRep procedure in the same module can have its own variable called `slsTax`. Both variables are independent of each other.

SIDEBAR   *Local Variables: With* `Dim` *or* `Static`?

When you declare a local variable with the `Dim` statement, the value of the variable is preserved only while the procedure in which it is declared is running. As soon as the procedure ends, the variable dies. The next time you execute the procedure, the variable is reinitialized.

When you declare a local variable with the `Static` statement, the value of the variable is preserved after the procedure in which the variable was declared has finished running. Static variables are reset when you quit the Microsoft Access application or when a runtime error occurs while the procedure is running.

Module-Level Variables

Often you want the variable to be available to other VBA procedures in the module after the procedure in which the variable was declared has finished running. This situation requires that you change the variable's scope to *module-level*.

Module-level variables are declared at the top of the module (above the first procedure definition) by using the `Dim` or `Private` statement. These variables are available to all of the procedures in the module in which they were declared, but are not available to procedures in other modules.

For instance, to make the `slsTax` variable available to any other procedure in the module, you could declare it by using the `Dim` or `Private` statement:

```
Option Explicit
Dim slsTax As Single ' module-level variable declared with
                     ' Dim statement

Sub CalcCost()
  ...Instructions of the procedure...
End Sub
```

Notice that the `slsTax` variable is declared at the top of the module, just below the `Option Explicit` statement and before the first procedure definition. You could also declare the `slsTax` variable like this:

```
Option Explicit
Private slsTax As Single ' module-level variable declared with
                         ' Private statement
Sub CalcCost()
 ...Instructions of the procedure...
End Sub
```

There is no difference between module-level variables declared with `Dim` or `Private` statements.

Before you can see how module-level variables actually work, you need another procedure that also uses the `slsTax` variable.

⊙ Hands-On 3.6. Understanding Module-Level Variables

This hands-on exercise requires the prior completion of Hands-On 3.4 and 3.5.

1. In the Code window, in the same module where you entered the CalcCost procedure, cut the declaration line **Dim slsTax As Single** and paste it at the top of the module sheet, below the `Option Explicit` statement.
2. Enter the following code of the **ExpenseRep** procedure in the same module where the **CalcCost** procedure is located (see Figure 3.1).

```
Sub ExpenseRep()
 Dim slsPrice As Currency
 Dim cost As Currency
 slsPrice = 55.99
 cost = slsPrice + (slsPrice * slsTax)
 MsgBox slsTax
 MsgBox cost
End Sub
```

The ExpenseRep procedure declares two Currency type variables: `slsPrice` and `cost`. The `slsPrice` variable is then assigned a value of 55.99. The `slsPrice` variable is independent of the `slsPrice` variable declared within the CalcCost procedure.

The ExpenseRep procedure calculates the cost of a purchase. The cost includes the sales tax. Because the sales tax is the same as the one used in the CalcCost procedure, the `slsTax` variable has been declared at the module level. After Visual Basic executes the CalcCost procedure, the contents of the `slsTax` variable equals 0.085. If `slsTax` were a local variable, the contents of this variable would be empty upon the termination of the CalcCost procedure. The ExpenseRep procedure ends by displaying the value of the `slsTax` and `cost` variables in two separate message boxes.

After running the CalcCost procedure, Visual Basic erases the contents of all the variables except for the `slsTax` variable, which was declared at a module level. As soon as you attempt to calculate the cost by running the ExpenseRep procedure, Visual Basic retrieves the value of the slsTax variable and uses it in the calculation.

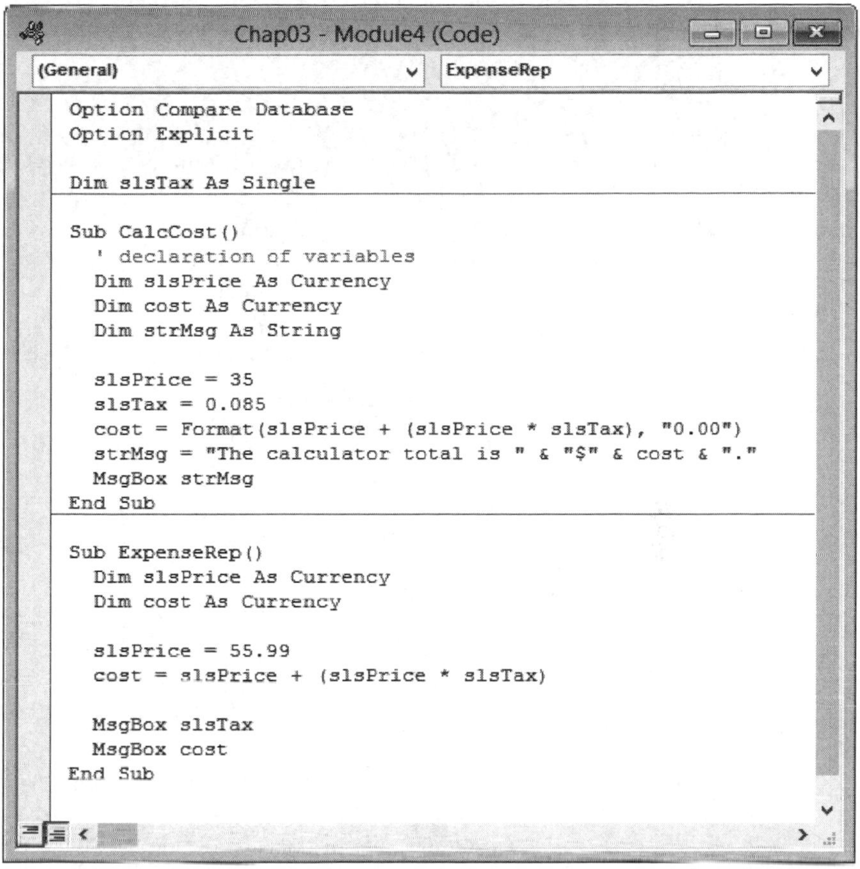

```
Chap03 - Module4 (Code)
(General)                          ExpenseRep

    Option Compare Database
    Option Explicit

    Dim slsTax As Single

    Sub CalcCost()
      ' declaration of variables
      Dim slsPrice As Currency
      Dim cost As Currency
      Dim strMsg As String

      slsPrice = 35
      slsTax = 0.085
      cost = Format(slsPrice + (slsPrice * slsTax), "0.00")
      strMsg = "The calculator total is " & "$" & cost & "."
      MsgBox strMsg
    End Sub

    Sub ExpenseRep()
      Dim slsPrice As Currency
      Dim cost As Currency

      slsPrice = 55.99
      cost = slsPrice + (slsPrice * slsTax)

      MsgBox slsTax
      MsgBox cost
    End Sub
```

FIGURE 3.1. Using module-level variables.

3. Click anywhere inside the revised CalcCost procedure and press **F5** to run it.
4. As soon as the CalcCost procedure finishes executing, run the ExpenseRep procedure.

Project-Level Variables

In the previous sections, you learned that declaring a variable with the Dim or Private keyword at the top of the module makes it available to other procedures in that module. Module-level variables that are declared with the Public keyword (instead of Dim or Private) have project-level scope. This means that they can be used in any Visual Basic for Applications module. When you want to work with a variable in all the procedures in all the open VBA projects, you must declare it with the `Public` keyword—for instance:

```
Option Explicit
Public gslsTax As Single
Sub CalcCost()
...Instructions of the procedure...
End Sub
```

Notice that the `gslsTax` variable declared at the top of the module with the `Public` keyword will now be available to any VBA modules that your code references.

A variable declared in the declaration section of a module using the `Public` keyword is called a *global variable*. This variable can be seen by all procedures in the database's modules. It is customary to use the prefix "g" to indicate this type of variable.

When using global variables, it's important to keep in mind the following:

■ The value of the global variable can be changed anywhere in your program. An unexpected change in the value of a variable is a common cause of problems. Be careful not to write a block of code that modifies a global variable. If you need to change the value of a variable within your application, make sure you are using a local variable.

■ Values of all global variables declared with the `Public` keyword are cleared when Access encounters an error. Since the release of the Access 2007 database format (ACCDB), you can use the TempVars collection for your global variable needs (see "Using Temporary Variables" later in this chapter).

■ Don't put your global variable declaration in a form class module. Variables in the code module behind the form are never global even if you declare them as such. You must use a standard code module (Insert | Module) to declare variables to be available in all modules and forms. Variables declared in a standard module can be used in the code for any form.

■ Use constants as much as possible whenever your application requires global variables. Constants are much more reliable because their values are static. Constants are covered later in this chapter.

SIDEBAR *Public Variables and the* `Option Private Module` *Statement*

Variables declared using the `Public` keyword are available to all procedures in all modules across all applications. To restrict a public module-level variable to the current database, include the `Option Private Module` statement in the declaration section of the standard or class module in which the variable is declared.

Understanding the Lifetime of Variables

In addition to scope, variables have a *lifetime*. The *lifetime* of a variable determines how long a variable retains its value. Module-level and project-level variables preserve their values as long as the project is open. Visual Basic, however, can reinitialize these variables if required by the program's logic. Local variables declared with the Dim statement lose their values when a procedure has finished. Local variables have a lifetime as long as a procedure is running, and they are reinitialized every time the program is run. Visual Basic allows you to extend the lifetime of a local variable by changing the way it is declared.

Using Temporary Variables

In the previous section, you learned that you can declare a global variable with the Public keyword and use it throughout your entire application. You also learned that these variables can be quite problematic, especially when you or another programmer accidentally changes the value of the variable or your application encounters an error and the values of the variables you have initially set for your application to use are completely wiped out. To avoid such problems, many programmers resort to using a separate global variables form to hold their global variables. And if they need certain values to be available the next time the application starts, they create a separate database table to store these values. A *global variables form* is simply a blank Access form where you can place both bound and unbound controls. Bound controls are used to pull the data from the table where global variables have been stored. You can use unbound controls on a form to store values of global variables that are not stored in a separate table. Simply set the ControlSource property of the unbound control by typing a value in it or use a VBA procedure to set the value of the ControlSource. The form set up as a global variables form must be open while the application is running for the values of the bound and unbound controls to be available to other forms, reports, and queries in the database. A global variables form can be hidden if the values of the global variables are pulled from a database table or set using VBA procedures or macro actions.

If your database is in the ACCDB format, instead of using a database table or a global variables form, you can use the TempVars collection to store the Variant values you want to reuse. TempVars stands for *temporary variables*. Temporary variables are global. You can refer to them in VBA modules, event procedures, queries, expressions, add-ins, and in any referenced databases. Access .ACCDB databases allow you to define up to 255 temporary variables at one time. These variables remain in memory until you close the database (unless you remove them when you are finished working with them). Unlike public variables, temporary variable values are not cleared when an error occurs.

Creating a Temporary Variable with a TempVars Collection Object

Let's look at some examples of using the `TempVars` collection first introduced in Access 2007. Assume your application requires three variables named `gtvUserName`, `gtvUserFolder`, and `gtvEndDate`.

To try this out, open the Immediate window and type the following statements. The variable is created as soon as you press Enter after each statement.

```
TempVars("gtvUserName").Value = "John Smith"
TempVars("gtvUserFolder").Value = Environ("HOMEPATH")
TempVars("gtvEndDate").Value = Format(now(),"mm/dd/yyyy")
```

Notice that to create a temporary variable all you have to do is specify its value. If the variable does not already exist, Access adds it to the `TempVars` collection. If the variable exists, Access modifies its value.

You can explicitly add a global variable to the `TempVars` collection by using the `Add` method, like this:

```
TempVars.Add "gtvCompleted", "true"
```

Retrieving Names and Values of TempVar Objects

Each `TempVar` object in the `TempVars` collection has Name and Value properties that you can use to access the variable and read its value from any procedure. By default, the items in the collection are numbered from zero (0), with the first item being zero, the second item being one, the third two, and so on. Therefore, to find the value of the second variable in the `TempVars` you have entered (`gtvUserFolder`), type the following statement in the Immediate window:

```
?TempVars(1).Value
```

When you press Enter, you will see the location of the user's private folder on the computer. In this case, it is your private folder. The folder information was returned by passing the "HOMEPATH" parameter to the built-in `Environ` function. Functions and parameter passing are covered in Chapter 4.

You can also retrieve the value of the variable from the `TempVars` collection by using its name, like this:

```
?TempVars("gtvUserFolder").Value
```

You can iterate through the `TempVars` collection to see the names and values of all global variables that you have placed in it. To do this from the Immediate window, you need to use the colon operator (:) to separate lines of code. Type the following statement all on one line to try this out:

```
For Each gtv in TempVars : Debug.Print gtv.Name & ":"
& gtv.Value : Next
```

When you press Enter, the `Debug.Print` statement will write to the Immediate window a name and value for each variable that is currently stored in the `TempVars` collection:

```
gtvUserName:John Smith
gtvUserFolder:\Documents and Settings\John
gtvEndDate:09/12/2015
gtvCompleted:true
```

The For Each...Next statement, a popular VBA programming construct, is covered in detail in Chapter 6. The "gtv" is an object variable used as an iterator. An *iterator* allows you to traverse through all the elements of a collection. You can use any variable name as an iterator as long as it is not a VBA keyword. Object variables are discussed later in this chapter. For more information on working with collections, see Chapter 8.

Using Temporary Global Variables in Expressions

You can use temporary global variables anywhere expressions can be used. For example, you can set the value of the unbound text box control on a form to display the value of your global variable by activating the property sheet and typing the following in the ControlSource property of the text box:

```
=[TempVars]![gtvCompleted]
```

You can also use a temporary variable to pass selection criteria to queries:

```
SELECT * FROM Orders WHERE Order_Date = TempVars!gtvEndDate
```

Removing a Temporary Variable from a TempVars Collection Object

When you are done using a variable, you can remove it from the TempVars collection with the Remove method, like this:

```
TempVars.Remove "gtvUserFolder"
```

To check the number of the TempVar objects in the TempVars collection, use the Count property in the Immediate window:

```
?TempVars.Count
```

Finally, to quickly remove all global variables (TempVar objects) from the TempVars collection, simply use the RemoveAll method, like this:

```
TempVars.RemoveAll
```

SIDEBAR *The* TempVars *Collection Is Exposed to Macros*

The following three macros allow macro users to set and remove TempVar objects:

■ SetTempVar—Sets a TempVar to a given value. You must specify the name of the temporary variable and the expression that will be used to set the value of this variable. Expressions must be entered without an equal sign (=).

- RemoveTempVar—Removes the `TempVar` from the `TempVars` collection. You must specify the name of the temporary variable you want to remove.
- RemoveAllTempVars—Clears the `TempVars` collection.

The values of `TempVar` *objects can be used in the arguments and in the condition columns of macros.*

Using Static Variables

A variable declared with the `Static` keyword is a special type of local variable. *Static variables* are declared at the procedure level. Unlike the local variables declared with the `Dim` keyword, static variables remain in existence and retain their values when the procedure in which they were declared ends.

The CostOfPurchase procedure (see Hands-On 3.7) demonstrates the use of the static variable `allPurchase`. The purpose of this variable is to keep track of the running total.

⊙ Hands-On 3.7. Using Static Variables

This hands-on exercise uses the C:\VBAPrimerAccess_ByExample\ Chap03.accdb database that you created in Hands-On 3.1.

1. In the Visual Basic window, choose **Insert | Module** to add a new module.
2. Enter the following **CostOfPurchase** procedure code in the new module's Code window.

```
Sub CostOfPurchase()
 ' declare variables
 Static allPurchase
 Dim newPurchase As String
 Dim purchCost As Single
 newPurchase = InputBox("Enter the cost of a purchase:")
 purchCost = CSng(newPurchase)
 allPurchase = allPurchase + purchCost
 ' display results
 MsgBox "The cost of a new purchase is: " & newPurchase
 MsgBox "The running cost is: " & allPurchase
End Sub
```

This procedure begins with declaring a static variable named `allPurchase` and two local variables named `newPurchase` and `purchCost`. The `InputBox` function is used to get a user's input while the procedure is running. As soon as the user inputs the value and clicks OK, Visual Basic assigns the value to the `newPurchase` variable. Because the result of the `InputBox` function is always a string, the `newPurchase` variable was declared as the String data type. You cannot use strings in mathematical calculations, so the next instruction uses a *type conversion* function (`CSng`) to translate the text value into a numeric value, which is stored as a Single data type in the variable `purchCost`. The `CSng` function requires only one argument: the value you want to translate. Refer to Chapter 4 for more information about converting data types.

The next instruction, `allPurchase = allPurchase + purchCost`, adds the new value supplied by the `InputBox` function to the current purchase value. When you run this procedure for the first time, the value of the `allPurchase` variable is the same as the value of the `purchCost` variable. During the second run, the value of the static variable is increased by the new value entered in the dialog box. You can run the CostOfPurchase procedure as many times as you want. The `allPurch` variable will keep the running total for as long as the project is open.

3. To run the procedure, position the insertion point anywhere within the CostOfPurchase procedure and press **F5**.
4. When the dialog box appears, enter a number. For example, type **100** and press **Enter**. Visual Basic displays the message "The cost of a new purchase is: 100."
5. Click **OK** in the message box. Visual Basic displays the second message "The running cost is: 100."
6. Rerun the same procedure.
7. When the input box appears, enter another number. For example, type **50** and press **Enter**. Visual Basic displays the message "The cost of a new purchase is: 50."
8. Click **OK** in the message box. Visual Basic displays the second message "The running cost is: 150."
9. Run the procedure a couple of times to see how Visual Basic keeps track of the running total.

SIDEBAR   *Type Conversion Functions*

To learn more about the `CSng` function, position the insertion point anywhere within the word `CSng` and press F1.

Using Object Variables

The variables you've learned about so far are used to store data, which is the main reason for using "normal" variables in your procedures. There are also special variables that refer to the Visual Basic objects. These variables are called *object variables*. Object variables don't store data; they store the location of the data. You can use them to reference databases, forms, and controls as well as objects created in other applications. Object variables are declared in a similar way as the variables you've already seen. The only difference is that after the `As` keyword, you enter the type of object your variable will point to—for instance:

```
Dim myControl As Control
```

This statement declares the object variable called `myControl` of type Control.

```
Dim frm As Form
```

This statement declares the object variable called `frm` of type Form.

You can use object variables to refer to objects of a generic type, such as Application, Control, Form, or Report, or you can point your object variable to specific object types, such as TextBox, ToggleButton, CheckBox, CommandButton, ListBox, OptionButton, Subform or Subreport, Label, BoundObjectFrame or UnboundObjectFrame, and so on. When you declare an object variable, you also have to assign it a specific value before you can use it in your procedure. You assign a value to the object variable by using the `Set` keyword followed by the equal sign and the value that the variable refers to—for example:

```
Set myControl = Me!CompanyName
```

The preceding statement assigns a value to the object variable called `myControl`. This object variable will now point to the CompanyName control on the active form. If you omit the word `Set`, Visual Basic will display the error message "Runtime error 91: *Object variable or With block variable not set.*"

Again, it's time to see a practical example. The HideControl procedure in Hands-On 3.8 demonstrates the use of the object variables `frm` and `myControl`.

(◉) Hands-On 3.8. Working with Object Variables

1. Close the currently open Access database **Chap03.accdb**. When prompted to save changes in the modules, click **OK**. Save the modules with the suggested default names Module1, Module2, and so on.
2. Copy the **HandsOn_03_8.accdb** database from the companion CD to your **C:\VBAPrimerAccess_ByExample** folder. This database contains a Customer table and a simple Customer form imported from the Northwind. mdb sample database that shipped with an earlier version of Microsoft Access.
3. Open Access and load the **C:\VBAPrimerAccess_ByExample\HandsOn_03_8.accdb** database file.
4. Open the **Customers** form in Form view.
5. Press **Alt+F11** to switch to the Visual Basic Editor window.
6. Choose **Insert | Module** to add a new module.
7. Enter the following **HideControl** procedure code in the new module's Code window.

```
Sub HideControl()
    ' this procedure is run against the open Customers form
    Dim frm As Form
    Dim myControl As Control
    Set frm = Forms!Customers
```

```
Set myControl = frm.CompanyName
myControl.Visible = False
End Sub
```

8. To run the procedure, click any line between the `Sub` and `End Sub` keywords and press **F5** or choose **Run | Run Sub/UserForm**.

The procedure begins with the declaration of two object variables called `frm` and `myControl`. The object variable `frm` is set to reference the Customers form. For the procedure to work, the referenced form must be open. Next, the `myControl` object variable is set to point to the Company-Name control located on the Customers form.

Instead of using the object's entire address, you can use the shortcut—the name of the object variable. For example, the statement

```
Set myControl = frm.CompanyName
```

is the same as

```
Set myControl = Forms!Customers.CompanyName
```

The purpose of this procedure is to hide the control referenced by the object variable `myControl`. After running the HideControl procedure, switch to the Microsoft Access window containing the open Customers form. The CompanyName control should not be visible on the form.

_____ *To make the CompanyName text box visible again, modify the last line of*
NOTE *this procedure by setting the Visible property of* `myControl` *to True and rerun the procedure.*

_____
SIDEBAR *Advantages of Using Object Variables*

The advantages of object variables are:

■ They can be used instead of the actual object.
■ They are shorter and easier to remember than the actual values they point to.
■ You can change their meaning while your procedure is running.

Disposing of Object Variables

When the object variable is no longer needed, you should assign Nothing to it. This frees up memory and system resources:

```
Set frm = Nothing
Set myControl = Nothing
```

Finding a Variable Definition

When you find an instruction that assigns a value to a variable in a VBA procedure, you can quickly locate the definition of the variable by selecting the variable name and pressing Shift+F2. Alternately, you can choose View | Definition. Visual Basic will jump to the variable declaration line. To return your mouse pointer to its previous position, press Ctrl+Shift+F2 or choose View | Last Position. Let's try it out.

⊙ Hands-On 3.9. Finding a Variable Definition

This hands-on exercise requires prior completion of Hands-On 3.8.

1. Locate the code of the procedure **HideControl** you created in Hands-On 3.8.
2. Locate the statement **myControl.Visible =** .
3. Right-click the **myControl** variable name and choose **Definition** from the shortcut menu.
4. Press **Ctrl+Shift+F2** to return to the previous location in the procedure code (myControl.Visible =).

Determining the Data Type of a Variable

Visual Basic has a built-in `VarType` function that returns an integer indicating the variable's type. Let's see how you can use this function in the Immediate window.

⊙ Hands-On 3.10. Asking Questions about the Variable Type

1. Open the Immediate window (**View | Immediate Window**) and type the following statements that assign values to variables:

```
age = 28
birthdate = #1/1/1981#
firstName = "John"
```

2. Now, ask Visual Basic what type of data each variable holds:

```
?varType(age)
```

When you press **Enter**, Visual Basic returns 2. The number 2 represents the Integer data type, as shown in Table 3.3.

```
?varType(birthdate)
```

Now Visual Basic returns 7 for Date. If you make a mistake in the variable name (let's say you type `birthday` instead of `birthdate`), Visual Basic returns zero (0).

```
?varType(firstName)
```

Visual Basic tells you that the value stored in the `firstName` variable is a String (8).

Table 3.3. Values returned by the `VarType` function.

Constant	Value	Description
vbEmpty	0	Empty (uninitialized)
vbNull	1	Null (no valid data)
vbInteger	2	Integer
vbLong	3	Long integer
vbSingle	4	Single-precision floating-point number
vbDouble	5	Double-precision floating-point number
vbCurrency	6	Currency value
vbDate	7	Date value
vbString	8	String
vbObject	9	Object
vbError	10	Error value
vbBoolean	11	Boolean value
vbVariant	12	Variant (used only with arrays of variants)
vbDataObject	13	Data access object
vbDecimal	14	Decimal value
vbByte	17	Byte value
vbLongLong	20	Long Long integer (on 64-bit platform only)
vbUserDefinedType	36	Variants that contain user-defined types
vbArray	8192	Array

USING CONSTANTS IN VBA PROCEDURES

The value of a variable can change while your procedure is executing. If your procedure needs to refer to unchanged values over and over again, you should use constants. A *constant* is like a named variable that always refers to the same value. Visual Basic requires that you declare constants before you use them.

You declare constants by using the Const statement, as in the following examples:

```
Const dialogName = "Enter Data" As String
Const slsTax = 8.5
Const Discount = 0.5
Const ColorIdx = 3
```

A constant, like a variable, has a scope. To make a constant available within a single procedure, you declare it at the procedure level, just below the name of the procedure—for instance:

```
Sub WedAnniv()
 Const Age As Integer = 25
 ...instructions...
End Sub
```

If you want to use a constant in all the procedures of a module, use the `Private` keyword in front of the `Const` statement—for instance:

```
Private Const dsk = "B: " As String
```

The `Private` constant has to be declared at the top of the module, just before the first `Sub` statement.

If you want to make a constant available to all modules in your application, use the `Public` keyword in front of the `Const` statement—for instance:

```
Public Const NumOfChar As Integer = 255
```

The `Public` constant has to be declared at the top of the module, just before the first `Sub` statement.

When declaring a constant, you can use any one of the following data types: Boolean, Byte, Integer, Long, Currency, Single, Double, Date, String, or Variant.

Like variables, constants can be declared on one line if separated by commas—for instance:

```
Const Age As Integer = 25, PayCheck As Currency = 350
```

Using constants makes your VBA procedures more readable and easier to maintain. For example, if you need to refer to a certain value several times in your procedure, use a constant instead of using a value. This way, if the value changes (e.g., the sales tax rate goes up), you can simply change the value in the declaration of the `Const` statement instead of tracking down every occurrence of the value.

Intrinsic Constants

Both Microsoft Access and Visual Basic for Applications have a long list of predefined (intrinsic) constants that do not need to be declared. These built-in constants can be looked up using the Object Browser window, which was discussed in detail in Chapter 2.

Let's open the Object Browser to take a look at the list of constants in Access.

Hands-On 3.11. Exploring Access's Constants

1. In the Visual Basic Editor window, choose **View | Object Browser**.
2. In the Project/Library list box, click the drop-down arrow and select the **Access** library.

3. Enter **constants** as the search text in the Search Text box and either press **Enter** or click the **Search** button. Visual Basic shows the results of the search in the Search Results area. The right side of the Object Browser window displays a list of all built-in constants available in the Microsoft Access Object Library (see Figure 3.2). Notice that the names of all the constants begin with the prefix "ac."

4. To look up VBA constants, choose **VBA** in the Project/Library list box. Notice that the names of the VBA built-in constants begin with the prefix "vb."

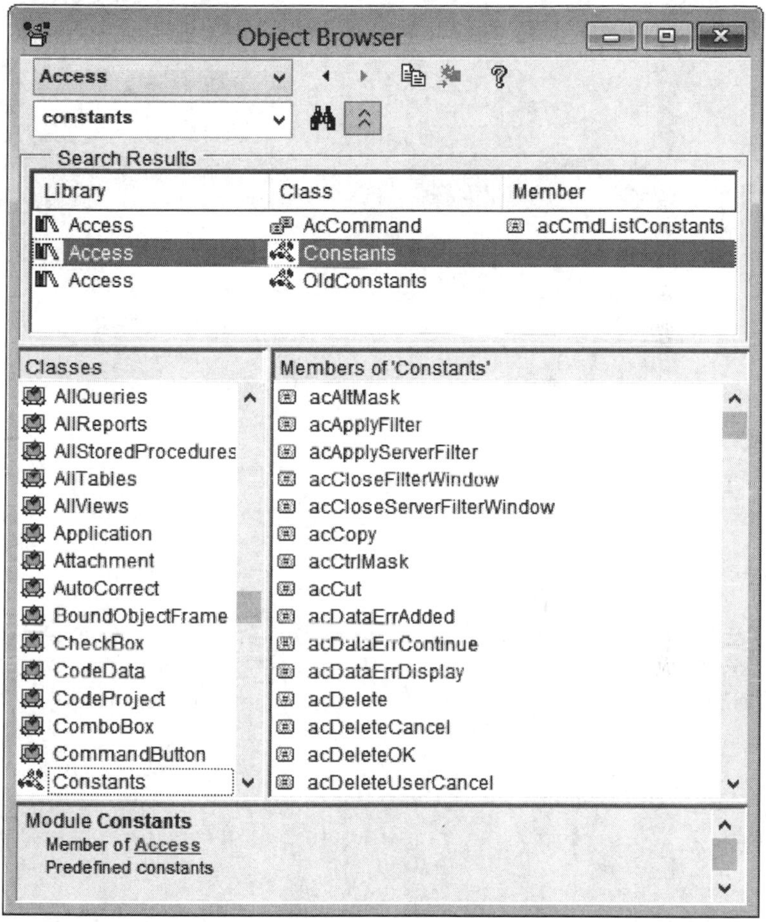

FIGURE 3.2. Use the Object Browser to look up any intrinsic constant.

Hands-On 3.12 illustrates how to use the intrinsic constants `acFilterByForm` and `acFilterAdvanced` to disable execution of filtering on a form.

⊙ Hands-On 3.12. Using Intrinsic Constants in a VBA Procedure

This hands-on exercise uses the HandsOn_03_8.accdb database file used in Hands-On 3.8.

1. Open the **Customers** form in Design view.
2. If the property sheet is not visible, activate it by pressing **Alt+Enter**.
3. In the property sheet, click the **Event** tab. Make sure that **Form** is selected in the drop-down box on the top of the property sheet.
4. Click to the right of the **On Filter** property and select the **Build** button (...).
5. In the Choose Builder dialog box, select **Code Builder** and click **OK**.
6. In the Code window, enter the following **Form_Filter** event procedure code.

```
Private Sub Form_Filter(Cancel As Integer, FilterType As Integer)
  If FilterType = acFilterByForm Or _
   FilterType = acFilterAdvanced Then
    MsgBox "You need authorization to filter records."
    Cancel = True
  End If
End Sub
```

7. Press **Alt+F11** to switch back to Design view in the Customers form.
8. Right-click the Customers form tab and choose **Form View**. You can also use the Views section of the Design tab to activate the Form view.
9. Choose **Home | Sort & Filter | Advanced Filter Options | Filter By Form**.

Access displays the message "You need authorization to filter records." The same message appears when you choose Advanced Filter/Sort from the Advanced Filter Options.

SUMMARY

This chapter has introduced you to several important VBA concepts such as data types, variables, and constants. You learned how to declare various types of variables and define their types. You also saw the difference between a variable and a constant.

In the next chapter, you will expand your knowledge of Visual Basic for Applications by writing procedures and functions with arguments. In addition, you will learn about built-in functions that allow your VBA procedures to interact with users.

CHAPTER 4

ACCESS VBA BUILT-IN AND CUSTOM FUNCTIONS

As you already know from Chapter 1, VBA subroutines and function procedures often require arguments to perform certain tasks. In this chapter, you learn various methods of passing arguments to procedures and functions.

WRITING FUNCTION PROCEDURES

Function procedures can perform calculations based on data received through arguments. When you declare a function procedure, you list the names of arguments inside a set of parentheses, as shown in Hands-On 4.1.

 Please note files for the hands-on project may be found on the companion CD-ROM.

⦿ Hands-On 4.1. Writing a Function Procedure with Arguments

1. Start Microsoft Access and create a new database named **Chap04.accdb** in your **C:\VBAPrimerAccess_ByExample** folder.
2. Once your new database is opened, press **Alt+F11** to switch to the Visual Basic Editor **window.**
3. Choose **Insert | Module** to add a new standard module and notice that Module1 appears under the Modules folder in the Project Explorer window.
4. In the Module1 (Code) window, enter the code of the **JoinText** function procedure as shown here.

```
Function JoinText(k, o)
  JoinText = k + " " + o
End Function
```

Note that there is a space character in quotation marks concatenated between the two arguments of the JoinText function's result: `JoinText = k + " " + o.`

A better way of adding a space is by using one of the following built-in functions:

```
JoinText = k + Space(1) + o
```

or:

```
JoinText = k + Chr(32) + o
```

The `Space` function returns a string of spaces as indicated by the number in the parentheses. The `Chr` function returns a string containing the character associated with the specified character code.

Other control characters you may need to use when writing your VBA procedures include:

Tab	Chr(9)
Linefeed	Chr(10)
Carriage Return	Chr(13)

VARIOUS METHODS OF RUNNING FUNCTION PROCEDURES

You can execute a function procedure from the Immediate window, or you can write a subroutine to call the function. See Hands-On 4.2 and 4.3 for instructions on how to run the JoinText function procedure using these two methods.

Hands-On 4.2. Executing a Function Procedure from the Immediate Window

This hands-on exercise requires prior completion of Hands-On 4.1.

1. Choose **View | Immediate Window** or press **Ctrl+G**, and enter the following statement:

```
?JoinText("function", " procedure")
```

Notice that as soon as you type the opening parenthesis, Visual Basic displays the arguments that the function expects. Type the value of the first argument, enter the comma, and supply the value of the second argument. Finish by entering the closing parenthesis.

2. Press **Enter** to execute this statement from the Immediate window. When you press Enter, the string "function procedure" appears in the Immediate window.

Hands-On 4.3. Executing a Function Procedure from a Subroutine

This hands-on exercise requires prior completion of Hands-On 4.1.

1. In the same module where you entered the JoinText function procedure, enter the following **EnterText** subroutine:

```
Sub EnterText()
  Dim strFirst As String, strLast As String, strFull As String
  strFirst = InputBox("Enter your first name:")
  strLast = InputBox("Enter your last name:")
  strFull = JoinText(strFirst, strLast)

  MsgBox strFull
End Sub
```

2. Place the cursor anywhere inside the code of the EnterText procedure and press **F5** to run it.

As Visual Basic executes the statements of the EnterText procedure, it uses the InputBox function to collect the data from the user, and then stores the data (the values of the first and last names) in the variables strFirst and strLast. Then these values are passed to the JoinText function. Visual Basic substitutes the variables' contents for the arguments of the JoinText function and assigns the result to the name of the function (JoinText). When Visual Basic returns to the EnterText procedure, it stores the function's value in the strFull variable. The MsgBox function then displays the contents of the strFull variable in a message box. The result is the full name of the user (first and last name separated by a space).

SIDEBAR *More about Arguments*

Argument names are like variables. Each argument name refers to whatever value you provide at the time the function is called. You write a subroutine to call a function procedure. When a subroutine calls a function procedure, the required arguments are passed to the procedure as variables. Once the function does something, the result is assigned to the function name. Notice that the function procedure's name is used as if it were a variable.

SPECIFYING THE DATA TYPE FOR A FUNCTION'S RESULT

Like variables, functions can have types. The data type of your function's result can be a String, Integer, Long, and so forth. To specify the data type for your function's result, add the As keyword and the name of the desired data type to the end of the function declaration line—for example:

```
Function MultiplyIt(num1, num2) As Integer
```

If you don't specify the data type, Visual Basic assigns the default type (Variant) to your function's result. When you specify the data type for your function's result, you get the same advantages as when you specify the data type for your variables—your procedure uses memory more efficiently, and therefore runs faster.

Let's take a look at an example of a function that returns an integer, even though the arguments passed to it are declared as Single in a calling subroutine.

◉ Hands-On 4.4. Calling a Function from a Procedure

1. In the Visual Basic Editor window, choose **Insert | Module** to add a new module.
2. Enter the following **HowMuch** subroutine in the Code window:

```
Sub HowMuch()
  Dim num1 As Single
  Dim num2 As Single
  Dim result As Single

  num1 = 45.33
  num2 = 19.24
  result = MultiplyIt(num1, num2)

  MsgBox result
End Sub
```

3. Enter the following **MultiplyIt** function procedure in the Code window below the HowMuch subroutine:

```
Function MultiplyIt(num1, num2) As Integer
  MultiplyIt = num1 * num2
End Function
```

4. Click anywhere within the HowMuch procedure and press **F5** to run it.

   Because the values stored in the variables num1 and num2 are not whole numbers, you may want to assign the Integer type to the result of the function to ensure that the result of the multiplication is a whole number. If you don't assign the data type to the MultiplyIt function's result, the HowMuch procedure will display the result in the data type specified in the declaration line of the result variable. Instead of 872, the result of the multiplication will be 872.1492.

   To make the MultiplyIt function more useful, instead of hard-coding the values to be used in the multiplication, you can pass different values each time you run the procedure by using the InputBox function.

5. Take a few minutes to modify the HowMuch procedure on your own, following the example of the EnterText subroutine that was created in Hands-On 4.3.

6. To pass a specific value from a function to a subroutine, assign the value to the function name. For example, the NumOfDays function shown here passes the value of 7 to the subroutine DaysInAWeek.

```
Function NumOfDays()
  NumOfDays = 7
End Function


Sub DaysInAWeek()
  MsgBox "There are " & NumOfDays & " days in a week."
End Sub
```

Subroutines or Functions: Which Should You Use?

Create a subroutine when you:

■ Want to perform some actions
■ Want to get input from the user
■ Want to display a message on the screen

Create a function when you:

■ Want to perform a simple calculation more than once
■ Must perform complex computations
■ Must call the same block of instructions more than once
■ Want to check whether a certain expression is true or false

PASSING ARGUMENTS TO BY REFERENCE AND BY VALUE

In some procedures, when you pass arguments as variables, Visual Basic can suddenly change the value of the variables. To ensure that the called function procedure does not alter the value of the passed arguments, you should precede the name of the argument in the function's declaration line with the `ByVal` keyword. Let's practice this in the following example.

(◉) **Hands-On 4.5. Passing Arguments to Subroutines and Functions**

1. In the Visual Basic Editor window, choose **Insert | Module** to add a new module.
2. In the Code window, type the following **ThreeNumbers** subroutine and the **MyAverage** function procedure:

```
Sub ThreeNumbers()
    Dim num1 As Integer, num2 As Integer, num3 As Integer
    num1 = 10
    num2 = 20
    num3 = 30

    MsgBox MyAverage(num1, num2, num3)
    MsgBox num1
    MsgBox num2
    MsgBox num3
End Sub

Function MyAverage(ByVal num1, ByVal num2, ByVal num3)
    num1 = num1 + 1
    MyAverage = (num1 + num2 + num3) / 3
End Function
```

3. Click anywhere within the ThreeNumbers procedure and press **F5** to run it.
   The ThreeNumbers procedure assigns values to three variables, and then calls the MyAverage function to calculate and return the average of the numbers stored

in these variables. The function's arguments are the names of the variables: num1, num2, and num3. Notice that all variable names are preceded with the ByVal keyword. Also, notice that prior to the calculation of the average, the MyAverage function changes the value of the num1 variable. Inside the function procedure, the num1 variable equals 11 (10 + 1). Therefore, when the function passes the calculated average to the ThreeNumbers procedure, the MsgBox function displays the result as 20.3333333333333 and not 20, as expected. The next three functions show the contents of each of the variables. The values stored in these variables are the same as the original values assigned to them: 10, 20, and 30.

What will happen if you omit the ByVal keyword in front of the num11 argument in the MyAverage function's declaration line? The function's result will still be the same, but the content of the num1 variable displayed by the MsgBox num1 is now 11. The MyAverage function has not only returned an unexpected result (20.3333333333333 instead of 20), but also modified the original data stored in the num1 variable. To prevent Visual Basic from permanently changing the values supplied to the function, use the ByVal keyword.

SIDEBAR   *Know Your Keywords: ByRef and ByVal*

Because any of the variables passed to a function procedure (or a subroutine) can be changed by the receiving procedure, it is important to know how to protect the original value of a variable. Visual Basic has two keywords that give or deny the permission to change the contents of a variable: ByRef *and* ByVal.

By default, Visual Basic passes information to a function procedure (or a subroutine) by reference (ByRef keyword), referring to the original data specified in the function's argument at the time the function is called. So, if the function alters the value of the argument, the original value is changed. You will get this result if you omit the ByVal keyword in front of the num1 argument in the MyAverage function's declaration line. If you want the function procedure to change the original value, you don't need to explicitly insert the ByRef keyword because passed variables default to ByRef.

When you use the ByVal keyword in front of an argument name, Visual Basic passes the argument by value, which means that Visual Basic makes a copy of the original data. This copy is then passed to a function. If the function changes the value of an argument passed by value, the original data does not change—only the copy changes. That's why when the MyAverage function changed the value of the num1 argument, the original value of the num1 variable remained the same.

USING OPTIONAL ARGUMENTS

At times, you may want to supply an additional value to a function. Let's say you have a function that calculates the price of a meal per person. Sometimes, however, you'd like the function to perform the same calculation for a group of two or more people. To indicate that a procedure argument isn't always required, precede the name of the argument with the `Optional` keyword. Arguments that are optional come at the end of the argument list, following the names of all the required arguments. Optional arguments must always be the Variant data type. This means that you can't specify the optional argument's type by using the `As` keyword.

In the preceding section, you created a function to calculate the average of three numbers. Suppose that sometimes you would like to use this function to calculate the average of two numbers. You could define the third argument of the MyAverage function as optional. To preserve the original MyAverage function, let's create the Avg function to calculate the average for two or three numbers.

(•) Hands-On 4.6. Using Optional Arguments

1. In the Visual Basic Editor window, choose **Insert | Module** to add a new module.
2. Type the following **Avg** function procedure in the Code window:

```
Function Avg(num1, num2, Optional num3)
    Dim totalNums As Integer

    totalNums = 3
    If IsMissing(num3) Then
    num3 = 0
    totalNums = totalNums - 1
    End If
    Avg = (num1 + num2 + num3) / totalNums
End Function
```

3. Call this function from the Immediate window by entering the following instruction and pressing **Enter**:

```
?Avg(2, 3)
```

As soon as you press Enter, Visual Basic displays the result: 2.5.
4. Now, type the following instruction and press **Enter**:

```
?Avg(2, 3, 5)
```

This time the result is: 3.3333333333333.

As you've seen, the Avg function is used to calculate the average of two or three numbers. You decide what values and how many values (two or three) you want to average. When you start typing the values for the function's arguments in the Immediate window, Visual Basic displays the name of the optional argument enclosed in square brackets.

Let's take a few minutes to analyze the Avg function. This function can take up to three arguments. Arguments `num1` and `num2` are required. Argument `num3` is optional. Notice that the name of the optional argument is preceded by the `Optional` keyword. The optional argument is listed at the end of the argument list. Because the types of the `num1`, `num2`, and `num3` arguments are not declared, Visual Basic treats all three arguments as Variants.

Inside the function procedure, the `totalNums` variable is declared as an Integer and then assigned a beginning value of 3. Because the function has to be capable of calculating an average of two or three numbers, the handy built-in function `IsMissing` checks for the number of supplied arguments. If the third (optional) argument is not supplied, the `IsMissing` function puts the value of zero (0) in its place, and deducts the value of 1 from the value stored in the `totalNums` variable. Hence, if the optional argument is missing, `totalNums` is 2. The next statement calculates the average based on the supplied data, and the result is assigned to the name of the function.

USING THE ISMISSING FUNCTION

The `IsMissing` function called from within Hands-On 4.6 allows you to determine whether the optional argument was supplied. This function returns the logical value of True if the third argument is not supplied, and returns False when the third argument is given. The `IsMissing` function is used here with the decision-making statement `If...Then` (discussed in Chapter 5). If the `num3` argument is missing (`IsMissing`), then Visual Basic supplies a zero (0) for the value of the third argument (`num3 = 0`), and reduces the value stored in the argument `totalNums` by 1 (`totalNums = totalNums - 1`).

USING VBA BUILT-IN FUNCTIONS FOR USER INTERACTION

VBA comes with numerous built-in functions that can be looked up in the Visual Basic online help. To access an alphabetical listing of all VBA functions, choose Help | Microsoft Visual Basic for Applications Help in the Visual Basic Editor window. In the Table of Contents, choose Visual Basic for Applications Language Reference | Visual Basic Language Reference | Functions. Each function is described in detail, and is often illustrated with a code fragment or a complete function procedure that shows how to use it in a specific context. After completing this chapter, be sure to launch the VBA help, and browse through the built-in functions to familiarize yourself with their names and usage. You can also search for the function name in your favorite browser to get more information.

> **NOTE**
> *If you are working with Access via the Office 365 subscription service, you will need an active Internet connection to access the Visual Basic for Applications language reference for Microsoft Office 2013 and later. You will find the list of all VBA functions under this link:*
> *http://msdn.microsoft.com/en-us/library/office/jj692811.aspx*
> *The following link will bring up the Office VBA language reference:*
> *http://msdn.microsoft.com/en-us/library/office/gg264383.aspx*

One of the features of a good program is its interaction with the user. When you work with Microsoft Access, you interact with the application by using various dialog boxes, such as message boxes and input boxes. When you write your own procedures, you can use the `MsgBox` function to inform users about an unexpected error or the result of a specific calculation. So far you have seen a simple implementation of this function. In the next section, you will find out how to control the appearance of your message. Then you will learn how to get information from the user with the `InputBox` function.

Using the MsgBox Function

The `MsgBox` function you have used thus far was limited to displaying a message to the user in a simple, one-button dialog box. You closed the message box by clicking the OK button or pressing the Enter key. You can create a simple message box by following the `MsgBox` function name with the text of the message enclosed in quotation marks. In other words, to display the message "The procedure is complete." you use the following statement:

```
MsgBox "The procedure is complete."
```

You can try this instruction by entering it in the Immediate window. When you type this instruction and press Enter, Visual Basic displays the message box shown in Figure 4.1.

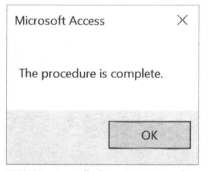

FIGURE 4.1. To display a message to the user, place the text as the argument of the MsgBox function.

The `MsgBox` function allows you to use other arguments that make it possible to determine the number of buttons that should be available in the message box or to change the title of the message box from the default. You can also assign your own help topic. The syntax of the `MsgBox` function is shown here.

```
MsgBox (prompt [, buttons] [, title], [, helpfile, context])
```

Notice that while the `MsgBox` function has five arguments, only the first one, `prompt`, is required. The arguments listed in square brackets are optional.

When you enter a long text string for the `prompt` argument, Visual Basic decides how to break the text so it fits the message box. Let's do some exercises in the Immediate window to learn various text formatting techniques.

 Hands-On 4.7. Formatting the Message Box

1. In the Visual Basic Editor window, activate the Immediate window and enter the following instruction. Be sure to enter the entire text string on one line, and then press **Enter**.

```
MsgBox "All done. Now open ""Test.doc"" and place an empty CD
or DVD in your computer's CD/DVD drive. The following procedure
will copy this file to the disc."
```

As soon as you press **Enter**, Visual Basic shows the resulting dialog box (see Figure 4.2). If you get a compile error, click **OK**. Then make sure that the name of the file is surrounded by double quotation marks (`""Test.doc""`).

Microsoft Access	✕

All done. Now open "Test.doc" and place an empty CD or DVD in your computer's CD/DVD drive. The following procedure will copy this file to the disc.

OK

FIGURE 4.2. This long message will look more appealing to the user when you take the text formatting into your own hands.

When the text of your message is particularly long, you can break it into several lines using the VBA `Chr` function. The `Chr` function's argument is a number from 0 to 255, which returns a character represented by this number. For example, `Chr(13)` returns a carriage return character (this is the same as pressing the Enter key), and `Chr(10)` returns a linefeed character (this is useful for adding spacing between the text lines).

2. Modify the instruction entered in the previous step in the following way and make sure it stays on the same line in the Immediate window:

```
MsgBox "All done." & Chr(13) & "Now open ""Test.doc"" and place
an empty" & Chr(13) & "CD or DVD in your computer's CD/DVD
drive." & Chr(13) & "The following procedure will copy this
file to the disc."
```

Your result should look like Figure 4.3.

FIGURE 4.3. You can break a long text string into several lines by using the Chr(13) function.

You must surround each text fragment with quotation marks. Quoted text embedded in a text string requires an additional set of quotation marks, as in `""Test.doc""`. The `Chr(13)` function indicates a place where you'd like to start a new line. The concatenate character (&) is used to combine the strings. When you enter exceptionally long text messages on one line, it's easy to make a mistake. An underscore (_) is a special line continuation character in VBA that allows you to break a long VBA statement into several lines. Unfortunately, the line continuation character cannot be used in the Immediate window. A better place to try out various formatting of your long strings for the MsgBox function is within a VBA procedure.

3. Add a new module by choosing **Insert | Module**.

4. In the Code window, enter the following **MyMessage** subroutine. Be sure to precede each line continuation character (_) with a space.

```
Sub MyMessage()
    MsgBox "All done." & Chr(13) _
    & "Now open ""Test.doc"" and place an empty" & Chr(13) _
    & "CD or DVD in your computer's CD/DVD drive." & Chr(13) _
    & "The following procedure will copy this file to the disc."
End Sub
```

5. Position the insertion point within the code of the MyMessage procedure and press **F5** to run it.

When you run the MyMessage procedure, Visual Basic displays the same message as the one illustrated earlier in Figure 4.3.

As you can see, the text entered on several lines is more readable, and the code is easier to maintain. To improve the readability of your message, you may want to add more spacing between the text lines by including blank lines. To do this, use two `Chr(13)` functions, as shown in the following step.

6. Enter the following **MyMessage2** procedure:

```
Sub MyMessage2()
    MsgBox "All done." & Chr(13) & Chr(13) _
    & "Now open ""Test.doc"" and place an empty" & Chr(13) _
    & "CD or DVD in your computer's CD/DVD drive." & Chr(13) _
    & Chr(13) & "The following procedure will copy this " & _
    "file to the disc."
End Sub
```

7. Position the insertion point within the code of the MyMessage2 procedure and press **F5** to run it. The result should look like Figure 4.4.

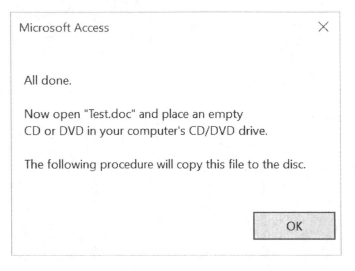

FIGURE 4.4. You can increase the readability of your message by increasing spacing between selected text lines.

Now that you have mastered the text formatting techniques, let's take a closer look at the next argument of the MsgBox function. Although the buttons argument is optional, it is frequently used. The buttons argument specifies how many and what types of buttons you want to appear in the message box. This argument can be a constant or a number (see Table 4.1). If you omit this argument, the resulting message box contains only the OK button, as you've seen in the preceding examples.

Table 4.1. The MsgBox buttons argument settings.

Constant	Value	Description
	Button settings	
vbOKOnly	0	Displays only an OK button. This is the default.
vbOKCancel	1	OK and Cancel buttons
vbAbortRetryIgnore	2	Abort, Retry, and Ignore buttons

Constant	Value	Description
vbYesNoCancel	3	Yes, No, and Cancel buttons
vbYesNo	4	Yes and No buttons
vbRetryCancel	5	Retry and Cancel buttons
Icon settings		
vbCritical	16	Displays the Critical Message icon
vbQuestion	32	Displays the Question Message icon
vbExclamation	48	Displays the Warning Message icon
vbInformation	64	Displays the Information Message icon
Default button settings		
vbDefaultButton1	0	The first button is default.
vbDefaultButton2	256	The second button is default.
vbDefaultButton3	512	The third button is default.
vbDefaultButton4	768	The fourth button is default.
Message box modality		
vbApplicationModal	0	The user must respond to the message before continuing to work in the current application.
vbSystemModal	4096	On Win16 systems, this constant is used to prevent the user from inter- acting with any other window until he or she dismisses the message box. On Win32 systems, this constant works like the vbApplication- Modal constant with the following exception: The message box always remains on top of any other programs you may have running.
Other MsgBox display settings		
vbMsgBoxHelpButton	16384	Adds the Help button to the message box
vbMsgBoxSetForeground	65536	Specifies the message box window as the foreground window
vbMsgBoxRight	524288	Text is right-aligned.
vbMsgBoxRtlReading	1048576	Text appears as right-to-left reading on Hebrew and Arabic systems.

When should you use the `buttons` argument? Suppose you want the user of your procedure to respond to a question with Yes or No. Your message box will then require two buttons. If a message box includes more than one button, one of them is considered a default button. When the user presses Enter, the default button is selected automatically.

Because you can display various types of messages (critical, warning, information), you can visually indicate the importance of the message by including the graphical representation (icon). In addition to the type of message, the `buttons` argument can include a setting to determine whether the message box must be closed before the user switches to another application. It's quite possible that the user may want to switch to another program or perform another task before he responds to the question posed in your message box. If the message box is application modal (`vbApplicationModal`), then the user must close the message box before continuing to use your application.

For example, consider the following message box:

```
MsgBox "How are you?", vbOKOnly + vbApplicationModal, "Please
Close Me"
```

If you type the preceding statement in the Immediate window and press Enter, a message box will pop up and you won't be able to work with your currently open Microsoft Access application until you respond to the message box.

On the other hand, if you want to keep the message box visible while the user works with other open applications, you must include the `vbSystemModal` setting in the `buttons` argument, like this:

```
MsgBox "How are you?", vbOKOnly + vbSystemModal, "System Modal"
```

_____ *Use the* `vbSystemModal` *constant when you want to ensure*
NOTE *that your message box is always visible (not hidden behind other windows).*

The `buttons` argument settings are divided into five groups: button settings, icon settings, default button settings, message box modality, and other `MsgBox` display settings (see Table 4.1). Only one setting from each group can be included in the `buttons` argument. To create a `buttons` argument, you can add up the values for each setting you want to include. For example, to display a message box with two buttons (Yes and No), the question mark icon, and the No button as the default button, look up the corresponding values in Table 4.1, and add them up. You should arrive at 292 (4 + 32 + 256).

To see the message box using the calculated message box argument, enter the following statement in the Immediate window:

```
MsgBox "Do you want to proceed?", 292
```

The resulting message box is shown in Figure 4.5.

FIGURE 4.5. You can specify the number of buttons to include, their text, and an icon in the message box by using the optional buttons argument.

When you derive the `buttons` argument by adding up the constant values, your procedure becomes less readable. There's no reference table where you can check the hidden meaning of 292. To improve the readability of your `MsgBox` function, it's better to use the constants instead of their values. For example, enter the following revised statement in the Immediate window:

```
MsgBox "Do you want to proceed?", vbYesNo + vbQuestion +
vbDefaultButton2
```

The preceding statement produces the result shown in Figure 4.5. The following example shows how to use the `buttons` argument inside a Visual Basic procedure.

⊙ Hands-On 4.8. Using the MsgBox Function with Arguments

1. In the Visual Basic Editor window, choose **Insert | Module** to add a new module.
2. In the Code window, enter the **MsgYesNo** subroutine shown here:

```
Sub MsgYesNo()
   Dim question As String
   Dim myButtons As Integer

   question = "Do you want to open a new report?"
   myButtons = vbYesNo + vbQuestion + vbDefaultButton2
   MsgBox question, myButtons
End Sub
```

3. Run the MsgYesNo procedure by pressing **F5**.

In this subroutine, the `question` variable stores the text of your message. The settings for the `buttons` argument are placed in the `myButtons` variable. Instead of using the names of constants, you can use their values, as in the following:

```
myButtons = 4 + 32 + 256
```

The `question` and `myButtons` variables are used as arguments for the `MsgBox` function. When you run the procedure, you see a result similar to the one shown in Figure 4.5. Note that the No button is selected, indicating that it's the default button for this dialog box. If you press Enter, Visual Basic removes the message box from the screen. Nothing happens because your procedure does not have any instructions following the `MsgBox` function. To change the default button, use the `vbDefaultButton1` setting instead.

The third argument of the `MsgBox` function is `title`. While this is also an optional argument, it's very handy because it allows you to create procedures that don't provide visual clues to the fact that you programmed them with Microsoft Access. Using this argument, you can set the titlebar of your message box to any text you want.

Suppose you want the MsgYesNo procedure to display the text "New report" in its title. The following MsgYesNo2 procedure demonstrates the use of the `title` argument.

```
Sub MsgYesNo2()
  Dim question As String
  Dim myButtons As Integer
  Dim myTitle As String

  question = "Do you want to open a new report?"
  myButtons = vbYesNo + vbQuestion + vbDefaultButton2
  myTitle = "New report"
  MsgBox question, myButtons, myTitle
End Sub
```

The text for the `title` argument is stored in the `myTitle` variable. If you don't specify the value for the `title` argument, Visual Basic displays the default text "Microsoft Access." Notice that the arguments are listed in the order determined by the `MsgBox` function.

If you would like to list the arguments in any order, you must precede the value of each argument with its name, as shown here:

```
MsgBox title:=myTitle, prompt:=question, buttons:=myButtons
```

The last two `MsgBox` arguments, `helpfile` and `context`, are used by more advanced programmers who are experienced with using help files in the Windows environment. The `helpfile` argument indicates the name of a special help file that contains additional information you may want to display to your VBA application user. When you specify this argument, the Help button will be added to your message box. When you use the `helpfile` argument, you must also use the `context` argument. This argument indicates which help subject in the specified help file you want to display. Suppose HelpX.hlp is the help file you created and 55 is the context topic you want to use. To include this information in your `MsgBox` function, you would use the following instruction:

```
MsgBox title:=myTitle, _
  prompt:=question, _
  buttons:=myButtons, _
```

```
helpfile:= "HelpX.hlp", _
context:=55
```

The preceding is a single VBA statement broken down into several lines using the line continuation character.

Returning Values from the MsgBox Function

When you display a simple message box dialog with one button, clicking the OK button or pressing the Enter key removes the message box from the screen. However, when the message box has more than one button, your procedure should detect which button was pressed. To do this, you must save the result of the message box in a variable. Table 4.2 lists values that the `MsgBox` function returns.

Table 4.2. Values returned by the `MsgBox` function.

Button Selected	Constant	Value
OK	vbOK	1
Cancel	vbCancel	2
Abort	vbAbort	3
Retry	vbRetry	4
Ignore	vbIgnore	5
Yes	vbYes	6
No	vbNo	7

The MsgYesNo3 procedure in Hands-On 4.9 is a revised version of MsgYesNo2. It demonstrates how to store the user's response in a variable.

Hands-On 4.9. Returning Values from the MsgBox Function

1. In the Visual Basic Editor window, choose **Insert | Module** to add a new module.
2. In the Code window, enter the following code of the **MsgYesNo3** procedure:

```
Sub MsgYesNo3()
    Dim question As String
    Dim myButtons As Integer
    Dim myTitle As String
    Dim myChoice As Integer

    question = "Do you want to open a new report?"
    myButtons = vbYesNo + vbQuestion + vbDefaultButton2
    myTitle = "New report"
    myChoice = MsgBox(question, myButtons, myTitle)
    MsgBox myChoice
End Sub
```

3. Position the insertion point within the MsgYesNo3 procedure and press **F5** to run it.

In this procedure, you assigned the result of the MsgBox function to the variable myChoice. Notice that the arguments of the MsgBox function are now listed in parentheses:

```
myChoice = MsgBox(question, myButtons, myTitle)
```

When you run the MsgYesNo3 procedure, a two-button message box is displayed. By clicking on the Yes button, the statement MsgBox myChoice displays the number 6. When you click the No button, the number 7 is displayed.

SIDEBAR *MsgBox Function—With or without Parentheses?*

Use parentheses around the MsgBox function argument list when you want to use the result returned by the function. By listing the function's arguments without parentheses, you tell Visual Basic that you want to ignore the function's result. Most likely, you will want to use the function's result when the message box contains more than one button.

Using the InputBox Function

The InputBox function displays a dialog box with a message that prompts the user to enter data. This dialog box has two buttons: OK and Cancel. When you click OK, the InputBox function returns the information entered in the text box. When you select Cancel, the function returns the empty string (""). The syntax of the InputBox function is as follows:

```
InputBox(prompt [, title] [, default] [, xpos] [, ypos]
  [, helpfile, context])
```

The first argument, prompt, is the text message you want to display in the dialog box. Long text strings can be entered on several lines by using the Chr(13) or Chr(10) functions. (See examples of using the MsgBox function earlier in this chapter.) All the remaining InputBox arguments are optional.

The second argument, title, allows you to change the default title of the dialog box. The default value is "Microsoft Access."

The third argument of the InputBox function, default, allows the display of a default value in the text box. If you omit this argument, the empty text box is displayed.

The following two arguments, xpos and ypos, let you specify the exact position where the dialog box should appear on the screen. If you omit these arguments, the input box appears in the middle of the current window. The xpos argument determines the horizontal position of the dialog box from the left edge of the screen. When omitted, the dialog box is centered horizontally. The ypos argument determines the vertical position from the top of the screen. If you omit this argument, the dialog box is positioned vertically approximately one-third of the way down the screen. Both xpos and ypos are measured in special units called *twips*. One twip is the equivalent of approximately 0.0007 inches.

The last two arguments, `helpfile` and `context`, are used in the same way as the corresponding arguments of the `MsgBox` function discussed earlier in this chapter.

Now that you know the meaning of the `InputBox` arguments, let's see some examples of using this function.

(⊙) Hands-On 4.10. Using the InputBox Function

1. In the Visual Basic Editor window, choose **Insert | Module** to add a new module.
2. In the Code window, type the following **Informant** subroutine:

```
Sub Informant()
  InputBox prompt:="Enter your place of birth:" & Chr(13) _
  & " (e.g., Boston, Great Falls, etc.) "
End Sub
```

3. Position the insertion point within the Informant procedure and press **F5** to run it.

This procedure displays a dialog box with two buttons. The input prompt is displayed on two lines (see Figure 4.6). Similar to using the `MsgBox` function, if you plan on using the data entered by the user in the dialog box, you should store the result of the `InputBox` function in a variable.

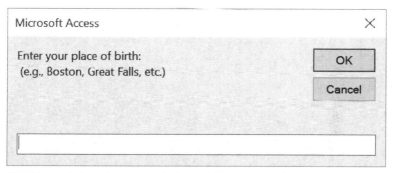

FIGURE 4.6. A dialog box generated by the Informant procedure.

4. Now, in the same module, enter the following code of the **Informant2** procedure:

```
Sub Informant2()
  Dim myPrompt As String
  Dim town As String

  Const myTitle = "Enter data"
  myPrompt = "Enter your place of birth:" & Chr(13) _
  & "(e.g., Boston, Great Falls, etc.)"
  town = InputBox(myPrompt, myTitle)

  MsgBox "You were born in " & town & ".", , "Your response"
End Sub
```

5. Position the insertion point within the Informant2 procedure and press **F5** to run it.

Notice that the Informant2 procedure assigns the result of the `InputBox` function to the `town` variable.

This time, the arguments of the `InputBox` function are listed in parentheses. Parentheses are required if you want to use the result of the `InputBox` function later in your procedure. The Informant2 subroutine uses a constant to specify the text to appear in the titlebar of the dialog box. Because the constant value remains the same throughout the execution of your procedure, you can declare the input box title as a constant. However, if you'd rather use a variable, you still can.

When you run a procedure using the `InputBox` function, the dialog box generated by this function always appears in the same area of the screen. To change the location of the dialog box, you must supply the `xpos` and `ypos` arguments, which were explained earlier.

6. To display the dialog box in the top left-hand corner of the screen, modify the `InputBox` function in the Informant2 procedure as follows:

```
town = InputBox(myPrompt, myTitle, , 1, 200)
```

Notice that the argument `myTitle` is followed by two commas. The second comma marks the position of the omitted `default` argument. The next two arguments determine the horizontal and vertical position of the dialog box. If you omit the second comma after the `myTitle` argument, Visual Basic will use the number 1 as the value of the `default` argument. If you precede the values of arguments by their names (e.g., `prompt:=myPrompt`, `title:=myTitle, xpos:=1, ypos:=200`), you won't have to remember to insert a comma in the place of each omitted argument.

What will happen if, instead of the name of a town, you enter a number? Because users often supply incorrect data in the input box, your procedure must verify that the data the user entered can be used in further data manipulations. The `InputBox` function itself does not provide a facility for data validation. To validate user input, you must use other VBA instructions, which are discussed in Chapter 5.

CONVERTING DATA TYPES

The result of the `InputBox` function is always a string. So if a user enters a number, its *string* value must be converted to a *numeric* value before your procedure can use the number in mathematical computations. Visual Basic is able to automatically convert many values from one data type to another.

⦿ Hands-On 4.11. Converting Data Types

1. In the Visual Basic Editor window, choose **Insert | Module** to add a new module.

2. In the Code window, enter the following **AddTwoNums** procedure:

```
Sub AddTwoNums()
    Dim myPrompt As String
    Dim value1 As String
    Dim mySum As Single

    Const myTitle = "Enter data"

    myPrompt = "Enter a number:"
    value1 = InputBox(myPrompt, myTitle, 0)
    mySum = value1 + 2

    MsgBox mySum & " (" & value1 & " + 2)"
End Sub
```

3. Place the cursor anywhere inside the code of the AddTwoNums procedure and press **F5** to run it.

This procedure displays the dialog box shown in Figure 4.7. Notice that this dialog box has two special features that are obtained by using the `InputBox` function's optional arguments: `title` and `default`. Instead of the default title "Microsoft Access," the dialog box displays a text string as defined by the contents of the `myTitle` constant. The zero (0) entered as the default value in the edit box suggests that the user enter a number instead of text. Once the user provides the data and clicks OK, the input is assigned to the variable `value1`.

```
value1 = InputBox(myPrompt, myTitle, 0)
```

FIGURE 4.7. To suggest that the user enter a specific type of data, you may want to provide a default value in the edit box.

The data type of the variable `value1` is String. You can check the data type easily if you follow the preceding instruction with this statement:

```
MsgBox varType(value1)
```

When Visual Basic runs this line, it will display a message box with the number 8. Recall that this number represents the String data type. The next line,

```
mySum = value1 + 2
```

adds 2 to the user's input and assigns the result of the calculation to the variable mySum. Because the value1 variable's data type is String, Visual Basic goes to work behind the scenes to perform the data type conversion. Visual Basic has the brains to understand the need for conversion. Without it, the two incompatible data types (text and number) would generate a Type Mismatch error.

The procedure ends with the MsgBox function displaying the result of the calculation and showing the user how the total was derived.

SIDEBAR *Define a Constant*

> To ensure that all the titlebars in a particular VBA procedure display the same text, assign the title text to a constant. By doing so, you will save yourself the time of typing the title text in more than one place.

SUMMARY

In this chapter, you learned the difference between subroutine procedures that perform actions and function procedures that return values. You saw examples of function procedures called from another Visual Basic procedure. You learned how to pass arguments to functions and how to determine the data type of a function's result. You increased your repertoire of VBA keywords with the ByVal, ByRef, and Optional keywords.

After working through this chapter, you should be able to create some custom functions of your own that are suited to your specific needs. You should also be able to interact easily with your users by employing the MsgBox and InputBox functions.

In the next chapter you learn how to make decisions in your VBA programs.

CHAPTER **5**

ADDING DECISIONS TO YOUR ACCESS VBA PROGRAMS

V isual Basic for Applications offers special statements called conditional statements, or "control structures," which allow you to include decision points in your procedures. In a conditional expression, a relational operator (see Table 5.1), a logical operator (see Table 5.2), or a combination of both evaluates the expression to determine whether it is true or false. If the answer is true, the procedure executes a specified block of instructions. If the answer is false, the procedure either executes a different block of instructions or simply doesn't do anything. In this chapter, you will learn how to use these VBA conditional statements to alter the flow of your program.

RELATIONAL AND LOGICAL OPERATORS

You can make decisions in your VBA procedures by using conditional expressions inside the special control structures. A *conditional expression* is an expression that uses a relational operator (see Table 5.1), a logical operator (see Table 5.2), or a combination of both. When Visual Basic encounters a conditional expression in your program, it evaluates the expression to determine whether it is true or false.

Table 5.1. Relational operators in VBA.

Operator	Description
=	Equal to
<>	Not equal to
>	Greater than
<	Less than

Operator	Description
>=	Greater than or equal to
<=	Less than or equal to

Table 5.2. Logical operators in VBA.

Operator	Description
AND	All conditions must be true before an action can be taken.
OR	At least one of the conditions must be true before an action can be taken.
NOT	If a condition is true, NOT makes it false. If a condition is false, NOT makes it true.

SIDEBAR *Boolean Expressions*

    Conditional expressions and logical operators are also known as Boolean. George Boole was a nineteenth-century British mathematician who made significant contributions to the evolution of computer programming. Boolean expressions can be evaluated as true or false.

For example:

One meter equals 10 inches.	False
Two is less than three.	True

IF...THEN STATEMENT

    The simplest way to get some decision making into your VBA procedure is by using the If...Then statement. Suppose you want to choose an action depending on a condition. You can use the following structure:

```
If condition Then statement
```

    For example, a quiz procedure might ask the user to guess the number of weeks in a year. If the user's response is other than 52, the procedure should display the message "Try Again."

 Please note files for the hands-on project may be found on the companion CD-ROM.

⊙ Hands-On 5.1. Using the If...Then Statement

1. Start Microsoft Access and create a new database named **Chap05.accdb** in your **C:\VBAPrimerAccess_ByExample** folder.
2. Once your new database is opened, press **Alt+F11** to switch to the Visual Basic Editor window.
3. Choose **Insert | Module** to add a new standard module.
   In the Module1 Code window, enter the following **Simple If Then** procedure:

```
Sub SimpleIfThen()
  Dim weeks As String

  weeks = InputBox("How many weeks are in a year:", "Quiz")
  If weeks<>52 Then MsgBox "Try Again"
End Sub
```

The SimpleIfThen procedure stores the user's answer in the weeks variable. The variable's value is then compared with the number 52. If the result
of the comparison is true (i.e., if the value stored in the variable weeks is not
equal to 52), Visual Basic will display the message "Try Again."
4. Run the SimpleIfThen procedure and enter a number other than 52.
5. Rerun the SimpleIfThen procedure and enter the number **52**. When you
enter the correct number of weeks, Visual Basic does nothing. The procedure
ends. It would be nice to also display a message when the user guesses right.
6. Enter the following instruction on a separate line before the End Sub keywords:

```
If weeks = 52 Then MsgBox "Congratulations!"
```

7. Run the SimpleIfThen procedure again and enter the number **52**. When you
enter the correct answer, Visual Basic does not execute the "Try Again" statement. When the procedure is executed, the statement to the right of the Then
keyword is ignored if the result from evaluating the supplied condition is false.
As you recall, a VBA procedure can call another procedure. Let's see if it can
also call itself.
8. Modify the first If statement in the SimpleIfThen procedure as follows:

```
If weeks <> 52 Then MsgBox "Try Again" : SimpleIfThen
```

We added a colon and the name of the SimpleIfThen procedure to the end
of the existing If...Then statement. If you enter the incorrect answer, you'll
see a message. After clicking the OK button in the message box, you'll get
another chance to supply the correct answer. You'll be able to keep on guessing
for a long time. In fact, you won't be able to exit the procedure gracefully until
you've supplied the correct answer. After clicking Cancel, you'll have to deal
with the unfriendly "Type Mismatch" error message. For now (until you learn
other ways of handling errors in VBA), let's revise your SimpleIfThen procedure as follows:

```
Sub SimpleIfThen()
  Dim weeks As String

  On Error GoTo VeryEnd

  weeks = InputBox("How many weeks are in a year:", "Quiz")
  If weeks <> 52 Then MsgBox "Try Again" : SimpleIfThen
  If weeks = 52 Then MsgBox "Congratulations!"

  VeryEnd:
End Sub
```

If Visual Basic encounters an error, it will jump to the `VeryEnd` label placed at the end of the procedure. The statements placed between `On Error GoTo VeryEnd` and the `VeryEnd` labels are ignored. Later in this chapter you will find other examples of trapping errors in your VBA procedures.

9. Run your revised SimpleIfThen procedure a few times by supplying incorrect answers. The error trap that you added to your procedure will allow you to quit guessing without having to deal with the ugly error message.

MULTILINE IF...THEN STATEMENT

Sometimes you may want to perform several actions when the condition is true. Although you could add other statements on the same line by separating them with colons, your code will look clearer if you use the multiline version of the `If`...Then statement, as shown here:

```
If condition Then
    statement1
    statement2
    statementN
End If
```

For example, let's modify the SimpleIfThen procedure to include additional statements.

(◉) Hands-On 5.2. Using the Multiline If...Then Statement

1. Insert a new module and enter the following **SimpleIfThen2** procedure:

```
Sub SimpleIfThen2()
    Dim weeks As String
    Dim response As String

    On Error GoTo VeryEnd
    weeks = InputBox("How many weeks are in a year?", "Quiz")
    If weeks <> 52 Then
    response = MsgBox("This is incorrect. Would you like " _
& " to try again?", vbYesNo + vbInformation _
        + vbDefaultButton1, _
        "Continue Quiz?")
    If response = vbYes Then
        Call SimpleIfThen2
    End If
    End If
    VeryEnd:
End Sub
```

2. Run the SimpleIfThen2 procedure and enter any number other than 52.

In this example, the statements between the first `Then` and the first `End If` keywords don't get executed if the variable `weeks` is equal to 52. Notice that the multiline If...Then statement must end with the keywords End If. How does Visual Basic make a decision? Simply put, it evaluates the condition it finds between the If...Then keywords.

Two Formats of the If...Then Statement

The If...Then statement has two formats: a single-line format and a multiline format. The short format is good for statements that fit on one line, like:

```
If secretCode <> "01W01" Then MsgBox "Access denied"
```

Or

```
If secretCode = "01W01" Then alpha = True : beta = False
```

In these examples, secretCode, alpha, and beta are the names of variables. In the first example, Visual Basic displays the message "Access denied" if the value of the secretCode variable is not equal to 01W01. In the second example, Visual Basic will set the value of the variable alpha to True and the value of the variable beta to False when the secretCode value is equal to 01W01. Notice that the second statement to be executed is separated from the first one by a colon. The multiline If...Then statement is more clear when there are more statements to be executed when the condition is true, or when the statement to be executed is extremely long.

DECISIONS BASED ON MORE THAN ONE CONDITION

The SimpleIfThen procedure you worked with earlier evaluated only a single condition in the If...Then statement. This statement, however, can take more than one condition. To specify multiple conditions in an If...Then statement, you use the logical operators AND and OR (see Table 5.2 at the beginning of the chapter). Here is the syntax of the If...Then statement with the AND operator:

```
If condition1 AND condition2 Then statement
```

In this syntax, both condition1 and condition2 must be true for Visual Basic to execute the statement to the right of the Then keyword—for example:

```
If sales = 10000 AND salary < 45000 Then SlsCom = sales * 0.07
```

In this example, condition1 is sales = 10000, and condition2 is salary < 45000.

When AND is used in the conditional expression, both conditions must be true before Visual Basic can calculate the sales commission (SlsCom). If any of these conditions is false or both are false, Visual Basic ignores the statement after Then. When it's good enough to meet only one of the conditions, you should use the OR operator. Here is the syntax:

```
If condition1 OR condition2 Then statement
```

The OR operator is more flexible. Only one of the conditions must be true before Visual Basic can execute the statement following the Then keyword. Let's look at this example:

```
If dept = "S" OR dept = "M" Then bonus = 500
```

In this example, if at least one condition is true, Visual Basic assigns 500 to the bonus variable. If both conditions are false, Visual Basic ignores the rest of the line.

Now, let's look at a complete procedure example. Suppose you can get a 10% discount if you purchase 50 units of a product priced at $7.00. The IfThenAnd procedure demonstrates the use of the AND operator.

Hands-On 5.3. Using the If...Then...AND Statement

1. Insert a new module and enter the following **IfThen And** procedure in the module's Code window:

```
Sub IfThenAnd()
  Dim price As Single
  Dim units As Integer
  Dim rebate As Single

  Const strMsg1 = "To get a rebate, buy an additional "
  Const strMsg2 = "Price must equal $7.00"

  units = 234
  price = 7

  If price = 7 And units >= 50 Then
  rebate = (price * units) * 0.1
  MsgBox "The rebate is: $" & rebate
  End If

  If price = 7 And units < 50 Then
  MsgBox strMsg1 & "50 - units."
  End If

  If price <> 7 And units >= 50 Then
  MsgBox strMsg2
  End If

  If price <> 7 And units < 50 Then
  MsgBox "You didn't meet the criteria."
  End If
End Sub
```

2. Run the IfThenAnd procedure.

The IfThenAnd procedure has four If...Then statements that are used to evaluate the contents of two variables: price and units. The AND operator between the keywords If...Then allows more than one condition to be tested. With the AND operator, all conditions must be true for Visual Basic to run the statements between the Then...End If keywords.

Indenting If Block Instructions

To make the If blocks easier to read and understand, use indentation. Compare the following:

If *condition* Then	If *condition* Then
action	action
End If	End If

Looking at the block statement on the right side, you can easily see where the block begins and where it ends.

IF...THEN...ELSE STATEMENT

Now you know how to display a message or take an action when one or more conditions are true or false. What should you do, however, if your procedure needs to take one action when the condition is true and another action when the condition is false? By adding the Else clause to the simple If...Then statement, you can direct your procedure to the appropriate statement depending on the result of the test.

The If...Then...Else statement has two formats: single-line and multiline. The single-line format is as follows:

```
If condition Then statement1 Else statement2
```

The statement following the Then keyword is executed if the condition is true, and the statement following the Else clause is executed if the condition is false—for example:

```
If sales > 5000 Then Bonus = sales * 0.05 Else MsgBox "No Bonus"
```

If the value stored in the variable sales is greater than 5000, Visual Basic will calculate the bonus using the following formula: sales * 0.05. However, if the variable sales is not greater than 5000, Visual Basic will display the message "No Bonus."

The If...Then...Else statement should be used to decide which of two actions to perform. When you need to execute more statements when the condition is true or false, it's better to use the multiline format of the If...Then...Else statement:

```
If condition Then
    statements to be executed if condition is True
Else
    statements to be executed if condition is False
End If
```

Notice that the multiline (block) If...Then...Else statement ends with the End If keywords. Use the indentation as shown to make this block structure easier to read.

```
If Me.Dirty Then
  Me!btnUndo.Enabled = True
Else
  Me!btnUndo.Enabled = False
End If
```

In this example, if the condition (Me.Dirty) is true, Visual Basic will execute the statements between Then and Else, and will ignore the statement between Else and End If. If the condition is false, Visual Basic will omit the statements between Then and Else, and will execute the statement between Else and End If. The purpose of this procedure fragment is to enable the Undo button when the data on the form has changed and keep the Undo button disabled if the data has not changed. Let's look at a procedure example.

⊙ Hands-On 5.4. Using the If...Then...Else Statement

1. Insert a new module and enter the following **WhatTypeOf Day** procedure in the module's Code window:

```
Sub WhatTypeOfDay()
  Dim response As String
  Dim question As String
  Dim strMsg1 As String, strMsg2 As String
  Dim myDate As Date

  question = "Enter any date in the format mm/dd/yyyy:" _
& Chr(13) & " (e.g., 07/06/2015)"
  strMsg1 = "weekday"
  strMsg2 = "weekend"
  response = InputBox(question)
  myDate = Weekday(CDate(response))

  If myDate >= 2 And myDate <= 6 Then
    MsgBox strMsg1
  Else
    MsgBox strMsg2
  End If
End Sub
```

2. Run the WhatTypeOfDay procedure.

This procedure asks the user to enter any date. The user-supplied string is then converted to the Date data type with the built-in CDate function. Finally, the Weekday function converts the date into an integer that indicates the day of the week (see Table 5.3). The integer is stored in the variable myDate. The conditional test is performed to check whether the value of the variable myDate is greater than or equal to 2 (>=2) and less than or equal to 6 (<=6). If the result of the test is true, the user is told that the supplied date is a weekday; otherwise, the program announces that it's a weekend.

3. Run the procedure a few more times, each time supplying a different date. Check the Visual Basic answers against your desktop or wall calendar.

Table 5.3. The **Weekday** function values.

Constant	Value
vbSunday	1
vbMonday	2
vbTuesday	3
vbWednesday	4
vbThursday	5
vbFriday	6
vbSaturday	7

IF...THEN...ELSEIF STATEMENT

Quite often you will need to check the results of several different conditions. To join a set of `If` conditions together, you can use the `ElseIf` clause. Using the `If...Then...ElseIf` statement, you can evaluate more conditions than is possible with the `If...Then...Else` statement that was the subject of the preceding section. Here is the syntax of the `If...Then...ElseIf` statement:

```
If condition1 Then
   statements to be executedif condition1 is True
ElseIf condition2 Then
   statements to be executedif condition2 is True
ElseIf condition3 Then
   statements to be executedif condition3 is True
ElseIf conditionN Then
   statements to be executedif conditionN is True
Else
   statements to be executedif all conditions are False
End If
```

The `Else` clause is optional; you can omit it if there are no actions to be executed when all conditions are false.

SIDEBAR *ElseIf Clause*

Your procedure can include any number of `ElseIf` statements and conditions. The `ElseIf` clause always comes before the `Else` clause. The statements in the `ElseIf` clause are executed only if the condition in this clause is true.

Let's look at the following procedure fragment:

```
If myNumber = 0 Then
  MsgBox "You entered zero."
ElseIf myNumber > 0 Then
  MsgBox "You entered a positive number."
ElseIf myNumber < 0 Then
```

```
    MsgBox "You entered a negative number."
End If
```

This example checks the value of the number entered by the user and stored in the variable myNumber. Depending on the number entered, an appropriate message (zero, positive, negative) is displayed. Notice that the Else clause is not used. If the result of the first condition (myNumber = 0) is false, Visual Basic jumps to the next ElseIf statement and evaluates its condition (myNumber > 0). If the value is not greater than zero, Visual Basic skips to the next ElseIf and the condition myNumber < 0 is evaluated.

NESTED IF...THEN STATEMENTS

You can make more complex decisions in your VBA procedures by placing an If...Then or If...Then...Else statement inside another If...Then or If...Then...Else statement. Structures in which an If statement is contained inside another If block are referred to as *nested* If statements. To understand how nested If...Then statements work, it's time for another hands-on exercise.

⊙ **Hands-On 5.5. Using Nested If...Then Statements**

1. In the database **Chap05.accdb**, create a blank form by choosing **Blank form** in the Forms section of the Create tab (Microsoft Access 2016window). When Access opens the new form in Layout view, switch to Design view.
2. Use the text box control in the Controls section of the Design tab to add two text boxes to the form (see Figure 5.1).

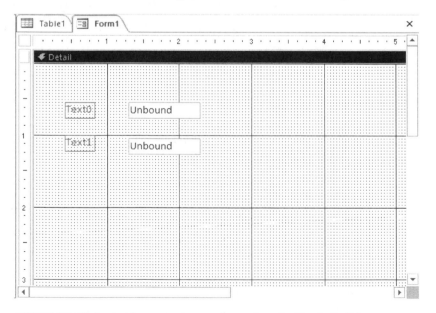

FIGURE 5.1. Placing text box controls on an Access form for Hands-On 5.5.

3. Click the **Property Sheet** button in the **Tools** section of the Design tab.

4. In the property sheet, change the Caption property for the label in front of the first text box to **User** and the Caption property for the label in front of the second text box to **Password**.

5. Click the Unbound text box to the right of the User label. In the property sheet on the Other tab, set the Name property of this control to **txtUser**. Click the Unbound text box to the right of the Password label. In the property sheet on the Other tab, set the Name property of this text box to **txtPwd**(see Figure 5.2).

6. In the property sheet on the Data tab, type **Password** next to the Input Mask property of the txtPwd text box control.

7. Click the **Button** (Form Control) in the **Controls** section of the Design tab, and add a button to the form. When the Command Button Wizard dialog box appears, click **Cancel**. With the Command button selected, set the Caption and Name properties of this button by typing the following values in the property sheet next to the shown property name (see Figure 5.3):

   Name property: **cmdOK**
   Caption property: **OK**

8. Right-click the **OK** button and choose **Build Event** from the shortcut menu. In the Choose Builder dialog box, select **Code Builder** and click **OK**.

9. Enter the following code for the **cmdOK_Click** event procedure. To make the procedure easier to understand, the conditional statements are shown with different formatting (bold and underlined).

```
Private Sub cmdOK_Click()
If txtPwd = "FOX" Then
    MsgBox "You're not authorized to run this report."
ElseIf txtPwd = "DOG" Then
If txtUser = "John" Then
        MsgBox "You're logged on with restricted privileges."
ElseIf txtUser = "Mark" Then
        MsgBox "Contact the Admin now."
ElseIf txtUser = "Anne" Then
        MsgBox "Go home."
Else
        MsgBox "Incorrect user name."
End If
Else
        MsgBox "Incorrect password or user name"
End If
  Me.txtUser.SetFocus
End Sub
```

FIGURE 5.2. **Setting the Name property of the text box control for Hands-On 5.5.**

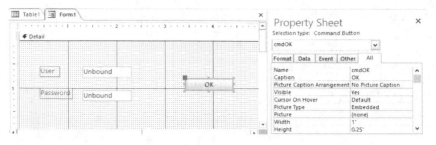

FIGURE 5.3. Setting the Command button properties for Hands-On 5.5.

10. Choose **File | Close and Return to Microsoft Access**. Save your form as **frmTestNesting**. When prompted to save standard modules you created in earlier exercises, save these objects with default names.

11. Switch to **Form** view. Enter any data in the User and Password text boxes, and then click **OK**.

The procedure first checks if the txtPwd text box on the form holds the text string "FOX." If this is true, the message is displayed, and Visual Basic skips over the ElseIf and Else clauses until it finds the matching End If (see the bolded conditional statement).

If the txtPwd text box holds the string "DOG," we use a nested If...Then... Else statement (underlined) to check if the content of the txtUser text box is set to John, Mark, or Anne, and then display the appropriate message. If the user name is not one of the specified names, then the condition is false and we jump to the underlined Else to display a message stating that the user entered an incorrect user name.

The first If block (in bold) is called the *outer* if statement. This outer statement contains one *inner* if statement (underlined).

<u>**SIDEBAR**</u>   *Nesting Statements*

Nesting means placing one type of control structure inside another control structure. You will see more nesting examples with the looping structures discussed in Chapter 6, "Adding Repeating Actions to Your Access VBA Programs."

SELECT CASE STATEMENT

To avoid complex nested If statements that are difficult to follow, you can use the Select Case statement instead. The syntax of this statement is as follows:

```
Select Case testExpression
  Case expressionList1
    statements to be executed
if expressionList1 matches testExpression
  Case expressionList2
    statements to be executed
```

```
if expressionList2 matches testExpression
  Case expressionListN
    statements to be executed
if expressionListN matches testExpression
  Case Else
    statements to be executed
if no values match testExpression
End Select
```

You can place any number of cases to test between the keywords `Select Case` and `End Select`. The `Case Else` clause is optional. Use it when you expect that there may be conditional expressions that return False. In the `Select Case` statement, Visual Basic compares each `expressionList` with the value of `testExpression`.

Here's the logic behind the `Select Case` statement. When Visual Basic encounters the `Select Case` clause, it makes note of the value of `testExpression`. Then it proceeds to test the expression following the first `Case` clause. If the value of this expression (`expressionList1`) matches the value stored in `testExpression`, Visual Basic executes the statements until another `Case` clause is encountered, and then jumps to the `End Select` statement. If, however, the expression tested in the first `Case` clause does not match `testExpression`, Visual Basic checks the value of each `Case` clause until it finds a match. If none of the `Case` clauses contain the expression that matches the value stored in `testExpression`, Visual Basic jumps to the `Case Else` clause and executes the statements until it encounters the `End Select` keywords. Notice that the `Case Else` clause is optional. If your procedure does not use `Case Else`, and none of the `Case` clauses contain a value matching the value of `testExpression`, Visual Basic jumps to the statements following `End Select` and continues executing your procedure.

Let's look at an example of a procedure that uses the `Select Case` statement. As you already know, the `MsgBox` function allows you to display a message with one or more buttons. You also know that the result of the `MsgBox` function can be assigned to a variable. Using the `Select Case` statement, you can decide which action to take based on the button the user pressed in the message box.

◉ Hands-On 5.6. Using the Select Case Statement

1. Press **Alt+F11** to switch from the Microsoft Access application window to the Visual Basic Editor window.
2. Insert a new module and enter the following **TestButtons** procedure in the module's Code window:

```
Sub TestButtons()
  Dim question As String
  Dim bts As Integer
  Dim myTitle As String
  Dim myButton As Integer
```

```
    question = "Do you want to preview the report now?"
    bts = vbYesNoCancel + vbQuestion + vbDefaultButton1
    myTitle = "Report"
    myButton = MsgBox(prompt:=question, buttons:=bts, _
    Title:=myTitle)

    Select Case myButton
      Case 6
        DoCmd.OpenReport "Sales by Year", acPreview
      Case 7
        MsgBox "You can review the report later."
      Case Else
        MsgBox "You pressed Cancel."
    End Select
End Sub
```

3. Run the TestButtons procedure three times, each time selecting a different button. (Because there is no Sales by Year report in the current database, an error message will pop up when you select Yes. Click **End** to exit the error message.)

The first part of the TestButtons procedure displays a message with three buttons: Yes, No, and Cancel. The value of the button selected by the user is assigned to the variable myButton.

If the user clicks Yes, the variable myButton is assigned the vbYes constant or its corresponding value 6. If the user selects No, the variable myButton is assigned the constant vbNo or its corresponding value 7. Lastly, if Cancel is pressed, the content of the variable myButton equals vbCancel, or 2.

The Select Case statement checks the values supplied after the Case clause against the value stored in the variable myButton. When there is a match, the appropriate Case statement is executed. The TestButtons procedure will work the same if you use constants instead of button values:

```
Select Case myButton
  Case vbYes
    DoCmd.OpenReport "Sales by Year", acPreview
  Case vbNo
    MsgBox "You can review the report later."
  Case Else
    MsgBox "You pressed Cancel."
End Select
```

You can omit the Else clause. Simply revise the Select Case statement as follows:

```
Select Case myButton
  Case vbYes
    DoCmd.OpenReport "Sales by Year", acPreview
  Case vbNo
    MsgBox "You can review the report later."
  Case vbCancel
    MsgBox "You pressed Cancel."
End Select
```

Capture Errors with Case Else

> Although using `Case Else` in the `Select Case` statement isn't required, it's always a good idea to include one just in case the variable you are testing has an unexpected value. The `Case Else` clause is a good place to put an error message.

Using Is with the Case Clause

Sometimes a decision is made based on whether the test expression uses the greater than, less than, equal to, or some other relational operator (see Table 5.1). The `Is` keyword lets you use a conditional expression in a `Case` clause. The syntax for the `Select Case` clause using the `Is` keyword is as follows:

```
Select Case testExpression
  Case Is condition1
    statements if condition1 is true
  Case Is condition2
    statements if condition2 is true
  Case Is conditionN
    statements if conditionN is true
End Select
```

Let's look at an example:

```
Select Case myNumber
  Case Is <= 10
    MsgBox "The number is less than or equal to 10."
  Case 11
    MsgBox "You entered 11."
  Case Is >= 100
    MsgBox "The number is greater than or equal to 100."
  Case Else
    MsgBox "The number is between 12 and 99."
End Select
```

Assuming that the variable myNumber holds 120, the third `Case` clause is true, and the only statement executed is the one between `Case Is >= 100` and the `Case Else` clause.

Specifying a Range of Values in a Case Clause

In the preceding example, you saw a simple `Select Case` statement that uses one expression in each `Case` clause. Many times, however, you may want to specify a range of values in a `Case` clause. You do this by using the `To` keyword between the values of expressions, as in the following example:

```
Select Case unitsSold
  Case 1 To 100
    Discount = 0.05
  Case Is <= 500
    Discount = 0.1
```

```
   Case 501 To 1000
      Discount = 0.15
   Case Is >1000
      Discount = 0.2
End Select
```

Let's analyze this `Select Case` block with the assumption that the variable `unitsSold` currently has a value of 99. Visual Basic compares the value of the variable `unitsSold` with the conditional expression in the `Case` clauses. The first and third `Case` clauses illustrate how to use a range of values in a conditional expression by using the `To` keyword.

Because `unitsSold` equals 99, the condition in the first `Case` clause is true; thus, Visual Basic assigns the value 0.05 to the variable `Discount`. Well, how about the second `Case` clause, which is also true? Although it's obvious that 99 is less than or equal to 500, Visual Basic does not execute the associated statement `Discount = 0.1`. The reason for this is that once Visual Basic locates a `Case` clause with a true condition, it doesn't bother to look at the remaining `Case` clauses. It jumps over them and continues to execute the procedure with the instructions that may follow the `End Select` statement.

For more practice with the Select Case statement, let's use it in a function procedure. As you recall from Chapter 4, function procedures allow you to return a result to a subroutine. Suppose a subroutine has to display a discount based on the number of units sold. You can get the number of units from the user and then run a function to figure out which discount applies.

◉ Hands-On 5.7. Using the Select Case Statement in a Function

1. Insert a new module and enter the following **DisplayDiscount** procedure in the Code window:

```
Sub DisplayDiscount()
  Dim unitsSold As Integer
  Dim myDiscount As Single

  unitsSold = InputBox("Units Sold:")
  myDiscount = GetDiscount(unitsSold)
  MsgBox myDiscount
End Sub
```

2. In the same module, enter the following **GetDiscount** function procedure:

```
Function GetDiscount(unitsSold As Integer)
  Select Case unitsSold
    Case 1 To 200
      GetDiscount = 0.05
    Case 201 To 500
      GetDiscount = 0.1
    Case 501 To 1000
      GetDiscount = 0.15
    Case Is > 1000
      GetDiscount = 0.2
  End Select
End Function
```

3. Place the insertion point anywhere within the code of the DisplayDiscount procedure and press **F5** to run it.

   The DisplayDiscount procedure passes the value stored in the variable units-Sold to the GetDiscount function. When Visual Basic encounters the `Select Case` statement, it checks whether the value of the first `Case` clause expression matches the value stored in the `unitsSold` parameter. If there is a match, Visual Basic assigns a 5% discount (0.05) to the function name, and then jumps to the `End Select` keywords. Because there are no more statements to execute inside the function procedure, Visual Basic returns to the calling procedure, DisplayDiscount. Here it assigns the function's result to the variable `myDiscount`. The last statement displays the value of the retrieved discount in a message box.

4. Choose **File | Save Chap05** and click OK when prompted to save the changes to the modules you created during the hands-on exercises.

5. Choose **File | Close and Return to Microsoft Access**.

6. Close the **Chap05.accdb** database and exit Microsoft Access.

Specifying Multiple Expressions in a Case Clause

You may specify multiple conditions within a single `Case` clause by separating each condition with a comma:

```
Select Case myMonth
   Case "January", "February", "March"
     Debug.Print myMonth & ": 1st Qtr."
   Case "April", "May", "June"
     Debug.Print myMonth & ": 2nd Qtr."
   Case "July", "August", "September"
     Debug.Print myMonth & ": 3rd Qtr."
   Case "October", "November", "December"
     Debug.Print myMonth & ": 4th Qtr."
End Select
```

Multiple Conditions within a Case Clause

NOTE   *The commas used to separate conditions within a* Case *clause have the same meaning as the OR operator used in the* If *statement. The* Case *clause is true if at least one of the conditions is true.*

SUMMARY

Conditional statements, introduced in this chapter, let you control the flow of your VBA procedure. By testing the truth of a condition, you can decide which statements should be run and which should be skipped over. In other words, instead of running your procedure from top to bottom, line by line, you can execute only certain lines. Here are a few guidelines to help you determine which conditional statement you should use:

■ If you want to supply only one condition, the simple `If...Then` statement is the best choice.

- If you need to decide which of two actions to perform, use the If...Then...Else statement.
- If your procedure requires two or more conditions, use the If...Then...ElseIf or Select Case statements.
- If your procedure has many conditions, use the Select Case statement. This statement is more flexible and easier to comprehend than the If...Then...ElseIf statement.

Sometimes decisions have to be repeated. The next chapter teaches you how your procedures can perform the same actions over and over again.

CHAPTER 6

ADDING REPEATING ACTIONS TO YOUR ACCESS VBA PROGRAMS

Now that you've learned how conditional statements can give your VBA procedures decision-making capabilities, it's time to get more involved. Not all decisions are easy. Sometimes you will need to perform a number of statements several times to arrive at a certain condition. On other occasions, however, after you've reached the decision, you may need to run the specified statements as long as a condition is true or until a condition becomes true. In programming, performing repetitive tasks is called *looping*. VBA has various looping structures that allow you to repeat a sequence of statements a number of times. In this chapter, you learn how to loop through your code.

SIDEBAR *What Is a Loop?*

A loop is a programming structure that causes a section of program code to execute repeatedly. VBA provides several structures to implement loops in your procedures: Do...While, Do...Until, For...Next, and For Each...Next.

USING THE DO...WHILE STATEMENT

Visual Basic has two types of Do loop statements that repeat a sequence of statements either as long as or until a certain condition is true: Do...While and Do...Until.

The Do...While statement lets you repeat an action as long as a condition is true. This statement has the following syntax:

```
Do While condition
   statement1
   statement2
   statementN
Loop
```

When Visual Basic encounters this loop, it first checks the truth value of the condition. If the condition is false, the statements inside the loop are not executed, and Visual Basic will continue to execute the program with the first statement after the `Loop` keyword or will exit the program if there are no more statements to execute. If the condition is true, the statements inside the loop are run one by one until the `Loop` statement is encountered. The `Loop` statement tells Visual Basic to repeat the entire process again as long as the testing of the condition in the `Do...While` statement is true.

Let's see how you can put the `Do...While` loop to good use in Microsoft Access. You will find out how to continuously display an input box until the user enters the correct password. The following hands-on exercise demonstrates this.

Please note files for the hands-on project may be found on the companion CD-ROM.

Hands-On 6.1. Using the Do...While Statement

1. Start Microsoft Access and create a new database named **Chap06.accdb** in your **C:\VBAPrimerAccess_ByExample** folder.
2. Once your new database is opened, press **Alt+F11** to switch to the Visual Basic Editor window.
3. Choose **Insert | Module** to add a new standard module.
4. In the Module1 Code window, enter the following **AskForPassword** procedure:

```
Sub AskForPassword()
  Dim pWord As String

  pWord = ""
  Do While pWord <> "DADA"
    pWord = InputBox("What is the report password?")
  Loop
  MsgBox "You entered the correct report password."
End Sub
```

5. Run the AskForPassword procedure.

In this procedure, the statement inside the `Do...While` loop is executed as long as the variable `pWord` is not equal to the string "DADA." If the user enters the correct password ("DADA"), Visual Basic leaves the loop and executes the `MsgBox` statement after the `Loop` keyword.

To allow the user to exit the procedure gracefully and cancel out of the input box if he does not know the correct password, add the following statement on an empty line before the `Loop` keyword:

```
If pWord = "" Then Exit Do
```

The `Exit Do` statement tells Visual Basic to exit the `Do` loop if the variable `pWord` does not hold any value (please see the section titled "Exiting Loops Early" later in this chapter). Therefore, when the input box appears, the user can leave the text field empty and click OK or Cancel to stop the procedure.

Without the `Exit Do` statement, the procedure will keep on asking the user to enter the password until the correct value is supplied.

To forgo displaying the informational message when the user has not provided the correct password, you may want to use the conditional statement `If...Then` that you learned in the previous chapter. Here is the revised AskForPassword procedure:

```
Sub AskForPassword() ' revised procedure
  Dim pWord As String

  pWord = ""
  Do While pWord <> "DADA"
    pWord = InputBox("What is the report password?")
    If pWord = "" Then
      MsgBox "You did not enter a password."
      Exit Do
    End If
  Loop
  If pWord <> "" Then
    MsgBox "You entered the correct report password."
  End If
End Sub
```

Another Approach to the Do...While Statement

The `Do...While` statement has another syntax that lets you test the condition at the bottom of the loop:

```
Do
    statement1
    statement2
    statementN
Loop While condition
```

When you test the condition at the bottom of the loop, the statements inside the loop are executed at least once. Let's try this in the next hands-on exercise.

 Hands-On 6.2. Using the Do...While Statement with a Condition at the Bottom of the Loop

1. In the Visual Basic Editor window, insert a new module and enter the following **SignIn** procedure:

```
Sub SignIn()
  Dim secretCode As String

  Do
    secretCode = InputBox("Enter your secret code:")
    If secretCode = "sp1045" Then Exit Do
  Loop While secretCode <> "sp1045"
End Sub
```

2. Run the SignIn procedure.

Notice that by the time the condition is evaluated, Visual Basic has already executed the statements one time. In addition to placing the condition at the end of the loop, the SignIn procedure shows again how to exit the loop when a condition is reached. When the `Exit Do` statement is encountered, the loop ends immediately.

To exit the loop in the SignIn procedure without entering the password, you may revise it as follows:

```
Sub SignIn() 'revised procedure
  Dim secretCode As String

  Do
    secretCode = InputBox("Enter your secret code:")
    If secretCode = "sp1045" Or secretCode = "" Then
      Exit Do
    End If
  Loop While secretCode <> "sp1045"
End Sub
```

SIDEBAR   *Avoid Infinite Loops*

If you don't design your loop correctly, you can get an infinite loop—a loop that never ends. You will not be able to stop the procedure by using the Esc key. The following procedure causes the loop to execute endlessly because the programmer forgot to include the test condition:

```
Sub SayHello()
  Do
    MsgBox "Hello."
  Loop
End Sub
```

To stop the execution of the infinite loop, you must press Ctrl+Break. When Visual Basic displays the message box "Code execution has been interrupted," click End to end the procedure.

USING THE DO...UNTIL STATEMENT

Another handy loop is `Do...Until`, which allows you to repeat one or more statements until a condition becomes true. In other words, `Do...Until` repeats a block of code as long as something is false. Here is the syntax:

```
Do Until condition
  statement1
  statement2
  statementN
Loop
```

Using the preceding syntax, you can now rewrite the AskForPassword procedure (written in Hands-On 6.1) as shown in the following hands-on exercise.

(◉) Hands-On 6.3. Using the Do...Until Statement

1. In the Visual Basic Editor window, insert a new module and type the **AskForPassword2** procedure:

```
Sub AskForPassword2()
  Dim pWord As String

  pWord = ""
  Do Until pWord = "DADA"
    pWord = InputBox("What is the report password?")
  Loop
End Sub
```

2. Run the AskForPassword2 procedure.

The first line of this procedure says: Perform the following statements until the variable `pWord` holds the value "DADA." As a result, until the correct password is supplied, Visual Basic executes the `InputBox` statement inside the loop. This process continues as long as the condition `pWord = "DADA"` evaluates to false.

You could modify this procedure to allow the user to cancel the input box without supplying the password, as follows:

```
Sub AskForPassword2() 'revised procedure
  Dim pWord As String

  pWord = ""
  Do Until pWord = "DADA"
    pWord = InputBox("What is the report password?")
    If pWord = "" Then Exit Do
  Loop
End Sub
```

SIDEBAR *Variables and Loops*

All variables that appear in a loop should be assigned default values before the loop is entered.

Another Approach to the Do...Until Statement

Similar to the `Do...While` statement, the `Do...Until` statement has a second syntax that lets you test the condition at the bottom of the loop:

```
Do
  statement1
  statement2
  statementN
Loop Until condition
```

If you want the statements to execute at least once, no matter what the value of the condition, place the condition on the line with the `Loop` statement. Let's try out the following example that prints 27 numbers to the Immediate window.

⊙ **Hands-On 6.4. Using the Do...Until Statement with a Condition at the Bottom of the Loop**

1. In the Visual Basic Editor window, insert a new module and type the **Print-Numbers** procedure shown here:

```
Sub PrintNumbers()
  Dim num As Integer

  num = 0
  Do
    num = num + 1
    Debug.Print num
  Loop Until num = 27
End Sub
```

2. Make sure the Immediate window is open in the Visual Basic Editor window (choose **View | Immediate Window** or press **Ctrl+G**).
3. Run the PrintNumbers procedure.

    The variable num is initialized at the beginning of the procedure to zero (0). When Visual Basic enters the loop, the content of the variable num is increased by one, and the value is written to the Immediate window with the `Debug.Print` statement. Next, the condition tells Visual Basic that it should execute the statements inside the loop until the variable num equals 27.
4. Return to the Microsoft Access application window by choosing **File | Close and Return to Microsoft Access.** When prompted, save the changes to all the modules.

SIDEBAR *Counters*

A *counter* is a numeric variable that keeps track of the number of items that have been processed. The preceding PrintNumbers procedure declares the variable num to keep track of numbers that were printed. A counter variable should be initialized (assigned a value) at the beginning of the program. This ensures that you always know the exact value of the counter before you begin using it. A counter can be incremented or decremented by a specified value.

USING THE FOR...NEXT STATEMENT

The `For...Next` statement is used when you know how many times you want to repeat a group of statements. The syntax of a `For...Next` statement looks like this:

```
For counter = start To end [Step increment]
    statement1
    statement2
    statementN
Next [counter]
```

The code in the brackets is optional. `Counter` is a numeric variable that stores the number of iterations. `Start` is the number at which you want to begin counting. `End` indicates how many times the loop should be executed. For example, if you want to repeat the statements inside the loop five times, use the following `For` statement:

```
For counter = 1 To 5
  statements
Next
```

When Visual Basic encounters the `Next` statement, it will go back to the beginning of the loop and execute the statements inside the loop again, as long as the counter hasn't reached the end value. As soon as the value of `counter` is greater than the number entered after the `To` keyword, Visual Basic exits the loop. Because the variable `counter` automatically changes after each execution of the loop, sooner or later the value stored in the counter exceeds the value specified in `end`.

By default, every time Visual Basic executes the statements inside the loop, the value of the variable `counter` is increased by one. You can change this default setting by using the `Step` clause. For example, to increase the variable `counter` by three, use the following statement:

```
For counter = 1 To 5 Step 3
  statements
Next counter
```

When Visual Basic encounters this statement, it executes the statements inside the loop twice. The first time the loop runs, the counter equals 1. The second time the loop runs, the counter equals 4 (1+3). The loop does not run a third time, because now the counter equals 7 (4+3), causing Visual Basic to exit the loop.

Note that the `Step` increment is optional. Optional statements are always shown in square brackets (see the syntax at the beginning of this section). The `Step` increment isn't specified unless it's a value other than 1. You can place a negative number after `Step` in order to decrement this value from the counter each time it encounters the `Next` statement. The name of the variable (`counter`) after the `Next` statement is also optional; however, it's good programming practice to make your `Next` statements explicit by including the `counter` variable's name.

How can you use the `For...Next` loop in Microsoft Access? Suppose you want to retrieve the names of the text boxes located on an active form. The procedure in the next hands-on exercise demonstrates how to determine whether a control is a text box and how to display its name if a text box is found.

Hands-On 6.5. Using the For...Next Statement

1. Make sure you have a copy of the Northwind 2007.accdb database from the companion CD in your VBAPrimerAccess_ByExample folder.

2. Import the **Customers** table from the **Northwind 2007.accdb** database. To do this, click **Access** in the Import & Link section of the External Data tab. In the File name text box of the Get External Data dialog box, enter **C:\VBAPrimerAccess_ByExample\Northwind 2007.accdb** and click **OK**. In the Import Objects dialog box, select the **Customers** table and click **OK**. Click **Close** to exit the Get External Data dialog box.

3. Now, create a simple **Customers** form based on the Customers table. To do this, select the Customers table in the navigation pane by clicking on its name. Next, click the **Form** button in the Forms section of the Create tab. Access creates a form as shown in Figure 6.1.

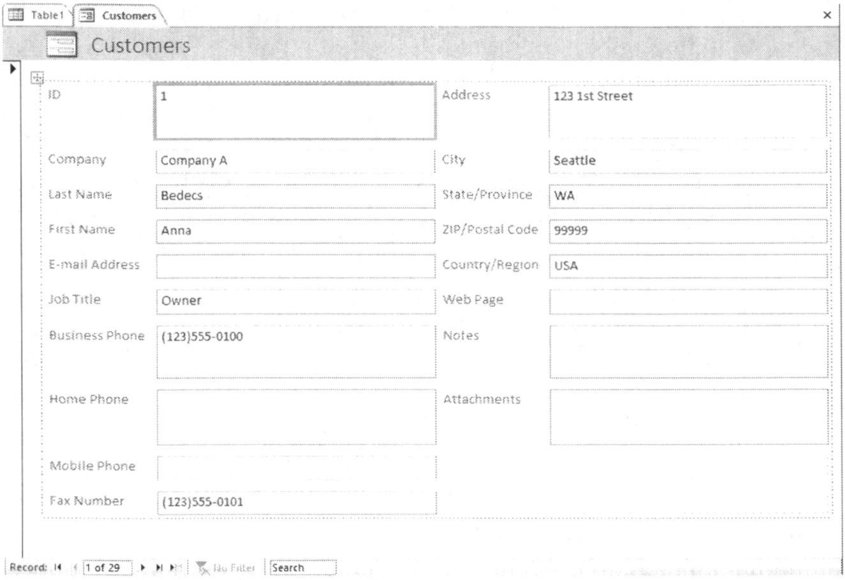

FIGURE 6.1. Automatic data entry form created by Microsoft Access.

4. Press **Alt+F11** to switch to the Visual Basic Editor window and insert a new module.

5. In the module's Code window, enter the following **GetTextBoxNames** procedure:

```
Sub GetTextBoxNames()
  Dim myForm As Form
  Dim myControl As Control
  Dim c As Integer

  Set myForm = Screen.ActiveForm
  Set myControl = Screen.ActiveControl

  For c = 0 To myForm.Count - 1
    If TypeOf myForm(c) Is TextBox Then
      MsgBox myForm(c).Name
    End If
  Next c
End Sub
```

The conditional statement (If...Then) nested inside the For...Next loop tells Visual Basic to display the name of the active control only if it is a text box.

6. Run the GetTextBoxNames procedure.

Paired Statements

For and Next must be paired. If one is missing, Visual Basic generates the following error message: "For without Next."

USING THE FOR EACH...NEXT STATEMENT

When your procedure needs to loop through all of the objects of a collection or all of the elements in an array (arrays are the subject of the next chapter), the For Each...Next statement should be used. This loop does not require a counter variable. Visual Basic can figure out on its own how many times the loop should execute. The For Each...Next statement looks like this:

```
For Each element In Group
   statement1
   statement2
   statementN
Next [element]
```

Element is a variable to which all the elements of an array or collection will be assigned. This variable must be of the Variant data type for an array and of the Object data type for a collection. Group is the name of a collection or an array. Let's now see how to use the For Each...Next statement to print the names of the controls in the Customers form to the Immediate window.

⊙ Hands-On 6.6. Using the For Each...Next Statement

This hands-on exercise requires the completion of Steps 1 and 2 of Hands-On 6.5.

1. Ensure that the Customers form you created in Hands-On 6.5 is still open in Form view.

2. Switch to the Visual Basic Editor window and insert a new module.

3. In the Code window, enter the **GetControls** procedure shown here:

```
Sub GetControls()
   Dim myControl As Control
   Dim myForm As Form

   DoCmd.OpenForm "Customers"
   Set myForm = Screen.ActiveForm

   For Each myControl In myForm
     Debug.Print myControl.Name
   Next
End Sub
```

4. Run the GetControls procedure.

5. The results of the procedure you just executed will be displayed in the Immediate window. If the window is not visible, press **Ctrl+G** in the Visual Basic Editor window to open the Immediate window or choose **View | Immediate Window**.

EXITING LOOPS EARLY

Sometimes you might not want to wait until the loop ends on its own. It's possible that a user will enter the wrong data, a procedure will encounter an error, or perhaps the task will complete and there's no need to do additional looping. You can leave the loop early without reaching the condition that normally terminates it. Visual Basic has two types of `Exit` statements:

- The Exit For statement is used to end either a For…Next or a For Each… Next loop early.
- The Exit Do statement immediately exits any of the VBA Do loops.

The following hands-on exercise demonstrates how to use the `Exit For` statement to leave the `For Each…Next` loop early.

Hands-On 6.7. Early Exit from a Loop

1. In the Visual Basic Editor window, choose **Insert | Module**.
2. In the module's Code window, enter the following **GetControls2** procedure:

```
Sub GetControls2()
  Dim myControl As Control
  Dim myForm As Form

  DoCmd.OpenForm "Customers"
  Set myForm = Screen.ActiveForm

  For Each myControl In myForm
    Debug.Print myControl.Name
    If myControl.Name = "Address" Then
      Exit For
    End If
  Next
End Sub
```

3. Run the GetControls2 procedure.
    The GetControls2 procedure examines the names of the controls in the open Customers form. If Visual Basic encounters the control named "Address," it exits the loop.
4. Return to the Microsoft Access application window by choosing **File | Close and Return to Microsoft Access**.

SIDEBAR *Exiting Procedures*

If you want to exit a subroutine earlier than normal, use the `Exit Sub` statement. If the procedure is a function, use the `Exit Function` statement instead.

NESTED LOOPS

So far in this chapter you have tried out various loops. Each procedure demonstrated the use of an individual looping structure. In programming practice, however, one loop is often placed inside another. Visual Basic allows you to "nest" various types of loops (For and Do loops) within the same procedure. When writing nested loops, you must make sure that each inner loop is completely contained inside the outer loop. Also, each loop must have a unique counter variable. When you use nesting loops, you can often execute specific tasks more effectively.

The GetFormsAndControls procedure shown in the following hands-on exercise illustrates how one For Each...Next loop is nested within another For Each...Next loop.

⊙ Hands-On 6.8. Using Nested Loops

1. Import the **Employees** table from the **Northwind 2007.accdb** database located in your VBAPrimerAccess_ByExample folder (see Hands-On 6.5). To do this, click **Access** in the Import section of the External Data tab. In the File name text box of the Get External Data dialog box, enter **C:\VBAPrimerAccess_ByExample\Northwind 2007.accdb** and click **OK**. In the Import Objects dialog box, select the **Employees** table and click **OK**. Click **Close** to exit the Get External Data dialog box.
2. Now, create a simple **Employees** form based on the Employees table. To do this, select the Employees table in the navigation pane by clicking on its name. Next, click the **Form** button in the Forms section of the Create tab. Access creates a simple Employees data entry form.
3. Leave the Employees form in Form view and press **Alt+F11** to switch to the Visual Basic Editor window.
4. Choose **Insert | Module** to add a new module. In the module's Code window, enter the **GetFormsAndControls** procedure shown here:

```
Sub GetFormsAndControls()
   Dim accObj As AccessObject
   Dim myControl As Control

   For Each accObj In CurrentProject.AllForms
     Debug.Print accObj.Name & " Form"
     If Not accObj.IsLoaded Then
       DoCmd.OpenForm accObj.Name
     End If
     For Each myControl In Forms(accObj.Name).Controls
       Debug.Print Chr(9) & myControl.Name
     Next
     DoCmd.Close , , acSaveYes
   Next
End Sub
```

5. Run the GetFormsAndControls procedure.

The GetFormsAndControls procedure uses two `For Each...Next` loops to print the name of each currently open form and its controls to the Immediate window. To enumerate through the form's controls, the form must be open. Notice the use of the Access built-in function `IsLoaded`. The procedure will open the form only if it is not yet loaded. The control names are indented in the Immediate window using the `Chr(9)` function. This is like pressing the Tab key once. To get the same result, you can replace `Chr(9)` with a VBA constant: `vbTab`.

After reading the names of the controls, the form is closed and the next form is processed in the same manner. The procedure ends when no more forms are found in the AllForms collection of CurrentProject.

6. Choose **File | Save Chap06** to save changes to the modules.
7. Choose **File | Close and Return to Microsoft Access**.
8. Close the **Chap06.accdb** database and click **Yes** when prompted to save changes. You do not need to save Table1 that Access automatically created for you when you chose to create a blank desktop database.
9. Exit Microsoft Access.

SUMMARY

In this chapter, you learned how to repeat certain groups of statements in VBA procedures by using loops. While working with several types of loops, you saw how each loop performs repetitions in a slightly different way. As you gain experience, you'll find it easier to choose the appropriate flow control structure for your task.

The next chapter shows you how to write procedures that require a large number of variables.

CHAPTER 7

KEEPING TRACK OF MULTIPLE VALUES USING ARRAYS

I n previous chapters, you worked with many VBA procedures that used variables to hold specific information about an object, property, or value. For each single value you wanted your procedure to manipulate, you declared a variable. But what if you have a series of values? If you had to write a VBA procedure to deal with larger amounts of data, you would have to create enough variables to handle all of the data. Can you imagine the nightmare of storing currency exchange rates for all the countries in the world in your program? To create a table to hold the necessary data, you'd need at least three variables for each country: country name, currency name, and exchange rate. Fortunately, Visual Basic has a way to get around this problem. By clustering the related variables together, your VBA procedures can manage a large amount of data with ease. In this chapter, you'll learn how to manipulate lists and tables of data with arrays.

UNDERSTANDING ARRAYS

In Visual Basic, an *array* is a special type of variable that represents a group of similar values that are of the same data type (String, Integer, Currency, Date, etc.). The two most common types of arrays are one-dimensional arrays (lists) and two-dimensional arrays (tables).

A one-dimensional array is sometimes referred to as a *list*. A shopping list, a list of the days of the week, and an employee list are examples of one-dimensional arrays or, simply, numbered lists. Each element in the list has an index value that allows you to access that element. For example, in the following illustration we have a one-dimensional array of six elements indexed from 0 to You can access the third element of this array by specifying index (2). By default, the first element of an array is indexed zero (0). You can change this behavior by using the Option Base 1 statement or by explicitly coding the lower bound of your array as explained later in this chapter.

| (0) | (1) | (2) | (3) | (4) | (5) |

All elements of the array should be of the same data type. In other words, if you declare an array to hold textual data you cannot store in it both strings and integers. If you want to store values of *different* data types in the same array, you must declare the array as Variant as discussed later. Following are two examples of one-dimensional arrays: an array named `cities` that is populated with text (String data type—$) and an array named `lotto` that contains six lottery numbers stored as integers (Integer data type—%).

A one-dimensional array: cities$		A one-dimensional array: lotto%	
cities(0)	Baltimore	lotto(0)	25
cities(1)	Atlanta	lotto(1)	4
cities(2)	Boston	lotto(2)	31
cities(3)	Washington	lotto(3)	22
cities(4)	New York	lotto(4)	11
cities(5)	Trenton	lotto(5)	5

As you can see, the contents assigned to each array element match the array type. Storing values of different data types in the same array requires that you declare the array as Variant. You will learn how to declare arrays in the next section.

A two-dimensional array may be thought of as a table or matrix. The position of each element in a table is determined by its row and column numbers. For example, an array that holds the yearly sales data for each product your company sells has two dimensions: the product name and the year. The following is a diagram of an empty two-dimensional array.

(0,0)	(0,1)	(0,2)	(0,3)	(0,4)	(0,5)
(1,0)	(1,1)	(1,2)	(1,3)	(1,4)	(1,5)
(2,0)	(2,1)	(2,2)	(2,3)	(2,4)	(2,5)
(3,0)	(3,1)	(3,2)	(3,3)	(3,4)	(3,5)
(4,0)	(4,1)	(4,2)	(4,3)	(4,4)	(4,5)
(5,0)	(5,1)	(5,2)	(5,3)	(5,4)	(5,5)

You can access the first element in the second row of this two-dimensional array by specifying indices (1, 0). Following are two examples of two-dimensional arrays: an array named `yearlyProductSales` that stores yearly product sales using the Currency data type (@) and an array named `exchange` (of Variant data type) that stores the name of the country, its currency, and the U.S. dollar exchange rate.

A two-dimensional array: yearlyProductSales@

Walking Cane (0,0)	$25,023 (0,1)
Pill Crusher (1,0)	$64,085 (1,1)
Electric Wheelchair (2,0)	$345,016 (2,1)
Folding Walker (3,0)	$85,244 (3,1)

A two-dimensional array: exchange (not actual rates)

Japan (0,0)	Japanese Yen (0,1)	122.856 (0,2)
Australia (1,0)	Australian Dollar (1,1)	1,38220 (1,2)
Canada (2,0)	Canadian Dollar (2,1)	1.33512 (2,2)
Norway (3,0)	Norwegian Krone (3,1)	8.63744 (3,2)
Europe (4,0)	Euro (4,1)	0.939350 (4,2)

In these examples, the yearlyProductSales array can hold a maximum of 8 elements (4 rows × 2 columns = 8) and the exchange array will allow a maximum of 15 elements (5 rows × 3 columns = 15).

Although VBA arrays can have up to 60 dimensions, most people find it difficult to picture dimensions beyond 3D. A three-dimensional array is an array of two-dimensional arrays (tables) where each table has the same number of rows and columns. A three-dimensional array is identified by three indices: table, row, and column. The first element of a three-dimensional array is indexed (0, 0, 0).

Declaring Arrays

Because an array is a variable, you must declare it in a similar way that you declare other variables (by using the keywords Dim, Private, or Public). For fixed-length arrays, the array bounds are listed in parentheses following the variable name. The *bounds* of an array are its lowest and highest indices. If a variable-length, or dynamic, array is being declared, the variable name is followed by an empty pair of parentheses.

The last part of the array declaration is the definition of the data type that the array will hold. An array can hold any of the following data types: Integer,

Long, Single, Double, Variant, Currency, String, Boolean, Byte, or Date. Let's look at some examples:

Array Declaration (one-dimensional)	Description
`Dim cities(5) as String`	Declares a 6-element array, indexed 0 to 5
`Dim lotto(1 To 6) as String`	Declares a 6-element array, indexed 1 to 6
`Dim supplies(2 To 11)`	Declares a 10-element array, indexed 2 to 11
`Dim myIntegers(-3 To 6)`	Declares a 10-element array, indexed −3 to 6
`Dim dynArray() as Integer`	Declares a variable-length array whose bounds will be determined at runtime (see examples later in this chapter)

Array Declaration (two-dimensional)	Description
`Dim exchange(4,2) as Variant`	Declares a two-dimensional array (five rows by three columns)
`Dim yearlyProductSales(3, 1) as Currency`	Declares a two-dimensional array (four rows by two columns)
`Dim my2Darray(1 To 3, 1 To 7) as Single`	Declares a two-dimensional array (three rows indexed 1 to 3 by seven columns indexed 1 to 7)

When you declare an array, Visual Basic automatically reserves enough memory space for it. The amount of memory allocated depends on the array's size and data type. For a one-dimensional array with six elements, Visual Basic sets aside 12 bytes—2 bytes for each element of the array (recall that the size of the Integer data type is 2 bytes—hence $2 \times 6 = 12$). The larger the array, the more memory space is required to store the data. Because arrays can eat up a lot of memory and impact your computer's performance, it's recommended that you declare arrays with only as many elements as you think you'll use.

___

SIDEBAR *What Is an Array Variable?*

An array is a group of variables that have a common name. While a typical variable can hold only one value, an array variable can store a large number of individual values. You refer to a specific value in the array by using the array name and an index number.

Subscripted Variables

The numbers inside the parentheses of the array variables are called subscripts, and each individual variable is called a subscripted variable or element. For example, `cities(5)` is the sixth subscripted variable (element) of the array `cities()`.

Array Upper and Lower Bounds

By default VBA assigns zero (0) to the first element of the array. Therefore, number 1 represents the second element of the array, number 2 represents the third, and so on. With numeric indexing starting at 0, the one-dimensional array `cities(5)` contains six elements numbered from 0 to 5. If you'd rather start counting your array's elements at 1, you can explicitly specify a lower bound of the array by using an `Option Base 1` statement. This instruction must be placed in the declaration section at the top of a VBA module before any `Sub` statements. If you don't specify `Option Base 1` in a procedure that uses arrays, VBA assumes that the statement `Option Base 0` is to be used and begins indexing your array's elements at 0. If you'd rather not use the `Option Base 1` statement and still have the array indexing start at a number other than 0, you must specify the bounds of an array when declaring the array variable. As mentioned in the previous section, the *bounds* of an array are its lowest and highest indices. Let's take a look at the following example:

```
Dim cities(3 To 6) As Integer
```

This statement declares a one-dimensional array with four elements. The numbers enclosed in parentheses after the array name specify the lower (3) and upper (6) bounds of the array. The index of the first element of this array is 3, the second 4, the third 5, and the fourth 6. Notice the keyword `To` between the lower and upper indices.

Initializing and Filling an Array

After you declare an array, you must assign values to its elements. This is often referred to as "initializing an array," "filling an array," or "populating an array." The three methods you can use to load data into an array are discussed in this section.

Filling an Array Using Individual Assignment Statements

Assume you want to store the names of your six favorite cities in a one-dimensional array named `cities`. After declaring the array with the `Dim` statement:

```
Dim cities(5) as String
```

or

```
Dim cities$(5)
```

you can assign values to the array variable like this:

```
cities(0)  =  "Baltimore"
cities(1)  =  "Atlanta"
cities(2)  =  "Boston"
cities(3)  =  "San Diego"
cities(4)  =  "New York"
cities(5)  =  "Denver"
```

Filling an Array Using the Array Function

VBA's built-in `Array` function returns an array of Variants. Because Variant is the default data type, the `As Variant` clause is optional in the array variable declaration:

```
Dim cities() as Variant
```

or

```
Dim cities()
```

Notice that you don't specify the number of elements between the parentheses.

Next, use the `Array` function as shown here to assign values to your `cities` array:

```
cities = Array("Baltimore", "Atlanta", "Boston", _
   "San Diego", "New York", "Denver")
```

When using the `Array` function to populate a six-element array like `cities`, the lower bound of the array is 0 or 1 and the upper bound is 5 or 6, depending on the setting of `Option Base` (see the previous section titled "Array Upper and Lower Bounds").

Filling an Array Using the For...Next Loop

The easiest way to learn how to use loops to populate an array is by writing a procedure that fills an array with a specific number of integer values. Let's look at the following example procedure:

```
Sub LoadArrayWithIntegers()
  Dim myIntArray(1 To 10) As Integer
  Dim i As Integer

  ' Initialize random number generator
  Randomize

  ' Fill the array with 10 random numbers between 1 and 100
  For i = 1 To 10
    myIntArray(i) = Int((100 * Rnd) + 1)
  Next

  ' Print array values to the Immediate window
  For i = 1 To 10
    Debug.Print myIntArray(i)
  Next
End Sub
```

This procedure uses a `For…Next` loop to fill `myIntArray` with 10 random numbers between 1 and 100. The second loop is used to print out the values from the array. Notice that the procedure uses the `Rnd` function to generate a random number. This function returns a value less than 1 but greater than or equal to 0. You can try it out in the Immediate window by entering:

```
x=rnd
?x
```

Before calling the `Rnd` function, the `LoadArrayWithIntegers` procedure uses the `Randomize` statement to initialize the random number generator. To become more familiar with the `Randomize` statement and `Rnd` function, be sure to follow up with the Access online help. For an additional example of using loops, `Randomize`, and `Rnd`, see Hands-On 7.4.

USING A ONE-DIMENSIONAL ARRAY

Having learned the basics of array variables, let's write a couple of VBA procedures to make arrays a part of your new skill set. The procedure in Hands-On 7.1 uses a one-dimensional array to programmatically display a list of six North American cities.

 Please note files for the hands-on project may be found on the companion CD-ROM.

(◉) Hands-On 7.1. Using a One-Dimensional Array

1. Start Microsoft Access and create a new database named **Chap07.accdb** in your **C:\VBAPrimerAccess_ByExample** folder.
2. Once your new database is opened, press **Alt+F11** to switch to the Visual Basic Editor window.
3. Choose **Insert | Module** to add a new standard module.
4. In the Module1 Code window, enter the following **FavoriteCities** procedure. Be sure to enter the `Option Base 1` statement at the top of the module.

```
Option Base 1

Sub FavoriteCities()
  ' declare the array
  Dim cities(6) As String

  ' assign the values to array elements
  cities(1) = "Baltimore"
  cities(2) = "Atlanta"
  cities(3) = "Boston"
  cities(4) = "San Diego"
  cities(5) = "New York"
  cities(6) = "Denver"
```

```
' display the list of cities
MsgBox cities(1) & Chr(13) & cities(2) & Chr(13) _
  & cities(3) & Chr(13) & cities(4) & Chr(13) _
  & cities(5) & Chr(13) & cities(6)
End Sub
```

5. Choose **Run | Run Sub/UserForm** to execute the FavoriteCities proce-
   dure.

   Before the FavoriteCities procedure begins, the default indexing for an array
   is changed. Notice the `Option Base 1` statement at the top of the module
   window before the `Sub` statement. This statement tells Visual Basic to assign
   the number 1 instead of the default 0 to the first element of the array. The array
   `cities()` is declared with six elements of the String data type. Each element
   of the array is then assigned a value. The last statement in this procedure uses
   the `MsgBox` function to display the list of cities in a message box. When you
   run this procedure, each city name will appear on a separate line (see Figure
   7.1). You can change the order of the displayed data by switching the index
   values.

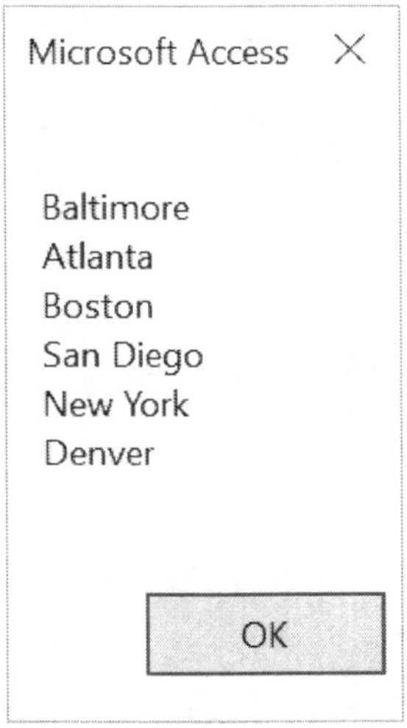

FIGURE 7.1. You can display the elements of a one-dimensional array with the MsgBox
function.

6. Click **OK** to close the message box.
7. On your own, modify the FavoriteCities procedure so that it displays the names
   of the cities in reverse order (from 6 to 1).

SIDEBAR   *The Range of the Array*

   The spread of the elements specified by the Dim statement is
   called the range of the array—for example: `Dim mktgCodes(5 To`
   `15)`.

ARRAYS AND LOOPING STATEMENTS

Several of the looping statements you learned about in Chapter 6 (For...Next and For Each...Next) will come in handy now that you're ready to perform such tasks as populating an array and displaying the elements of an array. It's time to combine the skills you've learned so far.

How can you rewrite the FavoriteCities procedure so each city name is shown in a separate message box? To answer this question, notice how in the FavoriteCities2 procedure in Hands-On 7.2 we are replacing the last statement of the original procedure with the For Each...Next loop.

⊙ **Hands-On 7.2. Using the For Each...Next Statement to List the Array Elements**

1. In the Visual Basic Editor window, insert a new module.
2. Enter the **FavoriteCities2** procedure in the Code window. Be sure to enter the Option Base 1 statement at the top of the module.

```
Option Base 1

Sub FavoriteCities2()
  ' declare the array
  Dim cities(6) As String
  Dim city As Variant

  ' assign the values to array elements
  cities(1) = "Baltimore"
  cities(2) = "Atlanta"
  cities(3) = "Boston"
  cities(4) = "San Diego"
  cities(5) = "New York"
  cities(6) = "Denver"

  ' display the list of cities in separate messages
  For Each city In cities
    MsgBox city
  Next
End Sub
```

3. Choose **Run | Run Sub/UserForm** to execute the FavoriteCities2 procedure.

Notice that the For Each...Next loop uses the variable city of the Variant data type. As you recall from the previous chapter, the For Each...Next loop allows you to loop through all of the objects in a collection or all of the elements of an array and perform the same action on each object or element. When you run the FavoriteCities2 procedure, the loop will execute as many times as there are elements in the array.

In Chapter 4, you practiced passing arguments as variables to subroutines and functions. The CityOperator procedure in Hands-On 7.3 demonstrates how you can pass elements of an array to another procedure.

⊙ Hands-On 7.3. Passing Elements of an Array to Another Procedure

1. In the Visual Basic Editor window, insert a new module.
2. Enter the following two procedures (**CityOperator** and **Hello**) in the module's Code window. Be sure to enter the Option Base 1 statement at the top of the module.

```
Option Base 1

Sub CityOperator()
  ' declare the array
  Dim cities(6) As String

  ' assign the values to array elements
  cities(1) = "Baltimore"
  cities(2) = "Atlanta"
  cities(3) = "Boston"
  cities(4) = "San Diego"
  cities(5) = "New York"
  cities(6) = "Denver"

  ' call another procedure and pass
  ' the array as argument
  Hello cities()
End Sub

Sub Hello(cities() As String)
  Dim counter As Integer

  For counter = 1 To 6
    MsgBox "Hello, " & cities(counter) & "!"
  Next
End Sub
```

Notice that the last statement in the CityOperator procedure calls the Hello procedure and passes to it the array cities() that holds the names of our favorite cities. Also notice that the declaration of the Hello procedure includes an array type argument—cities()—passed to this procedure as String. In order to iterate through the elements of an array, you need to know how many elements are included in the passed array. You can easily retrieve this information via two array functions— LBound and UBound. These functions are discussed later in this chapter. In this procedure example, LBound(cities()) will return 1 as the first element of the array, and UBound(cities()) will return 6 as the last element of the cities() array. Therefore, the statement For counter = LBound(cities()) To UBound(cities()) will boil down to For counter = 1 To 6.

3. Execute the CityOperator procedure (choose **Run | Run Sub/UserForm**).

Passing array elements from a subroutine to a subroutine or function procedure allows you to reuse the same array in many procedures without unnecessary duplication of the program code.

Here's how you can put to work your newly acquired knowledge about arrays and loops in real life. If you're an avid lotto player who is getting tired of picking your own lucky numbers, have Visual Basic do the picking. The Lotto procedure in Hands-On 7.4 populates an array with six numbers from 1 to 54. You can adjust this procedure to pick numbers from any range.

Hands-On 7.4. Using Arrays and Loops in Real Life

1. In the Visual Basic Editor window, insert a new module.
2. Enter the following **Lotto** procedure in the module's Code window:

```vba
Sub Lotto()
  Const spins = 6
  Const minNum = 1
  Const maxNum = 54
  Dim t As Integer ' looping variable in outer loop
  Dim i As Integer ' looping variable in inner loop
  Dim myNumbers As String ' string to hold all picks
  Dim lucky(spins) As String ' array to hold generated picks

  myNumbers = ""
  For t = 1 To spins
    Randomize
    lucky(t) = Int((maxNum - minNum + 1) * Rnd) + minNum

    ' check if this number was picked before
    For i = 1 To (t - 1)
      If lucky(t) = lucky(i) Then
        lucky(t) = Int((maxNum - minNum + 1) * Rnd) + minNum
        i = 0
      End If
    Next i
      MsgBox "Lucky number is " & lucky(t), , "Lucky number " & t
      myNumbers = myNumbers & " -" & lucky(t)
  Next t
  MsgBox "Lucky numbers are " & myNumbers, , "6 Lucky Numbers"
End Sub
```

The `Randomize` statement initializes the random number generator. The instruction `Int((maxNum – minNum + 1) * Rnd + minNum)` uses the `Rnd` function to generate a random value from the specified `minNum` to `maxNum`. The `Int` function converts the resulting random number to an integer. Instead of assigning constant values for `minNum` and `maxNum`, you can use the `InputBox` function to get these values from the user.

The inner `For...Next` loop ensures that each picked number is unique—it may not be any one of the previously picked numbers. If you omit the inner loop and run this procedure multiple times, you'll likely see some occurrences of duplicate numbers.

3. Execute the Lotto procedure (choose **Run | Run Sub/UserForm**) to get the computer-generated lottery numbers.

Initial Value of an Array Element

Until a value is assigned to an element of an array, the element retains its default value. Numeric variables have a default value of zero (0), and string variables have a default value of empty string ("").

Passing Arrays between Procedures

When an array is declared in a procedure, it is local to this procedure and unknown to other procedures. However, you can pass the local array to another procedure by using the array's name followed by an empty set of parentheses as an argument in the calling statement. For example, the statement `Hello cities()` calls the procedure named Hello and passes to it the array `cities`.

USING A TWO-DIMENSIONAL ARRAY

Now that you know how to programmatically produce a list (a one-dimensional array), it's time to take a closer look at how you can work with tables of data. The following procedure creates a two-dimensional array that will hold country name, currency name, and exchange rate for three countries.

Hands-On 7.5. Using a Two-Dimensional Array

1. In the Visual Basic Editor window, insert a new module.
2. Enter the **Exchange** procedure in the module's Code window:

```
Sub Exchange()
   Dim t As String
   Dim r As String
   Dim Ex(3, 3) As Variant

   t = Chr(9) & Chr(9) ' 2 Tabs
   r = Chr(13) ' Enter

   Ex(1, 1) = "Japan"
   Ex(1, 2) = "Yen"
   Ex(1, 3) = 122.856
   Ex(2, 1) = "Europe"
   Ex(2, 2) = "Euro"
   Ex(2, 3) = 0.939350
   Ex(3, 1) = "Canada"
   Ex(3, 2) = "Dollar"
   Ex(3, 3) = 1.33512

   MsgBox "Country " & t & "Currency" & t & _
      "1 USD" & r & r _
      & Ex(1, 1) & t & Ex(1, 2) & t & Ex(1, 3) & r _
      & Ex(2, 1) & t & Ex(2, 2) & t & Ex(2, 3) & r _
      & Ex(3, 1) & t & Ex(3, 2) & t & Ex(3, 3), , _
      "Exchange Rates"
End Sub
```

3. Execute the Exchange procedure (choose **Run | Run Sub/UserForm**).

When you run the Exchange procedure, you will see a message box with the information presented in three columns, as shown in Figure 7.2.

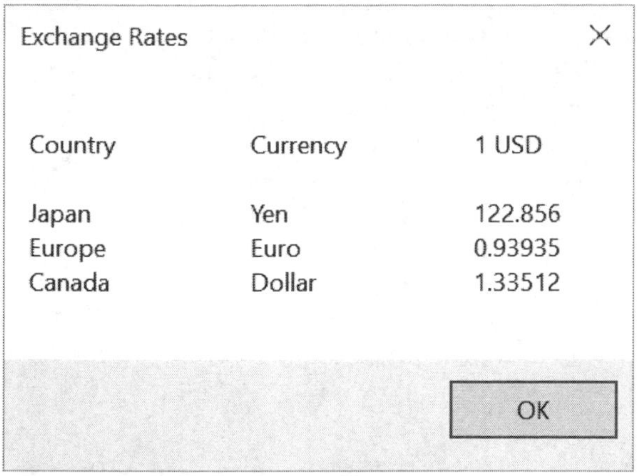

Exchange Rates		✕
Country	Currency	1 USD
Japan	Yen	122.856
Europe	Euro	0.93935
Canada	Dollar	1.33512
		OK

FIGURE 7.2. The text displayed in the message box can be custom formatted. (Note that these are fictitious exchange rates for demonstration only.)

4. Click **OK** to close the message box.

STATIC AND DYNAMIC ARRAYS

The arrays introduced thus far are static. A *static array* is an array of a specific size. You use a static array when you know in advance how big the array should be. The size of the static array is specified in the array's declaration statement. For example, the statement Dim Fruits(10) As String declares a static array called Fruits that is made up of 10 elements.

But what if you're not sure how many elements your array will contain? If your procedure depends on user input, the number of user-supplied elements might vary every time the procedure is executed. How can you ensure that the array you declare is not wasting memory?

You may recall that after you declare an array, VBA sets aside enough memory to accommodate the array. If you declare an array to hold more elements than what you need, you'll end up wasting valuable computer resources. The solution to this problem is making your arrays dynamic. A *dynamic array* is an array whose size can change. You use a dynamic array when the array size will be determined each time the procedure is run.

SIDEBAR   *Fixed-Dimension Arrays*

A static array contains a fixed number of elements. The number of elements in a static array will not change once it has been declared.

A dynamic array is declared by placing empty parentheses after the array name—for example:

```
Dim Fruits() As String
```

Before you use a dynamic array in your procedure, you must use the ReDim statement to dynamically set the lower and upper bounds of the array.

The ReDim statement redimensions arrays as the procedure code executes. The ReDim statement informs Visual Basic about the new size of the array. This statement can be used several times in the same procedure. Now let's write a procedure that demonstrates the use of a dynamic array.

(◉) Hands-On 7.6. Using a Dynamic Array

1. Insert a new module and enter the following **DynArray** procedure in the module's Code window:

```
Sub DynArray()
  Dim counter As Integer
  Dim myArray() As Integer ' declare a dynamic array
  ReDim myArray(5) ' specify the initial size of the array
  Dim myValues As String

  ' populate myArray with values
  For counter = 1 To 5
    myArray(counter) = counter + 1
    myValues = myValues & myArray(counter) & Chr(13)
  Next

  ' change the size of myArray to hold 10 elements
  ReDim Preserve myArray(10)

  ' add new values to myArray
  For counter = 6 To 10
    myArray(counter) = counter * counter
    myValues = myValues & myArray(counter) & Chr(13)
  Next counter

  MsgBox myValues
  For counter = 1 To 10
    Debug.Print myArray(counter)
  Next counter
End Sub
```

In the DynArray procedure, the statement Dim myArray() As Integer declares a dynamic array called myArray. Although this statement declares the array, it docs not allocate any memory to the array. The first ReDim statement specifies the initial size of myArray and reserves for it 10 bytes of memory to hold its five elements. As you know, every Integer value requires 2 bytes of memory. The For...Next loop populates myArray with data and writes the array's elements to the variable myValues. The value of the variable counter equals 1 at the beginning of the loop.

The first statement in the loop (`myArray(counter) = counter +1`) assigns the value 2 to the first element of `myArray`. The second statement (`myValues = myValues & myArray(counter) & Chr(13)`) enters the current value of `myArray`'s element followed by a carriage return (`Chr(13)`) into the variable `myValues`. The statements inside the loop are executed five times. Visual Basic places each new value in the variable `myValues` and proceeds to the next statement: `ReDim Preserve myArray(10)`.

Normally, when you change the size of the array, you lose all the values that were in that array. When used alone, the `ReDim` statement reinitializes the array. However, you can append new elements to an existing array by following the `ReDim` statement with the `Preserve` keyword. In other words, the `Preserve` keyword guarantees that the redimensioned array will not lose its existing data.

The second `For...Next` loop assigns values to the 6th through 10th elements of `myArray`. This time the values of the array's elements are obtained by multiplication: `counter * counter`.

2. Execute the **DynArray** procedure (choose **Run | Run Sub/UserForm**).

<hr>

SIDEBAR   *Dimensioning Arrays*

You can't assign a value to an array element until you have declared the array with the `Dim` or `ReDim` statement. (An exception to this is if you use the `Array` function discussed in the next section.)

ARRAY FUNCTIONS

You can manipulate arrays with five built-in VBA functions: `Array`, `IsArray`, `Erase`, `LBound`, and `UBound`. The following sections demonstrate the use of each of these functions in VBA procedures.

The Array Function

The `Array` function allows you to create an array during code execution without having to first dimension it. This function always returns an array of Variants. You can quickly place a series of values in a list by using the `Array` function.

The CarInfo procedure in the following hands-on exercise creates a fixed-size, one-dimensional, three-element array called `auto`.

⊙ Hands-On 7.7. Using the Array Function

1. Insert a new module and enter the following **CarInfo** procedure in the module's Code window:

```
Option Base 1

Sub CarInfo()
  Dim auto As Variant
```

```
auto = Array("Ford", "Black", "2015")
MsgBox auto(2) & " " & auto(1) & ", " & auto(3)

auto(2) = "4-door"
MsgBox auto(2) & " " & auto(1) & ", " & auto(3)
End Sub
```

2. Run the **CarInfo** procedure and examine the results.

   When you run this procedure, you get two message boxes. The first one displays the following text: "Black Ford, 2015." After changing the value of the second array element, the second message box will say: "4-door Ford, 2015."

   _____ *Be sure to enter* `Option Base 1` *at the top of the module before run-*
   NOTE *ning the CarInfo procedure. If this statement is missing in your module, Visual Basic will display runtime error 9—"Subscript out of range."*

The IsArray Function

The `IsArray` function lets you test whether a variable is an array. The `IsArray` function returns True if the variable is an array or False if it is not an array. Let's do another hands-on exercise.

(⊙) Hands-On 7.8. Using the IsArray Function

1. Insert a new module and enter the code of the **IsThisArray** procedure in the module's Code window:

```
Sub IsThisArray()
  ' declare a dynamic array
  Dim tblNames() As String
  Dim totalTables As Integer
  Dim counter As Integer
  Dim db As Database

  Set db = CurrentDb

  ' count the tables in the open database
  totalTables = db.TableDefs.Count

  ' specify the size of the array
  ReDim tblNames(1 To totalTables)

  ' enter and show the names of tables
  For counter = 1 To totalTables - 1
    tblNames(counter) = db.TableDefs(counter).Name
    Debug.Print tblNames(counter)
  Next counter

  ' check if this is indeed an array
  If IsArray(tblNames) Then
  MsgBox "The tblNames is an array."
  End If
End Sub
```

2. Run the IsThisArray procedure to examine its results.

When you run this procedure, the list of tables in the current database is written to the Immediate window. A message box displays whether the `tblNames` array is indeed an array.

The Erase Function

When you want to remove the data from an array, you should use the `Erase` function. This function deletes all the data held by static or dynamic arrays. In addition, the `Erase` function reallocates all of the memory assigned to a dynamic array. If a procedure has to use the dynamic array again, you must use the `ReDim` statement to specify the size of the array. The next hands-on exercise demonstrates how to erase the data from the array `cities`.

(◉) Hands-On 7.9. Removing Data from an Array

1. Insert a new module and enter the code of the **FunCities** procedure in the module's Code window:

```
' start indexing array elements at 1
Option Base 1

Sub FunCities()
  ' declare the array
  Dim cities(1 To 5) As String

  ' assign the values to array elements
  cities(1) = "Las Vegas"
  cities(2) = "Orlando"
  cities(3) = "Atlantic City"
  cities(4) = "New York"
  cities(5) = "San Francisco"

  ' display the list of cities
  MsgBox cities(1) & Chr(13) & cities(2) & Chr(13) _
    & cities(3) & Chr(13) & cities(4) & Chr(13) _
    & cities(5)

  Erase cities

  ' show all that was erased
  MsgBox cities(1) & Chr(13) & cities(2) & Chr(13) _
    & cities(3) & Chr(13) & cities(4) & Chr(13) _
    & cities(5)
End Sub
```

2. Run the FunCities procedure to examine its results.
3. Click **OK** to close the message box.

Visual Basic should now display an empty message box because all values were deleted from the array by the `Erase` function.

4. Click **OK** to close the empty message box.

The LBound and UBound Functions

The LBound and UBound functions return whole numbers that indicate the lower bound and upper bound indices of an array.

◉ Hands-On 7.10. Finding the Lower and Upper Bounds of an Array

1. Insert a new module and enter the code of the **FunCities2** procedure in the module's Code window:

```
Sub FunCities2()
  ' declare the array
  Dim cities(1 To 5) As String

  ' assign the values to array elements
  cities(1) = "Las Vegas"
  cities(2) = "Orlando"
  cities(3) = "Atlantic City"
  cities(4) = "New York"
  cities(5) = "San Francisco"

  ' display the list of cities
  MsgBox cities(1) & Chr(13) & cities(2) & Chr(13) _
    & cities(3) & Chr(13) & cities(4) & Chr(13) _
    & cities(5)

  ' display the array bounds
  MsgBox "The lower bound: " & LBound(cities) & Chr(13) _
    & "The upper bound: " & UBound(cities)
End Sub
```

2. Run the FunCities2 procedure.
3. Click **OK** to close the message box that displays the favorite cities.
4. Click **OK** to close the message box that displays the lower and upper bound indices.

To determine the upper and lower indices in a two-dimensional array, you may want to add the following statements at the end of the Exchange procedure that was prepared in Hands-On 7.5 (add these lines just before the End Sub keywords):

```
MsgBox "The lower bound (first dimension) is " & LBound(Ex, 1) & "."
MsgBox "The upper bound (first dimension) is " & UBound(Ex, 1) & "."
MsgBox "The lower bound (second dimension) is " & LBound(Ex, 2) & "."
MsgBox "The upper bound (second dimension) is " & UBound(Ex, 2) & "."
```

_____ *When determining the lower and upper bound indices of a two-dimen-*
NOTE *sional array, you must specify the dimension number: 1 for the first di-*
mension and 2 for the second dimension.

ERRORS IN ARRAYS

When working with arrays, it's easy to make a mistake. If you try to assign more values than there are elements in the declared array, Visual

Basic will display the error message "Subscript out of range" (see Figure 7.3).

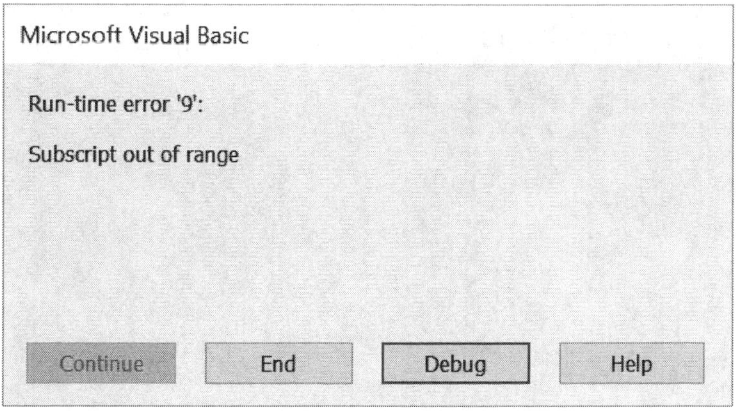

```
Microsoft Visual Basic


Run-time error '9':

Subscript out of range




    [ Continue ]        [ End ]         [ Debug ]         [ Help ]
```

FIGURE 7.3. This error was caused by an attempt to access a nonexistent array element.

Suppose you declared a one-dimensional array that consists of three elements, and you are trying to assign a value to the fourth element. When you run the procedure, Visual Basic can't find the fourth element, so it displays the error message shown in Figure 7.3. If you click the Debug button, Visual Basic will highlight the line of code that caused the error (see Figure 7.4).

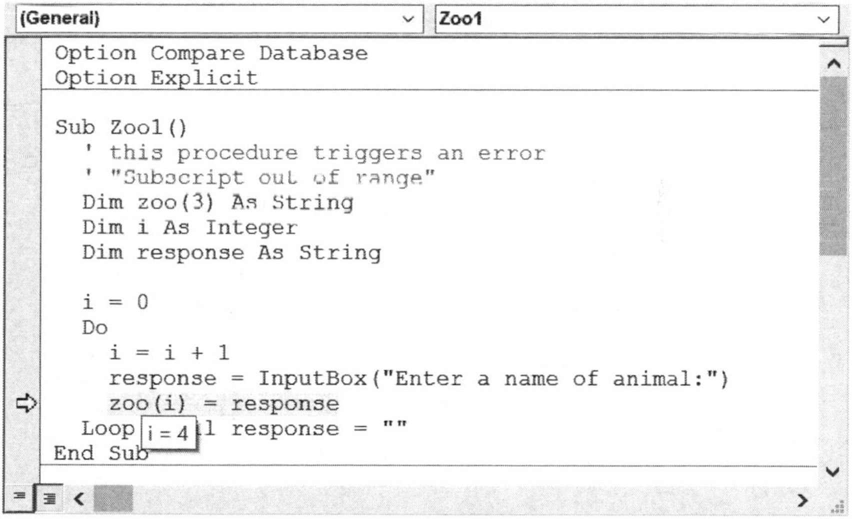

```
(General)                           v   Zoo1                          v

   Option Compare Database
   Option Explicit

   Sub Zoo1()
   ' this procedure triggers an error
   ' "Subscript out of range"
   Dim zoo(3) As String
   Dim i As Integer
   Dim response As String

   i = 0
   Do
      i = i + 1
      response = InputBox("Enter a name of animal:")
⇨    zoo(i) = response
   Loop i = 4 l response = ""
   End Sub
```

FIGURE 7.4. The statement that triggered the error shown in Figure 7.3. is highlighted.

The error *Subscript out of range* is often triggered in procedures using loops. The procedure Zoo1 shown in Hands-On 7.11 serves as an example of such a situation.

⊙ Hands-On 7.11. Understanding Errors in Arrays

1. Insert a new module and enter the following **Zoo1** and **Zoo2** procedures in the module's Code window:

```
Sub Zoo1()
  ' this procedure triggers an error
  ' "Subscript out of range"
  Dim zoo(3) As String
  Dim i As Integer
  Dim response As String

  i = 0
  Do
    i = i + 1
    response = InputBox("Enter a name of animal:")
    zoo(i) = response
  Loop Until response = ""
End Sub

Sub Zoo2()
  ' this procedure avoids the error
  ' "Subscript out of range"
  Dim zoo(3) As String
  Dim i As Integer
  Dim response As String

  i = 1
  Do While i >= LBound(zoo) And i <= UBound(zoo)
    response = InputBox("Enter a name of animal:")
    If response = "" Then Exit Sub
      zoo(i) = response
      Debug.Print zoo(i)
      i = i + 1
  Loop
End Sub
```

2. Run the Zoo1 procedure and enter your favorite animal names when prompted. Do not cancel the procedure until you see the error.

   While executing this procedure, when the variable i equals 4, Visual Basic will not be able to find the fourth element in a three-element array, so the error message will appear.

3. Click the **Debug** button in the error message.

   Visual Basic will highlight the code that caused the error.

4. Position the cursor over the variable i in the highlighted line of code to view the variable's value.

   Visual Basic displays: i=4

   Notice that at the top of the Zoo1 procedure zoo has been declared as an array containing only three elements:

```
Dim zoo(3) As String
```

   Because Visual Basic could not find the fourth element, it displayed the "Subscript out of range" error.

The Zoo2 procedure demonstrates how, by using the LBound and UBound functions introduced in the preceding section, you can avoid errors caused by an attempt to access a nonexistent array element.

5. Choose **Run** | **Reset** to terminate the debugging session and exit the procedure. You will learn more about debugging procedures in Chapter 9.

Another frequent error you may encounter while working with arrays is a *Type Mismatch* error. To avoid this error, keep in mind that each element of an array must be of the same data type. Therefore, if you attempt to assign to an element of an array a value that conflicts with the data type of the array, you will get a Type Mismatch error during the code execution. If you need to hold values of different data types in an array, declare the array as Variant.

PARAMETER ARRAYS

In Chapter 4, you learned that values can be passed between subroutines or functions as either required or optional arguments. If the passed argument is not absolutely required for the procedure to execute, the argument's name is preceded by the keyword Optional. Sometimes, however, you don't know in advance how many arguments you want to pass. A classic example is addition. One time you may want to add 2 numbers together, another time you may want to add 3, 10, or 15 numbers.

Using the keyword ParamArray, you can pass an array consisting of any number of elements to your subroutines and functions. The following hands-on exercise uses the AddMultipleArgs function to add as many numbers as you may require. This function begins with the declaration of an array myNumbers. Notice the use of the ParamArray keyword.

The array must be declared as type Variant, and it must be the last argument in the procedure definition.

(◉) Hands-On 7.12. Working with Parameter Arrays

1. Insert a new module and enter the following **AddMultipleArgs** function procedure in the module's Code window:

```
Function AddMultipleArgs(ParamArray myNumbers() As Variant)
    Dim mySum As Single
    Dim myValue As Variant

    For Each myValue In myNumbers
    mySum = mySum + myValue
    Next
    AddMultipleArgs = mySum
End Function
```

2. Choose **View** | **Immediate Window** and type the following instruction, and then press **Enter** to execute it:

```
AddMultipleArgs(1, 23.24, 3, 24, 8, 34)
```

you press Enter, Visual Basic returns the total of all the numbers in the parentheses: 93.24. You can supply an unlimited number of arguments. To add more values, enter additional values in the parentheses after the function name in the Immediate window, and then press Enter. Notice that each function argument must be separated by a comma.

PASSING ARRAYS TO FUNCTION PROCEDURES

You can pass an array to a function procedure and return an array from a function. For example, let's assume you have a list of countries. You want to convert the country names stored in your array to uppercase and keep the original array intact. You can delegate the conversion process to a function procedure. When the array is passed using the `ByVal` keyword, the function will work with the copy of the original array. Any modifications performed within the function will affect only the copy. Therefore, the array in the calling procedure will not be modified.

(◉) Hands-On 7.13. Passing an Array to a Function Procedure

1. Insert a new module and enter the following procedure and function in the module's Code window:

```
Sub ManipulateArray()
  Dim countries(1 To 6) As Variant
  Dim countriesUCase As Variant
  Dim i As Integer

' assign the values to array elements
  countries(1) = "Bulgaria"
  countries(2) = "Argentina"
  countries(3) = "Brazil"
  countries(4) = "Sweden"
  countries(5) = "New Zealand"
  countries(6) = "Denmark"

  countriesUCase = ArrayToUCase(countries)

  For i = 1 To 6
    Debug.Print countriesUCase(i)
    Debug.Print countries(i) & " (Original Entry)"
  Next i
End Sub

Public Function ArrayToUCase(ByVal myValues _
 As Variant) As String()
  Dim i As Integer
  Dim Temp() As String
  If IsArray(myValues) Then
    ReDim Temp(LBound(myValues) To UBound(myValues))
    For i = LBound(myValues) To UBound(myValues)
      Temp(i) = CStr(UCase(myValues(i)))
```

```
      Next i
      ArrayToUCase = Temp
    End If
End Function
```

2. Run the ManipulateArray procedure and check its results in the Immediate window.

SORTING AN ARRAY

We all find it easier to work with sorted data. Some operations on arrays, like finding maximum and minimum values, require that the array is sorted. Once it is sorted, you can find the maximum value by assigning the upper bound index to the sorted array, as in the following:

```
y = myIntArray(UBound(myIntArray))
```

The minimum value can be obtained by reading the first value of the sorted array:

```
x = myIntArray(1)
```

So how can you sort an array? Hands-On 7.14 demonstrates how to delegate the sorting task to a classic bubble sort routine. A *bubble sort* is a comparison sort. To create a sorted set, you step through the list to be sorted, compare each pair of adjacent items, and swap them if they are in the wrong order. As a result of this sorting algorithm, the smaller values "bubble" to the top of the list. In the next procedure, we will sort the list of countries alphabetically in ascending order.

⊙ Hands-On 7.14. Sorting an Array

This hands-on exercise requires prior completion of Hands-On 7.13.

1. In the same module where you entered the ArrayToUCase function procedure, enter the following BubbleSort function procedure:

```
Sub BubbleSort(myArray As Variant)
  Dim i As Integer
  Dim j As Integer
  Dim uBnd As Integer
  Dim Temp As Variant
  uBnd = UBound(myArray)
    For i = LBound(myArray) To uBnd - 1
      For j = i + 1 To uBnd
        If UCase(myArray(i)) > UCase(myArray(j)) Then
          Temp = myArray(j)
          myArray(j) = myArray(i)
          myArray(i) = Temp
        End If
      Next j
    Next i
End Sub
```

2. Add the following statements to the ManipulateArray procedure, placing them just above the `For...Next` statement block (see Figure 7.5):

```
' call function to sort the array
  BubbleSort countriesUCase
```

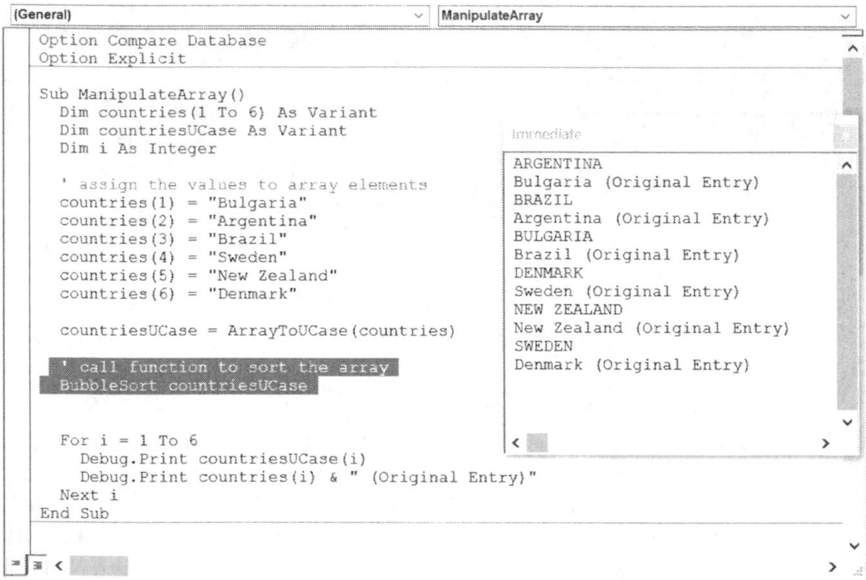

FIGURE 7.5. Calling the BubbleSort function procedure from the ManipulateArray procedure.

3. Run the ManipulateArray procedure and check its results in the Immediate window. Notice that the countries that appear in uppercase letters are shown in alphabetic order.
4. Choose **File | Save Chap07** and save changes to the modules when prompted.
5. Choose **File | Close and Return to Microsoft Access**.
6. Close the **Chap07.accdb** database and exit Microsoft Access.

SUMMARY

In this chapter, you learned how, by creating an array, you can write procedures that require a large number of variables. You worked with examples of procedures that demonstrated how to declare and use a one-dimensional array (list) and a two-dimensional array (table). You learned the difference between static and dynamic arrays. This chapter introduced you to five built-in VBA functions that are frequently used with arrays (`Array`, `IsArray`, `Erase`, `LBound`, and `UBound`), as well as the `ParamArray` keyword. You also learned how to pass one array and return another array from a function procedure. Finally, you saw how to sort an array. You now know all the VBA control structures that can make your code more intelligent: conditional statements, loops, and arrays.

In the next chapter, you will learn how to use collections instead of arrays to manipulate large amounts of data.

CHAPTER 8

KEEPING TRACK OF MULTIPLE VALUES USING OBJECT COLLECTIONS

Microsoft Access offers a large number of built-in objects that you can access from your VBA procedures to automate many aspects of your databases. You are not limited to using these built-in objects, however. VBA allows you to create your own objects and collections of objects, complete with their own methods and properties. While writing your own VBA procedures, you may come across a situation where there's no built-in collection to handle the task at hand. The solution is to create a custom collection object. You already know from the previous chapter how to work with multiple items of data by using static and dynamic arrays. Because collections have built-in properties and methods that allow you to add, remove, and count their elements, they make working with multiple data items much easier. In this chapter, you learn how to work with collections, including how to declare a custom Collection object. Using class modules to create user-defined objects will also be discussed. Before diving into theory and this chapter's hands-on examples, let's review the following terms:

Collection—An object that contains a set of related objects.
Class—A definition of an object that includes its name, properties, methods, and events. The class acts as a sort of object template from which an instance of an object is created at runtime.
Class module—A module that contains the definition of a class, including its property and method definitions.
Event—An action recognized by an object, such as a mouseclick or a keypress, for which you can define a response. Events can be triggered by a user action, a VBA statement, or the system.
Event procedure—A procedure that is automatically executed in response to an event triggered by the user, program code, or the system.

Form module—A module that contains the VBA code for all event procedures triggered by events occurring in a user form or its controls. A form module is a type of class module.

Instance—A specific object that belongs to a class is referred to as an *instance of the class*. When you create an instance, you create a new object that has the properties and methods defined by the class.

Module—A structure containing subroutine and function procedures that are available to other VBA procedures and are not related to any object in particular.

WORKING WITH COLLECTIONS OF OBJECTS

Collections are objects that contain other similar objects. For example, a Microsoft Access database has a collection of Tables, and each table has a collection of Fields and Indexes. In Microsoft Excel, all open workbooks belong to the Workbooks collection, and all the sheets in a particular workbook are members of the Worksheets collection. In Microsoft Word, all open documents belong to the Documents collection, and each paragraph in a document is a member of the Paragraphs collection.

No matter what collection you want to work with, you can do the following:

■ Insert new items into the collection by using the `Add` method.

The following example uses the Immediate window to create a collection named myTestCollection and adds three items to the collection. To try out these examples, type the statements in the Immediate window, and then press Enter after each line:

```
set myTestCollection = New Collection
myTestCollection.Add "first member"
myTestCollection.Add "second member"
myTestCollection.Add "third member"
```

■ Determine the number of items in the collection by using the Count property.

For example, when you type this statement in the Immediate window, and then press Enter:

```
?myTestCollection.Count
```

it returns the total number of items stored in the `myTestCollection` object variable.

■ Refer to a specific object in a collection by using an index value.

For example, to find out the names of the collection members, you can type the following statement in the Immediate window, and then press Enter:

```
?myTestCollection.Item(1)
```

Because the `Item` method is a default method of the collection, you may omit it from the statement, as shown here:

```
?myTestCollection(1)
```

■ Remove an object from a collection by using the `Remove` method.

For example, to remove the first object from the `myTestCollection` object variable, enter the following statement, and then press Enter:

```
myTestCollection.Remove 1
```

■ Cycle through every object in the collection by using the `For  Each...  Next` loop.

For example, to remove all objects from the `myTestCollection` object variable, type the following looping structure in the Immediate window, and then press Enter:

```
For Each m in myTestCollection : myTestCollection.Remove 1 : Next
```

Note that a colon is used to separate one statement from the next. You can write two or more statements on a single line by separating them with a colon (:). This is very convenient when testing statements in the Immediate window. Because collections are reindexed, the preceding statement will remove the first member of the collection on each iteration. When you press Enter, `myTestCollection` should have zero objects. However, to be sure, type the following statement in the Immediate window, and then press Enter:

```
?myTestCollection.Count
```

Now that you have learned the basics of working with built-in collections, let's move on to declaring and using custom collections.

DECLARING A CUSTOM COLLECTION

To create a user-defined collection, you should begin by declaring an object variable of the Collection type. This variable is declared with the `New` keyword in the `Dim` statement:

```
Dim collection Fruits As New Collection
```

ADDING OBJECTS TO A CUSTOM COLLECTION

After you've declared the Collection object, you can insert new items into the collection by using the `Add` method. The objects with which you populate your collection do not have to be of the same data type. The `Add` method looks as follows:

```
object.Add item[, key, before, after]
```

For example, the following statement adds a new item to the previously declared Fruits collection:

```
Fruits.Add "apples"
```

You are required only to specify `object` and `item`. `object` is the collection name, such as Fruits. This is the same name that was used in the declaration of the Collection object. The Item, such as "apples," is the object you want to add to the collection (Fruits).

Although the other arguments are optional, they are quite useful. It's important to understand that the items in a collection are automatically assigned numbers starting with 1. However, they can also be assigned a unique key value. Instead of accessing a specific item with an index (1, 2, 3, and so on) at the time an object is added to a collection, you can assign a key for that object. For instance, to identify an individual in a collection of students or employees, you could use Social Security numbers as a key. If you want to specify the position of the object in the collection, you should use either the `before` or `after` argument (but not both). The `before` argument is the object before which the new object is added. The `after` argument is the object after which the new object is added.

The NewEmployees procedure in the following hands-on exercise declares the custom Collection object called `colEmployees`.

Please note files for the Hands-On project may be found on the companion CD-ROM.

Hands-On 8.1. Creating a Custom Collection

1. Start Microsoft Access and create a new database named **Chap08.accdb** in your **C:\VBAPrimerAccess_ByExample** folder.
2. Once your new database is opened, press **Alt+F11** to switch to the Visual Basic Editor window.
3. Choose **Insert | Module** to add a new standard module.
4. In the Module1 Code window, enter the following **NewEmployees** procedure. Be sure to enter the `Option Base 1` statement before this procedure.

```
Option Base 1                ' ensure that there is only one
                             ' Option Base 1 statement
                             ' at the top of the module
Sub NewEmployees()
 ' declare the employees collection
 Dim colEmployees As New Collection
 ' declare a variable to hold each element of a collection
 Dim emp As Variant
 ' Add 3 new employees to the collection
 With colEmployees
   .Add Item:="John Collins", Key:="128634456"
   .Add Item:="Mary Poppins", Key:="223998765"
   .Add Item:="Karen Loza", Key:="120228876", Before:=2
 End With
 ' list the members of the collection
 For Each emp In colEmployees
  Debug.Print emp
 Next
```

```
MsgBox "There are " & colEmployees.Count & " employees."
End Sub
```

Note that the control variable used in the `For Each...Next` loop must be declared as Variant or Object. When you run this procedure, you will notice that the order of employee names stored in the `colEmployees` collection (as displayed in the Immediate window) may be different from the order in which these employees were entered in the program code. This is the result of using the optional `before` argument with Karen Loza's entry. This argument's value tells Visual Basic to place Karen before the second item in the collection.

5. Choose **Run | Run Sub/UserForm** to execute the NewEmployees procedure.

REMOVING OBJECTS FROM A CUSTOM COLLECTION

Removing an item from a custom collection is as easy as adding an item. To remove an item, use the `Remove` method in the following format:

```
object.Remove index
```

`object` is the name of the custom collection that contains the object you want to remove. `index` is an expression specifying the position of the object in the collection.

To demonstrate the process of removing an item from a collection, let's work with the following hands-on exercise that modifies the NewEmployees procedure that you prepared in Hands-On 8.1.

⊙ Hands-On 8.2. Removing Objects from a Collection

This hands-on exercise requires the prior completion of Hands-On 8.1.

1. Add the following lines to the **NewEmployees** procedure just before the `End Sub` keywords:

```
' remove the third item from the collection
colEmployees.Remove 3
MsgBox colEmployees.Count & " employees remain."
```

2. Rerun the NewEmployees procedure.

SIDEBAR *Reindexing Collections*

Collections are reindexed automatically when an item is removed. Therefore, to remove all items from a custom collection you can use 1 for the `Index` argument, as in the following example:

```
Do While myCollection.Count > 0
 myCollection.Remove Index:=1
Loop
```

CREATING CUSTOM OBJECTS IN CLASS MODULES

There are two module commands available in the Visual Basic Editor's Insert menu: Module and Class Module. So far you've used a standard module to create subprocedures and function procedures. You'll use the class module for the first time in this chapter to create a custom object and define its properties and methods.

Creating a new VBA object involves inserting a class module into your project and adding code to that module. However, before you do so you need a basic understanding of what a class is.

If you refer back to the list of terms at the beginning of this chapter, you will find out that the *class* is a sort of object template. A frequently used analogy is comparing an object class to a cookie cutter. Just like a cookie cutter defines what a particular cookie will look like, the definition of the class determines how a particular object should look and how it should behave. Before you can actually use an object class, you must first create a new *instance* of that class. Object instances are the cookies. Each object instance has the characteristics (properties and methods) defined by its class. Just as you can cut out many cookies using the same cookie cutter, you can create multiple instances of a class. You can change the properties of each instance of a class independently of any other instance of the same class.

A *class module* lets you define your own custom classes, complete with custom properties and methods. A *property* is an attribute of an object that defines one of its characteristics, such as shape, position, color, title, and so forth. A *method* is an action that the object can perform. You can create the properties for your custom objects by writing property procedures in a class module. The object methods are also created in a class module by writing subprocedures or function procedures.

After building your object in the class module, you can use it in the same way you use other built-in objects. You can also export the object class outside the VBA project to other VBA-capable applications.

Creating a Class

The following sections of this chapter walk you through the process of creating and working with a custom object called CEmployee. This object will represent an employee. It will have properties such as ID, FirstName, LastName, and Salary. It will also have a method to modify the current salary.

◉ Custom Project 8.1. (Step 1) Creating a Class Module

1. In the Visual Basic Editor window, choose **Insert | Class Module**.
2. In the Project Explorer window, highlight the **Class1** module and use the Properties window to rename the class module **CEmployee** (see Figure 8.1).

SIDEBAR *Naming a Class Module*

Every time you create a new class module, give it a meaningful name. Set the name of the class module to the name you want to use in your VBA procedures using the class. The name you choose for your class should be easily understood and should identify the "thing" the object class represents. As a rule, the object class name is prefaced with an uppercase "C."

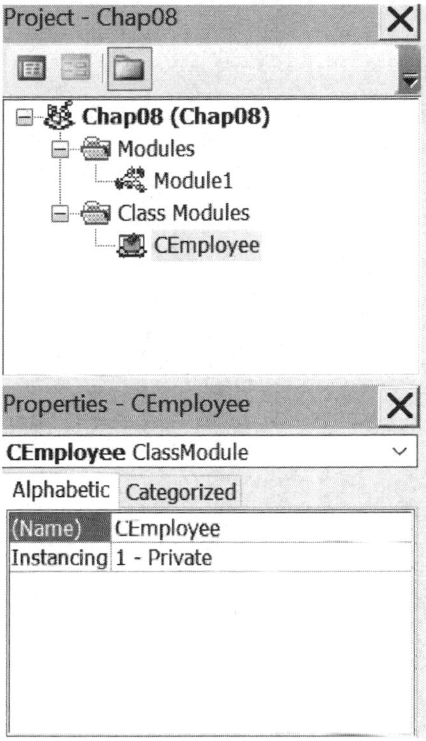

FIGURE 8.1. Use the Name property in the Properties window to rename the Class module.

Variable Declarations

After adding and renaming the class module, the next step is to declare the variables that will hold the data you want to store in the custom CEmployee object. Each item of data you want to store in an object should be assigned a variable. Class variables are called *data members* and are declared with the `Private` keyword. Using the `Private` keyword in a class module hides the data members and prevents other parts of the application from referencing them. Only the procedures within the class module in which the private variables were defined can modify the value of these variables.

Because the name of a variable also serves as a property name, use meaningful names for your object's data members. It's traditional to preface the class variable names with "m_" to indicate that they are data members of a class.

⊙ **Custom Project 8.1. (Step 2) Declaring Class Members**

1. Type the following declaration lines at the top of the **CEmployee** class module's code window:

```
Option Explicit
' declarations
Private m_LastName As String
Private m_FirstName As String
Private m_Salary As Currency
Private m_ID As String
```

Notice that the name of each data member variable begins with the prefix "m_."

Defining the Properties for the Class

Declaring the variables with the `Private` keyword ensures that they cannot be directly accessed from outside the object. This means that the VBA procedures outside the class module will not be able to set or read data stored in those variables. To enable other parts of your VBA application to set or retrieve the employee data, you must add special property procedures to the CEmployee class module. There are three types of property procedures:

- **Property Let**—This type of procedure allows other parts of the application to set the value of a property.
- **Property Get**—This type of procedure allows other parts of the application to get or read the value of a property.
- **Property Set**—This type of procedure is used instead of Property Let when setting the reference to an object.

Property procedures are executed when an object property needs to be set or retrieved. The Property Get procedure can have the same name as the Property Let procedure. You should create property procedures for each property of the object that can be accessed by another part of your VBA application.

The easiest of the three types of property statements to understand is the Property Get procedure. Let's examine the syntax of the property procedures by taking a close look at the Property Get LastName procedure.

Property procedures contain the following parts:

- A procedure declaration line
- An assignment statement
- The `End Property` keywords

A procedure declaration line specifies the name of the property and the data type:

```
Property Get LastName() As String
```

LastName is the name of the property and `As String` determines the data type of the property's return value.

An assignment statement is similar to the one used in a function procedure:

```
LastName = m_LastName
```

LastName is the name of the property and m_LastName is the data member variable that holds the value of the property you want to retrieve or set. The m_LastName variable should be defined with the Private keyword at the top of the class module. Here's the complete Property Get procedure:

```
Property Get LastName() As String
 LastName = m_LastName
End Property
```

The Property Get procedure can return a result from a calculation, like this:

```
Property Get Royalty()
 Royalty = (Sales * Percent) - Advance
End Property
```

The End Property keywords specify the end of the property procedure.

<hr>

SIDEBAR *Immediate Exit from Property Procedures*

Just as the Exit Sub and Exit Function keywords allow you to exit early from a subroutine or a function procedure, the Exit Property keywords give you a way to immediately exit from a property procedure. Program execution will continue with the statements following the statement that called the Property Get, Property Let, or Property Set procedure.

Creating the Property Get Procedures

The CEmployee class object has four properties that need to be exposed to VBA procedures that we will write later in a standard module named EmpOperations. When working with the CEmployee object, you would certainly like to get information about the employee ID, first and last name, and current salary.

⊙ Custom Project 8.1. (Step 3) Writing Property Get Procedures

1. Type the following Property Get procedures in the **CEmployee** class module, just below the declaration section that you entered in step 2 of this custom project:

```
Property Get ID() As String
 ID = m_ID
End Property
Property Get LastName() As String
 LastName = m_LastName
End Property
Property Get FirstName() As String
 FirstName = m_FirstName
End Property
```

```
Property Get Salary() As Currency
  Salary = m_Salary
End Property
```

Notice that each employee information type requires a separate Property Get procedure. Each of the preceding Property Get procedures returns the current value of the property. Notice also how a Property Get procedure is similar to a function procedure. Similar to function procedures, the Property Get procedures contain an assignment statement. As you recall from Chapter 4, to return a value from a function procedure, you must assign it to the function's name.

Creating the Property Let Procedures

In addition to retrieving values stored in data members (private variables) with Property Get procedures, you must prepare corresponding Property Let procedures to allow other procedures to change the values of these variables as needed. The only time you don't define a Property Let procedure is when the value stored in a private variable is meant to be *read-only*.

Suppose you don't want the user to change the employee ID. To make the ID read-only, you simply don't write a Property Let procedure for it. Hence, the CEmployee class will have only three properties (LastName, FirstName, and Salary). Each of these properties will require a separate Property Let procedure. The employee ID will be assigned automatically with a return value from a function procedure.

Let's continue with our project and write the required Property Let procedures for our custom CEmployee object.

◉ Custom Project 8.1. (Step 4) Writing Property Let Procedures

1. Type the following Property Let procedures in the **CEmployee** class module below the Property Get procedures:

```
Property Let LastName(L As String)
  m_LastName = L
End Property

Property Let FirstName(F As String)
  m_FirstName = F
End Property

Property Let Salary(ByVal dollar As Currency)
  m_Salary = dollar
End Property
```

The Property Let procedures require at least one parameter that specifies the value you want to assign to the property. This parameter can be passed by *value* (note the `ByVal` keyword in the preceding Property Let Salary procedure) or by *reference* (`ByRef` is the default). If you need a refresher on the meaning of these keywords, see the section titled "Passing Arguments by Reference and by Value" in Chapter 4.

The data type of the parameter passed to the Property Let procedure must be exactly the same data type as the value returned from the Property Get or Set procedure with the same name. Notice that the Property Let procedures have the same names as the Property Get procedures prepared in the preceding section. By skipping the Property Letprocedure for the ID property, you created a read-only ID property that can be retrieved but not set.

SIDEBAR *Defining the Scope of Property Procedures*

You can place the `Public`, `Private`, or `Static` keyword before the name of a property procedure to define its scope. To indicate that the Property Get procedure is accessible to procedures in all modules, use the following statement format:

```
Public Property Get FirstName() As String
```

To make the Property Get procedure accessible only to other procedures in the module where it is declared, use the following statement format:

```
Private Property Get FirstName() As String
```

To preserve the Property Get procedure's local variables between procedure calls, use the following statement format:

```
Static Property Get FirstName() As String
```

If not explicitly specified using either `Public` or `Private`, property procedures are public by default. Also, if the `Static` keyword is not used, the values of local variables are not preserved between procedure calls.

Creating the Class Methods

Apart from properties, objects usually have one or more methods. A *method* is an action that the object can perform. Methods allow you to manipulate the data stored in a class object. Methods are created with subroutines or function procedures. To make a method available outside the class module, use the `Public` keyword in front of the sub or function definition. The CEmployee object that you create in this chapter has one method that allows you to calculate the new salary. Assume that the employee salary can be increased or decreased by a specific percentage or amount.

Let's continue with our project by writing a class method that calculates the employee salary.

⊙ **Custom Project 8.1. (Step 5) Writing Class Methods**

1. Type the following **CalcNewSalary** function procedure in the **CEmployee** class module:

```
Public Function CalcNewSalary(choice As Integer, _
```

```
    curSalary As Currency, amount As Long) As Currency
    Select Case choice
     Case 1 ' by percent
      CalcNewSalary = curSalary + ((curSalary * amount) / 100)
     Case 2 ' by amount
      CalcNewSalary = curSalary + amount
    End Select
End Function
```

The CalcNewSalary function defined with the `Public` keyword in a class module serves as a method for the CEmployee class. To calculate a new salary, a VBA procedure from outside the class module must pass three arguments: `choice`, `CurSalary`, and `amount`. The `choice` argument specifies the type of the calculation. Suppose you want to increase the employee salary by 5% or by $5.00. The first option will increase the salary by the specified percentage, and the second option will add the specified amount to the current salary. The `curSalary` argument is the current salary figure for an employee, and `amount` determines the value by which the salary should be changed.

SIDEBAR   *About Class Methods*

- Only those methods that will be accessed from outside of the class should be declared as `Public`. All others should be declared as `Private`.
- Methods perform some operation on the data contained within the class.
- If a method needs to return a value, write a function procedure. Otherwise, create a subprocedure.

Creating an Instance of a Class

After typing all the necessary Property Get, Property Let, sub, or function procedures for your VBA application in the class module, you are ready to create a new instance of a class, which is called an *object*. Before an object can be created, an object variable must be declared in a standard module to store the reference to the object. If the name of the class module is CEmployee, then a new instance of this class can be created with the following statement:

```
Dim emp As New CEmployee
```

The `emp` variable will represent a reference to an object of the CEmployee class. When you declare the object variable with the `New` keyword, VBA creates the object and allocates memory for it. However, the object isn't instanced until you refer to it in your procedure code by assigning a value to its property or by running one of its methods.

You can also create an instance of the object by declaring an object variable with the data type defined to be the class of the object, as in the following:

```
Dim emp As CEmployee
Set emp = New CEmployee
```

If you don't use the New keyword with the Dim statement, VBA does not allocate memory for your custom object until your procedure actually needs it.

⊙ Custom Project 8.1. (Step 6) Creating an Instance of a Class

1. Activate the Visual Basic Editor window and choose **Insert | Module** to add a standard module to your application.
2. Use the Name property in the Properties window to change the name of the new module to **EmpOperations**.
3. Type the following declarations at the top of the EmpOperations module:

```
Dim emp As New CEmployee
Dim CEmployee As New Collection
```

The first declaration statement (Dim) declares the variable emp as a new instance of the CEmployee class. The second statement declares a custom collection. The CEmployee collection will be used to store all employee data.

Event Procedures in the Class Module

An *event* is basically an action recognized by an object. Custom classes recognize only two events: Initialize and Terminate. These events are triggered when an instance of the class is created and destroyed, respectively. The Initialize event is generated when an object is created from a class (see the preceding section on creating an instance of a class).In the CEmployee class example, the Initializeevent will also fire the first time that you use the empvariable in code. Because the statements included inside the Initializeevent are the first ones to be executed for the object before any properties are set or any methods are executed, the Initializeevent is a good place to perform initialization of the objects created from the class. As you recall, we made the ID read-only in the CEmployee class. You can use the Initializeevent to assign a unique five-digit number to the m_IDvariable.

The Class_Initialize procedure uses the following syntax:

```
Private Sub Class_Initialize()
 [code to perform tasks as the object is created goes here]
End Sub
```

The Terminate event occurs when all references to an object have been released. This is a good place to perform any necessary cleanup tasks. The Class_Terminate procedure uses the following syntax:

```
Private Sub Class_Terminate()
 [cleanup code goes here]
End Sub
```

To release an object variable from an object, use the following syntax:

```
Set objectVariable = Nothing
```

When you set the object variable to Nothing, the Terminate event is generated. Any code in this event is executed then.

CREATING THE USER INTERFACE

Implementing our custom CEmployee object requires that you design a form to enter and manipulate employee data.

⊙ Custom Project 8.1. (Step 7) Designing a User Form

1. Choose **File | Close and Return to Microsoft Access**.
2. Click the **Blank form** in the Forms section of the Create tab. Access will display a blank form in the Form view.
3. Switch to the form's Design view by choosing **Design View** from the Views section.
4. Save the form as **frmEmployeeSalaries**.
5. Use the tools in the Controls section of the Design tab to place controls on the form as shown in Figure 8.2.

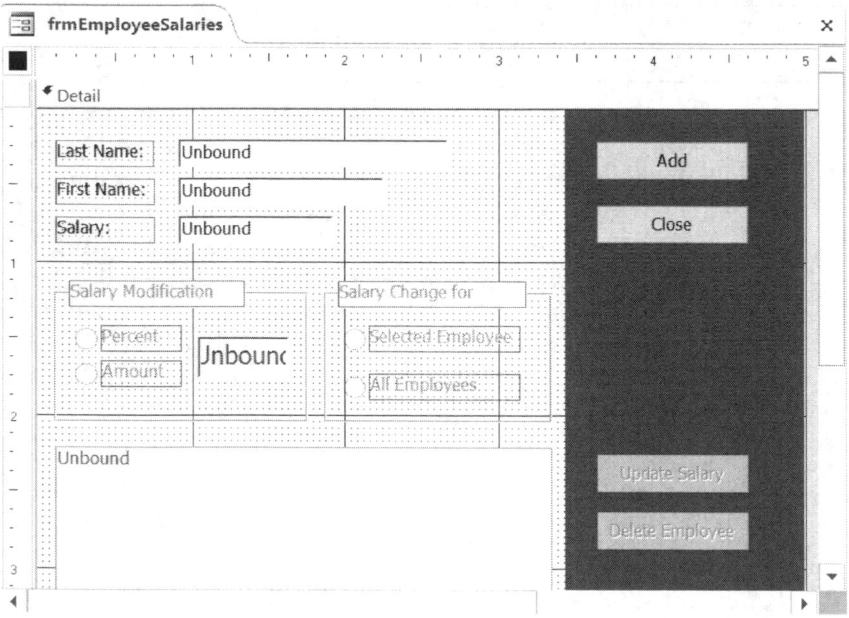

FIGURE 8.2. This form demonstrates the use of the CEmployee custom object.

6. Activate the property sheet and set the following properties for the form controls. To set the specified property, first click the control on the form to select it. Then, in the property sheet type the information shown in the Setting column next to the property indicated in the Property column.

Object	Property	Setting
Label1	Caption	Last Name
Text box next to the Last Name label	Name	txtLastName
Label2	Caption	First Name
Text box next to the First Name label	Name	txtFirstName
Label3	Caption	Salary
Text box next to the Salary label	Name	txtSalary
Option group 1	Name	frSalaryMod
	Caption	Salary Modification
Text box in the option group titled "Salary Modification"	Name	txtRaise
Option button 1	Name	optPercent
	Caption	Percent
Option button 2	Name	optAmount
	Caption	Amount
Option group 2	Name	frSalaryFor
	Caption	Salary Change for
Option button 3	Name	optSelected
	Caption	Selected Employee
Option button 4	Name	optAll
	Caption	All Employees
Listbox	Name	lboxPeople
	Row Source Type	Value List
	Column Count	4
	Column Widths	0.5";0.9";0.7";0.5"
Command Button 1	Name	cmdAdd
	Caption	Add
Command Button 2	Name	cmdClose
	Caption	Close
Command Button 3	Name	cmdUpdate
	Caption	Update Salary
Command Button 4	Name	cmdDelete
	Caption	Delete Employee

Now that the form is ready, you need to write a few event procedures to handle various events, such as clicking a command button or loading the form.

⊙ Custom Project 8.1. (Step 8) Writing Event Procedures

1. Activate the Code window behind the form by choosing the **View Code** button in the **Tools** section of the **Design** tab.
2. Enter the following variable declarations at the top of the form's Code window:

```
' variable declarations
Dim choice As Integer
Dim amount As Long
```

NOTE *Please ensure that the* Option Explicit *statement appears at the top of the module, above the variable declaration statements.*

3. Type the following **UserForm_Initialize** procedure to enable or disable controls on the form:

```
Private Sub UserForm_Initialize()
  txtLastName.SetFocus
  cmdUpdate.Enabled = False
  cmdDelete.Enabled = False
  lboxPeople.Enabled = False
  frSalaryFor.Enabled = False
  frSalaryFor.Value = 0
  frSalaryMod.Enabled = False
  frSalaryMod.Value = 0
  txtRaise.Enabled = False
  txtRaise.Value = ""
End Sub
```

4. Type the following **Form_Load** event procedure:

```
Private Sub Form_Load()
 Call UserForm_Initialize
End Sub
```

When the form loads, the UserForm_Initialize procedure will run.

5. Enter the following **cmdAdd_Click** procedure to add the employee to the collection:

```
Private Sub cmdAdd_Click()
 Dim strLast As String
 Dim strFirst As String
 Dim curSalary As Currency

 ' Validate data entry
 If IsNull(txtLastName.Value) Or txtLastName.Value = "" _
 Or IsNull(txtFirstName.Value) Or txtFirstName.Value = "" _
 Or IsNull(txtSalary.Value) Or txtSalary.Value = "" Then
  MsgBox "Enter Last Name, First Name and Salary."
  txtLastName.SetFocus
  Exit Sub
 End If
 If Not IsNumeric(txtSalary) Then
  MsgBox "You must enter a value for the Salary."
```

```
    txtSalary.SetFocus
    Exit Sub
  End If
  If txtSalary < 0 Then
    MsgBox "Salary cannot be a negative number."
    Exit Sub
  End If

  ' assign text box values to variables
  strLast = txtLastName
  strFirst = txtFirstName
  curSalary = txtSalary

  ' enable buttons and other controls
  cmdUpdate.Enabled = True
  cmdDelete.Enabled = True
  lboxPeople.Enabled = True
  frSalaryFor.Enabled = True
  frSalaryMod.Enabled = True
  txtRaise.Enabled = True
  txtRaise.Value = ""
  lboxPeople.Visible = True

  ' enter data into the CEmployees collection
  EmpOperations.AddEmployee strLast, strFirst, curSalary

  ' update listbox
  lboxPeople.RowSource = GetValues

  ' delete data from text boxes
  txtLastName = ""
  txtFirstName = ""
  txtSalary = ""
  txtLastName.SetFocus
End Sub
```

The cmdAdd_Click procedure starts off by validating the user's input in the Last Name, First Name, and Salary text boxes. If the user entered correct data, the text box values are assigned to the variables strLast, strFirst, and curSalary. Next, a number of statements enable buttons and other controls on the form so that the user can work with the employee data. The following statement calls the AddEmployee procedure in the EmpOperations standard module and passes the required parameters to it:

```
EmpOperations.AddEmployee strLast, strFirst, curSalary
```

Once the employee is entered into the collection, the employee data is added to the listbox (see Figure 8.3) with the following statement:

```
lboxPeople.RowSource = GetValues
```

GetValues is the name of a function procedure in the EmpOperations module (see step 12 further on). This function cycles through the CEmployee collection to create a string of values for the listbox row source.

The cmdAdd_Click procedure ends by clearing the text boxes, and then setting the focus to the Last Name text box so the user can enter new employee data.

6. Enter the following **cmdClose_Click** procedure to close the form:

```
Private Sub cmdClose_Click()
 DoCmd.Close
End Sub
```

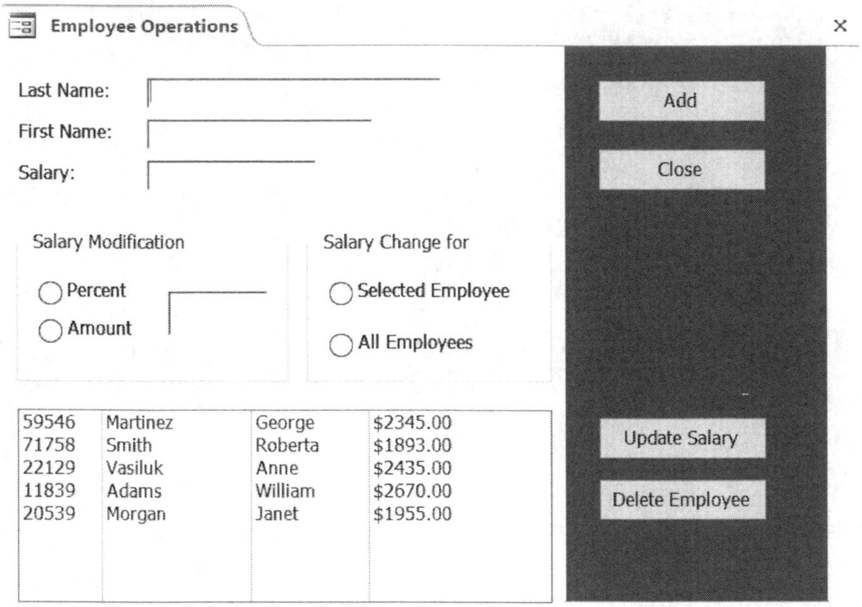

FIGURE 8.3. The listbox control displays employee data as entered in the custom collection CEmployee.

7. Write the following **Click** procedure for the cmdUpdate button:

```
Private Sub cmdUpdate_Click()
  Dim numOfPeople As Integer
  Dim colItem As Integer

  'validate user selections
  If frSalaryFor.Value = 0 Or frSalaryMod.Value = 0 Then
    MsgBox "Please choose appropriate option button in " & _
      vbCr & "the 'Salary Modification' and " & _
      "'Change the Salary for' areas.", vbOKOnly, _
      "Insufficient selection"
    Exit Sub
  ElseIf Not IsNumeric(txtRaise) Or txtRaise = "" Then
    MsgBox "You must enter a number."
```

```
    txtRaise.SetFocus
    Exit Sub
  ElseIf frSalaryMod.Value = 1 And _
    lboxPeople.ListIndex = -1 Then
    MsgBox "Click the employee name.", , _
      "Missing selection in the List box"
    Exit Sub
  End If

  If frSalaryMod.Value = 1 And lboxPeople.ListIndex = -1 Then
   MsgBox "Enter data or select an option."
   Exit Sub
  End If
  'get down to calculations
  amount = txtRaise
  colItem = lboxPeople.ListIndex + 1
  If frSalaryFor.Value = 1 And frSalaryMod.Value = 1 Then
   'by percent, one employee
   choice = 1
   numOfPeople = 1
  ElseIf frSalaryFor.Value = 2 And frSalaryMod.Value = 1 Then
   'by amount, one employee
   choice = 2
   numOfPeople = 1
  ElseIf frSalaryFor.Value = 1 And frSalaryMod.Value = 2 Then
   'by percent, all employees
   choice = 1
   numOfPeople = 2
  ElseIf frSalaryFor.Value = 2 And frSalaryMod.Value = 2 Then
   'by amount, all employees
   choice = 2
   numOfPeople = 2
  End If
  UpdateSalary choice, amount, numOfPeople, colItem
  lboxPeople.RowSource = GetValues
End Sub
```

When the Update Salary button is clicked, the procedure checks to see whether the user selected the appropriate option buttons and entered the adjusted figure in the text box. The update can be done for the selected employee or for all the employees listed in the listbox control and collection. You can increase the salary by the specified percentage or amount (see Figure 8.4). Depending on which options are specified, values are assigned to the variables choice, amount, numOfpeople, and colItem. These variables serve as parameters for the UpdateSalary procedure located in the EmpOperations module (see step 13 further on). The last statement in the cmdUpdate_Click procedure sets the row source property of the listbox control to the result obtained from the GetValues function, which is located in the EmpOperations standard module.

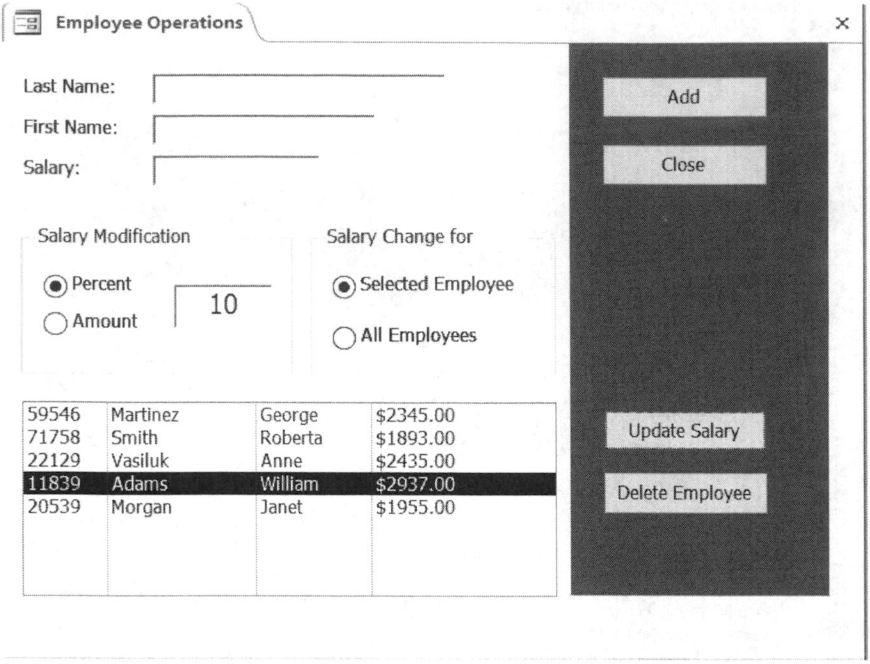

FIGURE 8.4. The employee salary can be increased or decreased by the specified percentage or amount.

8. Enter the following **cmdDelete_Click** procedure:

```
Private Sub cmdDelete_Click()
 ' make sure an employee row is highlighted
 ' in the listbox control
 If lboxPeople.ListIndex > -1 Then
  DeleteEmployee lboxPeople.ListIndex + 1
  If lboxPeople.ListCount = 1 Then
   lboxPeople.RowSource = GetValues
   UserForm_Initialize
  Else
   lboxPeople.RowSource = GetValues
  End If
 Else
  MsgBox "Click the item you want to remove."
 End If
End Sub
```

The cmdDelete_Click procedure lets you remove an employee from the custom collection CEmployee. If you click an item in the listbox and then click the Delete Employee button, the DeleteEmployee procedure is called. This procedure requires an argument that specifies the index number of the item selected in the listbox. After the employee is removed from the collection, the row source of the listbox control is reset to display the remaining employees. When the last employee is removed from the collection, the UserForm_

Initialize procedure is called to tackle the task of disabling controls that cannot be used until at least one employee is entered into the `CEmployee` collection.

9. To activate the **EmpOperations** module that you created earlier, double-click its name in the Project Explorer window. The top of the module should contain the following declaration lines, the first two automatically added by Access:

```
Option Compare Database
Option Explicit

Dim emp As New CEmployee
Dim CEmployee As New Collection
```

10. In the **EmpOperations** standard module, enter the following **AddEmployee** procedure:

```
Sub AddEmployee(empLast As String, empFirst As String, _
 empSalary As Currency)
 With emp
  .ID = SetEmpId
  .LastName = empLast
  .FirstName = empFirst
  .Salary = CCur(empSalary)
  If .Salary = 0 Then Exit Sub
  CEmployee.Add emp
 End With
End Sub
```

The AddEmployee procedure is called from the cmdAdd_Click procedure attached to the form's Add button. This procedure takes three arguments. When Visual Basic for Applications reaches the `With emp` construct, a new instance of the CEmployee class is created. The LastName, FirstName, and Salary properties are set with the values passed from the cmdAdd_Click procedure. The ID property is set with the number generated by the result of the SetEmpId function (see the following step). Each time VBA sees the reference to the instanced emp object, it will call upon the appropriate Property Let procedure located in the class module. (The next section of this chapter demonstrates how to walk through this procedure step by step to see exactly when the Property procedures are executed.) The last statement inside the `With emp` construct adds the user-defined object emp to the custom collection called `CEmployee`.

11. In the **EmpOperations** standard module, enter the following **SetEmpID** function procedure:

```
Function SetEmpID() As String
 Dim ref As String

 Randomize
 ref = Int((99999 - 10000) * Rnd + 10000)
 SetEmpId = ref
End Function
```

This function will assign a unique five-digit number to each new employee. To generate a random integer between two given integers where ending_number = 99999 and beginning_number = 10000, the following formula is used:

```
= Int((ending_number - beginning_number) * Rnd + beginning_number)
```

The SetEmpId function procedure also uses the Randomize statement to reinitialize the random number generator. For more information on using the Rnd and Integer functions, as well as the Randomize statement, refer to the online help.

12. Enter the following **GetValues** function procedure. This function, which is called from the cmdAdd_Click, cmdUpdate_Click, and cmdDelete_Click procedures, provides the values for the listbox control to synchronize it with the current values in the CEmployee collection.

```
Function GetValues()
 Dim myList As String

 myList = ""
 For Each emp In CEmployee
  myList = myList & emp.ID & ";" & _
  emp.LastName & ";" & _
  emp.FirstName & "; $" & _
  Format(emp.Salary, "0.00") & ";"
 Next emp
 GetValues = myList
End Function
```

13. Enter the following **UpdateSalary** procedure:

```
Sub UpdateSalary(choice As Integer, myValue As Long, _
 peopleCount As Integer, colItem As Integer)
 Set emp = New CEmployee

 If choice = 1 And peopleCount = 1 Then
  CEmployee.Item(colItem).Salary = _
  emp.CalcNewSalary(1, CEmployee.Item( _ colItem).Salary,
myValue)
 ElseIf choice = 1 And peopleCount = 2 Then
  For Each emp In CEmployee
   emp.Salary = emp.Salary + ((emp.Salary * myValue) _   / 100)
  Next emp
 ElseIf choice = 2 And peopleCount = 1 Then
  CEmployee.Item(colItem).Salary = _
  CEmployee.Item(colItem).Salary + myValue
 ElseIf choice = 2 And peopleCount = 2 Then
  For Each emp In CEmployee
   emp.Salary = emp.Salary + myValue
  Next emp
 Else
  MsgBox "Enter data or select an option."
 End If
End Sub
```

The UpdateSalary procedure is called from the cmdUpdate_Click procedure, which is assigned to the Update Salary button on the form. The click procedure passes four parameters that the UpdateSalary procedure uses for the salary calculations. When a salary for the selected employee needs to be updated by a percentage or amount, the CalcNewSalary method residing in the class module is called. For modification of salary figures for all the employees, we iterate over the CEmployee collection to obtain the value of the Salary property of each emp object, and then perform the required calculation by using a formula. By entering a negative number in the form's txtRaise text box, you can decrease the salary by the specified percentage or amount.

14. Enter the **DeleteEmployee** procedure:

```
Sub DeleteEmployee(colItem As Integer)
 Dim getcount As Integer

 CEmployee.Remove colItem
End Sub
```

The DeleteEmployee procedure uses the Remove method to delete the selected employee from the CEmployee custom collection. Recall that the Remove method requires one argument, which is the position of the item in the collection. The value of this argument is obtained from the cmdDelete_ Click procedure. The class module procedures were called from the standard module named EmpOperations. This was done to avoid creating a new instance of a user-defined class every time we needed to call it.

RUNNING THE CUSTOM APPLICATION

Now that you have finished writing the necessary VBA code, let's load frmEmployeeSalaries to enter and modify employee information.

Custom Project 8.1. (Step 9) Running the Custom Project

1. Choose **File | Save Chap08** to save all the objects in the VBA project.
2. Switch to the Microsoft Office Access window and activate **frmEmployeeSalaries** in the Form view.
3. Enter the employee last and first name and salary, and click the **Add** button.
   The employee information now appears in the listbox. Notice that an employee ID is automatically entered in the first column. All the disabled form controls are now enabled.
4. Enter data for another employee, and then click the **Add** button.
5. Enter information for at least three more people.
6. Increase the salary of the third employee in the listbox by 10%. To do this, click the employee name in the listbox, click the **Percent** option button, and type **10** in the text box in the Salary Modification section of the form. In the Change the Salary for section of the form, click the **Selected Employee** option button. Finally, click the **Update Salary** button to perform the update operation.
7. Now increase the salary of all the employees by **$5**.
8. Remove the fourth employee from the listbox. To do this, select the employee in the listbox and click the **Delete Employee** button.
9. Close frmEmployeeSalaries by clicking the **Close** button.

WATCHING THE EXECUTION OF YOUR VBA PROCEDURES

To help you understand what's going on when your code runs and how the custom object works, let's walk through the cmdAdd_Click procedure. Treat this exercise as a brief introduction to the debugging techniques that are covered in detail in the next chapter.

⊙ Custom Project 8.1. (Step 10) Custom Project Code Walkthrough

1. Open **frmEmployeeSalaries** in Design view and click **View Code** in theToolssection of theDesigntab.
2. Select **cmdAdd** from the combo box at the top left of the Code window.
3. Set a breakpoint by clicking in the left margin next to the following line of code, as shown in Figure 8.5:

```
If IsNull(txtLastName.Value) Or txtLastName.Value = "" _
 Or IsNull(txtFirstName.Value) Or txtFirstName.Value = "" _
 Or IsNull(txtSalary.Value) Or txtSalary.Value = "" Then
```

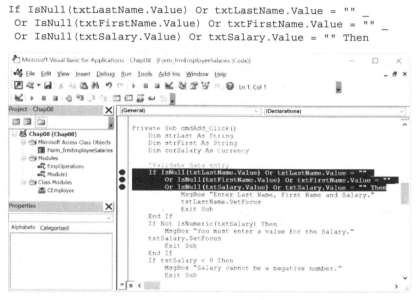

FIGURE 8.5. A red circle in the margin indicates a breakpoint. The statement with a breakpoint is displayed as white text on a red background.

4. Press **Alt+F11** to return to the form **frmEmployeeSalaries**, and then switch to the Form view.
5. Enter data in the Last Name, First Name, and Salary text boxes, and then click the form's **Add** button. Visual Basic should now switch to the Code window because it came across the breakpoint in the first line of the cmdAdd_Click procedure (see Figure 8.6).
6. Step through the code one statement at a time by pressing **F8**. Visual Basic runs the current statement, then automatically advances to the next statement and suspends execution. The current statement is indicated by a yellow arrow in the margin and a yellow background. Keep pressing **F8** to execute the procedure step by step. After Visual Basic switches to the EmpOperations

module to run the AddEmployee procedure and encounters the With emp statement, it will run the function to set the employee ID and will go out to execute the Property Let procedures in the CEmployee class module (see Figure 8.7).

```
cmdAdd                                    v   Click                              v

    Private Sub cmdAdd_Click()
        Dim strLast As String
        Dim strFirst As String
        Dim curSalary As Currency

        'Validate data entry
        If IsNull(txtLastName.Value) Or txtLastName.Value = "" _
            Or IsNull(txtFirstName.Value) Or txtFirstName.Value = "" _
            Or IsNull(txtSalary.Value) Or txtSalary.Value = "" Then
                MsgBox "Enter Last Name, First Name and Salary."
                txtLastName.SetFocus
                Exit Sub
        End If
        If Not IsNumeric(txtSalary) Then
            MsgBox "You must enter a value for the Salary."
        txtSalary.SetFocus
            Exit Sub
        End If
        If txtSalary < 0 Then
            MsgBox "Salary cannot be a negative number."
            Exit Sub
```

FIGURE 8.6. When Visual Basic encounters a breakpoint while running a procedure, it switches to the Code window and displays a yellow arrow in the margin to the left of the statement at which the procedure is suspended.

```
(General)                                 v   ID [PropertyLet]                   v

    Property Get FirstName() As String
       FirstName = m_FirstName
    End Property

    Property Get Salary() As Currency
       Salary = m_Salary
    End Property

⇨  Property Let ID(ref As String)
       m_ID = ref
    End Property

    Property Let LastName(L As String)
       m_LastName = L
    End Property

    Property Let FirstName(F As String)
       m_FirstName = F
    End Property
```

FIGURE 8.7. Setting the properties of your custom object is accomplished through the Property Let procedures.

7. Using the **F8** key, continue executing the cmdAdd_Click procedure code to the end. When VBA encounters the end of the procedure (End Sub), the yellow highlighter will be turned off. At this time, press **F5** to finish execution of the remaining code. Next, switch back to the active form by pressing **Alt+F11**.

NOTE *To activate the form, you may need to first click the Table1 tab and then reselect the Employee Operations tab (see Figure 8.3).*

8. Enter data for a new employee, and then click the **Add** button. When Visual Basic displays the Code window, choose **Debug | Clear All Breakpoints**. Now press **F5** to run the remaining code without stepping through it.

9. In the Visual Basic Editor window, choose **File | Save Chap08**, and then save changes to the modules when prompted.

10. Choose **File | Close and Return to Microsoft Access**.

11. Close the **Chap08.accdb** database and exit Microsoft Access.

SIDEBAR *VBA Debugging Tools*
_____

Visual Basic provides a number of debugging tools to help you analyze how your application operates, as well as to locate the source of errors in your procedures. See the next chapter for details on working with these tools.

SUMMARY

In this chapter, you learned how to create and use your own objects and collections in VBA procedures. You used a class module to create a user-defined (custom) object. You saw how to define your custom object's properties using the Property Get and Property Let procedures. You also learned how to write a method for your custom object and saw how to make the class module available to the user with a custom form. Finally, you learned how to analyze your VBA application by stepping through its code.

As your procedures become more complex, you will need to start using special tools for tracing errors, which are covered in the next chapter.

CHAPTER 9

GETTING TO KNOW BUILT-IN TOOLS FOR TESTING AND DEBUGGING

In the course of writing or editing VBA procedures, no matter how careful you are, you're likely to make some mistakes. For example, you may misspell a word, misplace a comma or quotation mark, or forget a period or ending parenthesis. These kinds of mistakes are known as *syntax errors*. Fortunately, Visual Basic for Applications is quite helpful in spotting these kinds of errors. To have VBA automatically check for correct syntax after you enter a line of code, choose Tools | Options in the VBE window. Make sure the Auto Syntax Check setting is selected on the Editor tab, as shown in Figure 9.1.

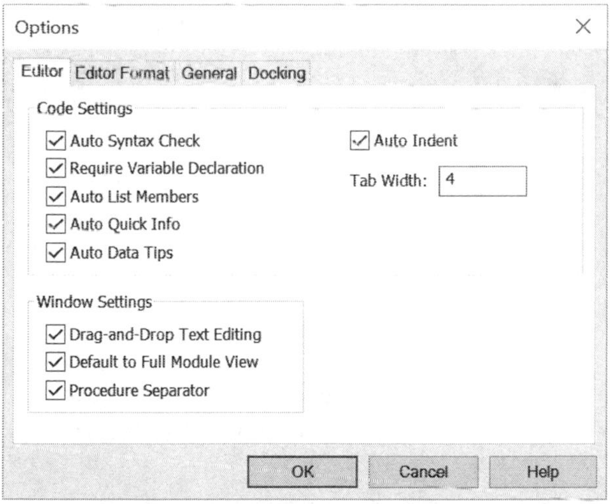

FIGURE 9.1. The Auto Syntax Check setting on the Editor tab of the Options dialog box helps you find typos in your VBA procedures.

When VBA finds a syntax error, it displays an error message box and changes the color of the incorrect line of code to red, or another color as indicated on the Editor Format tab in the Options dialog box.

If the explanation of the error in the error message isn't clear, you can click the Help button for more help. If Visual Basic for Applications cannot point you in the right direction, you must return to your procedure and carefully examine the offending instruction for missed letters, quotation marks, periods, colons, equal signs, and beginning and ending parentheses. Finding syntax errors can be aggravating and time-consuming. Certain syntax errors can be caught only during the execution of the procedure. While attempting to run your procedure, VBA can find errors that were caused by using invalid arguments or omitting instructions that are used in pairs, such as `If...End` statements and looping structures.

You've probably heard that computer programs are "full of bugs." In programming, errors are called bugs, and *debugging* is a process of eliminating errors from your programs. Visual Basic for Applications provides a myriad of tools for tracking down and eliminating bugs. The first step in debugging a procedure is to correct all syntax errors. In addition to syntax errors, there are two other types of errors: runtime and logic. *Runtime errors*, which occur while the procedure is running, are often caused by unexpected situations the programmer did not think of while writing the code. For example, the program may be trying to access a drive or a file that does not exist on the user's computer. Or it may be trying to copy a file to a CD-ROM disc without first determining whether the user had inserted a CD.

The third type of error, a logic error, often does not generate a specific error message. Even though the procedure has no flaws in its syntax and runs without errors, it produces incorrect results. *Logic errors* happen when your procedure simply does not do what you want it to do. Logic errors are usually very difficult to locate. Those that happen intermittently are sometimes so well concealed that you can spend long hours—even days—trying to locate the source of the error.

STOPPING A PROCEDURE

VBA offers four methods of stopping your procedure and entering into a so-called *break mode*:

- Pressing Ctrl+Break
- Setting one or more breakpoints
- Inserting the `Stop` statement
- Adding a watch expression

A break occurs when execution of your VBA procedure is temporarily suspended. Visual Basic remembers the values of all variables and the statement from which the execution of the procedure should resume when you decide to continue.

You can resume a suspended procedure in one of the following ways:

- Click the Run Sub/UserForm button on the toolbar
- Choose Run | Run Sub/UserForm from the menu bar
- Click the Continue button in the error message box (see Figure 9.2)

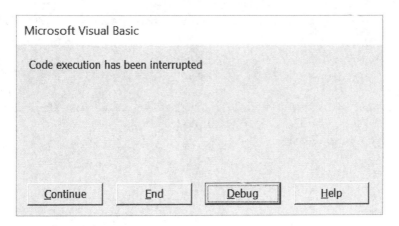

FIGURE 9.2. This message appears when you press Ctrl+Break while your VBA procedure is running.

TABLE 9.1. Error message box buttons.

Button Name	Description
Continue	Click this button to resume code execution. This button will be grayed out if an error was encountered.
End	Click this button if you do not want to troubleshoot the procedure at this time. VBA will stop code execution.
Debug	Click this button to enter break mode. The Code window will appear, and VBA will highlight the line at which the procedure execution was suspended. You can examine, debug, or step through the code.
Help	Click this button to view the online help that explains the cause of this error message.

USING BREAKPOINTS

If you know more or less where there may be a problem in your procedure code, you should suspend code execution at that location (on a given line). Set a breakpoint by pressing F9 when the cursor is on the desired line of code. When VBA gets to that line while running your procedure, it will display the Code window immediately. At this point you can step through the procedure code line by line by pressing F8 or choosing Debug | Step Into.

To see how this works, let's look at the following scenario. Assume that during the execution of the ListEndDates function procedure (see Custom Project 9.1) the following line of code could get you into trouble:

```
ListEndDates = Format(((Now() + intOffset) - 35) + 7 * row, _
    "MM/DD/YYYY")
```

Please note files for the Hands-On project may be found on the companion CD-ROM.

 **Custom Project 9.1. Debugging a Function Procedure**

1. Start Microsoft Access and create a new database named **Chap09.accdb** in your **C:\VBAPrimerAccess_ByExample** folder.
2. Create the form shown in Figure 9.3.

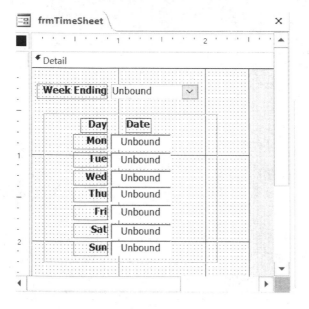

FIGURE 9.3. The combo box control shown on this form will be filled with the result of the ListEndDates function.

3. Use the property sheet to set the following control properties:

Control Name	Property Name	Property Setting
combo box	Name	cboEndDate
	Row Source Type	ListEndDates
	Column Count	1
text box controls	Name	txt1
		txt2
		txt3
		txt4
		txt5
		txt6
		txt7

4. Save the form as **frmTimeSheet**.
5. In the property sheet, select **Form** from the drop-down listbox. Click the **Event** tab. Choose **[Event Procedure]** from the drop-down list next to

the **On Load** property, and then click the **Build** button (…). Complete the following **Form_Load** procedure when the Code window appears:

```
Private Sub Form_Load()
  With Me.cboEndDate
    .SetFocus
    .ListIndex = 5 ' Select current end date
  End With
End Sub
```

6. Select the combo box control (cboEndDate) on the form. In the property sheet, click the **Event** tab. Choose **[Event Procedure]** from the drop-down list next to the **On Change** property, and then click the **Build** button (…). Enter the following code:

```
Private Sub cboEndDate_Change()
  Dim endDate As Date

  endDate = Me.cboEndDate.Value
  With Me
    .txt1 = Format(endDate - 6, "mm/dd")
    .txt2 = Format(endDate - 5, "mm/dd")
    .txt3 = Format(endDate - 4, "mm/dd")
    .txt4 = Format(endDate - 3, "mm/dd")
    .txt5 = Format(endDate - 2, "mm/dd")
    .txt6 = Format(endDate - 1, "mm/dd")
    .txt7 = Format(endDate - 0, "mm/dd")
  End With
End Sub
```

7. In the Visual Basic Editor window, choose **Insert | Module** to add a new standard module.
8. In the Properties window, change the Name property of Module1 to **TimeSheetProc**.
9. Enter the **ListEndDates** function procedure in the TimeSheetProc module:

```
Function ListEndDates(fld As Control, id As Variant, _
 row As Variant, col As Variant, _
 code As Variant) As Variant

  Dim intOffset As Integer

  Select Case code
    Case acLBInitialize
      ListEndDates = True
    Case acLBOpen
      ListEndDates = Timer
    Case acLBGetRowCount
      ListEndDates = 11
    Case acLBGetColumnCount
      ListEndDates = 1
    Case acLBGetColumnWidth
      ListEndDates = -1
    Case acLBGetValue
      ' days till end date
      intOffset = Abs((8 - Weekday(Now)) Mod 7)
```

```
' start 5 weeks prior to current week end date
' (7 days * 5 weeks = 35 days before next end date)
' and show 11 dates

        ListEndDates = Format(((Now() + intOffset) - 35) _
            + 7 * row, "MM/DD/YYYY")
    End Select
End Function
```

10. In the ListEndDates function procedure, click anywhere on the line containing the following statement:

```
ListEndDates = Format(((Now() + intOffset) - 35) _
    + 7 * row, "MM/DD/YYYY")
```

11. Press **F9** (or choose **Debug | Toggle Breakpoint**) to set a breakpoint on the line where the cursor is located.

When you set the breakpoint, Visual Basic displays a red dot in the margin. At the same time, the line that has the breakpoint will change to white text on a red background (see Figure 9.4). The color of the breakpoint can be changed on the Editor Format tab in the Options dialog box (choose Tools | Options).

Another way of setting a breakpoint is to click in the margin indicator to the left of the line on which you want to stop the procedure.

```
(General)                                      ListEndDates

    Option Compare Database
    Option Explicit

    Function ListEndDates(fld As Control, id As Variant, _
        row As Variant, col As Variant, _
        code As Variant) As Variant

        Dim intOffset As Integer

        Select Case code
            Case acLBInitialize
                ListEndDates = True
            Case acLBOpen
                ListEndDates = Timer
            Case acLBGetRowCount
                ListEndDates = 11
            Case acLBGetColumnCount
                ListEndDates = 1
            Case acLBGetColumnWidth
                ListEndDates = -1
            Case acLBGetValue
                ' days till end date
                intOffset = Abs((8 - Weekday(Now)) Mod 7)
                ' start 5 weeks prior to current week end date
                ' (7 days * 5 weeks = 35 days before next end date)
                ' and show 11 dates
                ListEndDates = Format(((Now() + intOffset) - 35)
                    + 7 * row, "MM/DD/YYYY")
        End Select
    End Function
```

FIGURE 9.4. **The line of code where the breakpoint is set is displayed in the color specified on the Editor Format tab in the Options dialog box.**

12. Press Alt+F11 to switch to the Microsoft Access application window and open the form **frmTimeSheet** in the Form view.

When the form is opened, Visual Basic for Applications will call the ListEndDates function to fill the combo box, executing all the statements until it encounters the breakpoint you set in steps 10–11. Once the breakpoint is reached, the code is suspended and the screen displays the Code window in break mode (notice the word "break" surrounded by square brackets in the Code window's titlebar), as shown in Figure 9.5. VBA displays a yellow arrow in the margin to the left of the statement at which the procedure was suspended. At the same time, the statement appears inside a box with a yellow background. The arrow and the box indicate the current statement, or the statement that is about to be executed. If the current statement also contains a breakpoint, the margin displays both indicators overlapping one another (the circle and the arrow).

FIGURE 9.5. Code window in break mode. A yellow arrow appears in the margin to the left of the statement at which the procedure was suspended. Because the current statement also contains a breakpoint (indicated by a red circle), the margin displays both indicators overlapping one another (the circle and the arrow).

13. Finish running the ListEndDates function procedure by pressing **F5** to continue without stopping, or press **F8** to execute the procedure line by line.

When you step through your procedure code line by line by pressing F8, you can use the Immediate window to further test your procedure (see the section titled "Using the Immediate Window in Break Mode"). To learn more about stepping through a procedure, refer to the section titled "Stepping through VBA Procedures" later in this chapter.

You can set any number of breakpoints in a procedure. This way you can suspend and continue the execution of your procedure as you please. Press F5 to quickly move between the breakpoints. You can analyze the code of your procedure and check the values of variables while code execution is suspended. You can also perform various tests by typing statements in the Immediate window. Consider setting a breakpoint if you suspect that your procedure never executes a certain block of code.

Removing Breakpoints

When you finish running the procedure in which you had set breakpoints, VBA does not automatically remove them. To remove the breakpoint, choose Debug | Clear All Breakpoints or press Ctrl+Shift+F9. All the breakpoints are removed. If you had set several breakpoints in a given procedure and would like to remove only some of them, click on the line containing the breakpoint you want to remove and press F9 (or choose Debug | Clear Breakpoint). You should clear the breakpoints when they are no longer needed. The breakpoints are automatically removed when you exit Microsoft Access.

NOTE *Remove the breakpoint you set in Custom Project 9.1.*

USING THE IMMEDIATE WINDOW IN BREAK MODE

When the procedure execution is suspended, the Code window appears in break mode. This is a good time to activate the Immediate window and type VBA instructions to find out, for instance, the name of the open form or the value of a certain control. You can also use the Immediate window to change the contents of variables in order to correct values that may be causing errors. By now, you should be an expert when it comes to working in the Immediate window. Figure 9.6 shows the suspended ListEndDates function procedure and the Immediate window with the questions that were asked of Visual Basic for Applications while in break mode.

In break mode, you can also hold the mouse pointer over any variable in a running procedure to see the variable's value. For example, in the ListEndDates function procedure shown in Figure 9.7, the breakpoint has been set on the statement just before the `End Select` keywords. When Visual Basic for Applications encounters this statement, the Code window appears in break mode. Because the statement that stores the value of the variable `intOffset` has already been executed, you can quickly find out the value of this variable by resting the mouse pointer over its name. The name of the variable and its current value appear in a floating frame. To show the values of several variables used in a procedure, you should use the Locals window, which is discussed later in this chapter.

FIGURE 9.6. When code execution is suspended, you can check current values of variables and expressions by entering appropriate statements in the Immediate window.

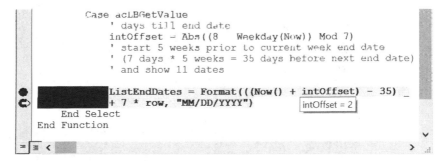

FIGURE 9.7. In break mode, you can find out the value of a variable by resting the mouse pointer on that variable.

SIDEBAR　*Working in a Code Window in Break Mode*

While in break mode, you can change code, add new statements, execute the procedure one line at a time, skip lines, set the next statement, use the Immediate window, and more. When the procedure is in break mode, all of the options on the Debug menu are available. You can enter break mode by pressing Ctrl+Break or F8 or by setting a breakpoint. In break mode, if you change a certain line of code, VBA will prompt you to reset the project by displaying the message "This action will reset your project, proceed anyway?" Click OK to stop the program's execution and proceed editing your code, or click Cancel to delete the new changes and continue running the code from the point where it was suspended. For example, change the variable declaration. As you press F5 to resume code execution, you'll be prompted to reset your project.

USING THE STOP STATEMENT

Sometimes you won't be able to test your procedure right away. If you set up your breakpoints and then close the database file, the breakpoints will be removed; next time, when you are ready to test your procedure, you'll have to begin by setting up your breakpoints again. If you need to postpone the task of testing your procedure until later, you can take a different approach by inserting a `Stop` statement into your code wherever you want to halt a procedure.

Figure 9.8 shows the `Stop` statement before the `With...End With` construct. VBA will suspend the execution of the cboEndDate_Change event procedure when it encounters the `Stop` statement, and the screen will display the Code window in break mode. Although the `Stop` statement has exactly the same effect as setting a breakpoint, it does have one disadvantage: All `Stop` statements stay in the procedure until you remove them. When you no longer need to stop your procedure, you must locate and remove all the `Stop` statements.

```
cboEndDate                          Change

Option Compare Database

Private Sub cboEndDate_Change()
    Dim endDate As Date
    endDate = Me.cboEndDate.Value
⇨   Stop
    With Me
        .txt1 = Format(endDate - 6, "mm/dd")
        .txt2 = Format(endDate - 5, "mm/dd")
        .txt3 = Format(endDate - 4, "mm/dd")
        .txt4 = Format(endDate - 3, "mm/dd")
        .txt5 = Format(endDate - 2, "mm/dd")
        .txt6 = Format(endDate - 1, "mm/dd")
        .txt7 = Format(endDate - 0, "mm/dd")
    End With
End Sub
```

FIGURE 9.8. You can insert a Stop statement anywhere in your VBA procedure code. The procedure will halt when it gets to the Stop statement, and the Code window will appear with the code line highlighted.

USING THE ASSERT STATEMENT

A very powerful and easy-to-apply debugging technique is utilizing `Debug.Assert` statements. Assertions allow you to write code that checks itself while running. By including assertions in your programming code you can verify that a particular condition or assumption is true. Assertions give you immediate feedback when an error occurs. They are great for detecting logic errors early in the development phase instead of hearing about them later from your end users. Just because your procedure ran on your system without generating an error does not mean that there are no bugs in that procedure. Don't assume anything—always test for validity of expressions and variables in your code. The `Debug.Assert` statement takes any expression that evaluates to True or False and activates the break mode when that expression evaluates to False. The syntax for `Debug.Assert` is as follows:

```
Debug.Assert condition
```

where *condition* is a VBA code or expression that returns True or False. If *condition* evaluates to False or 0 (zero), VBA will enter break mode. For example, when running the following looping structure, the code will stop executing when the variable i equals 50:

```
Sub TestDebugAssert()
   Dim i As Integer
   For i = 1 To 100
      Debug.Assert i <> 50
   Next
End Sub
```

Keep in mind that `Debug.Assert` does nothing if the condition is False or zero (0). The execution simply stops on that line of code and the VBE screen opens with the line containing the false statement highlighted so that you can start debugging your code. You may need to write an error handler to handle the identified error. Error-handling procedures are covered later in this chapter. While you can stop the code execution by using the `Stop` statement (see the previous section), `Debug.Assert` differs from the `Stop` statement in its conditional aspect; it will stop your code only under specific conditions. Conditional breakpoints can also be set by using the Watches window (see the next section). After you have debugged and tested your code, comment out or remove the `Debug.Assert` statements from your final code. The easiest way to do this is to use Edit | Replace in the VBE editor screen. To comment out the statements, in the Find What box, enter `Debug.Assert.` In the Replace With box, enter an apostrophe followed by `Debug.Assert.`

NOTE *To remove the `Debug.Assert` statements from your code, enter `Debug.Assert` in the Find What box. Leave the Replace With box empty, but be sure to mark the Use Pattern Matching checkbox.*

USING THE ADD WATCH WINDOW

Many errors in procedures are caused by variables that assume unexpected values. If a procedure uses a variable whose value changes in various locations, you may want to stop the procedure and check the current value of that variable. VBA offers a special Watches window that allows you to keep an eye on variables or expressions while your procedure is running. To add a watch expression to your procedure, select the variable whose value you want to monitor in the Code window, and then choose Debug | Add Watch. The screen will display the Add Watch dialog box, as shown in Figure 9.9.

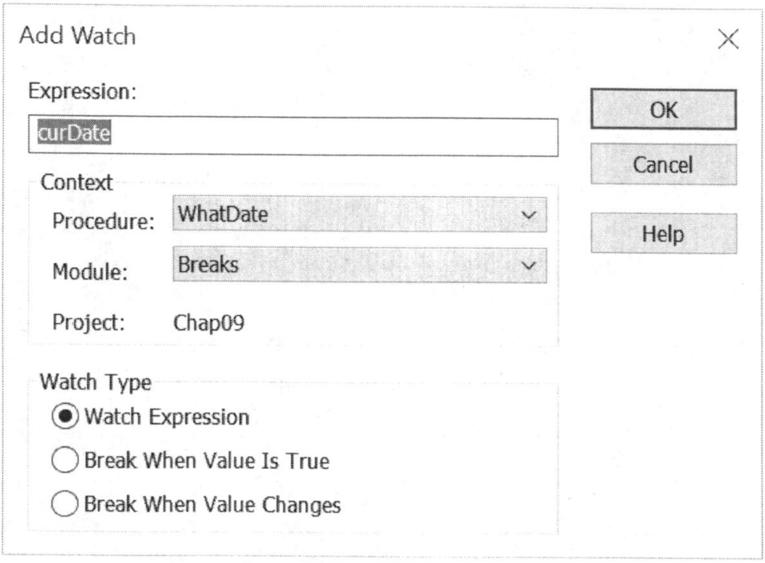

FIGURE 9.9. The Add Watch dialog box allows you to define conditions you want to monitor while a VBA procedure is running.

The Add Watch dialog box contains three sections, which are described in Table 9.2.

TABLE 9.2. Add Watch dialog box sections.

Section	Description
Expression	Displays the name of a variable you have highlighted in your procedure. If you opened the Add Watch dialog box without selecting a variable name, type the name of the variable you want to monitor in the Expression text box.
Context	In this section, indicate the name of the procedure that contains the variable and the name of the module where this procedure is located.

Section	Description
Watch Type	Specifies how to monitor the variable. If you choose:

- The Watch Expression option button, you can read the value of the variable in the Add Watch window while in break mode.
- Break When Value Is True, Visual Basic will automatically stop the procedure when the variable evaluates to True (nonzero).
- Break When Value Changes, Visual Basic will automatically stop the procedure each time the value of the variable or expression changes.

You can add a watch expression before running a procedure or after suspending the execution of your procedure.

The difference between a breakpoint and a watch expression is that the breakpoint always stops a procedure in a specified location, but the watch stops the procedure only when the specified condition (Break When Value Is True or Break When Value Changes) is met. Watches are extremely useful when you are not sure where the variable is being changed. Instead of stepping through many lines of code to find the location where the variable assumes the specified value, you can put a watch breakpoint on the variable and run your procedure as normal. Let's see how this works.

Hands-On 9.1. Watching the Values of VBA Expressions

1. In the Visual Basic Editor window, choose **Insert | Module** to insert a new standard module.
2. Use the Properties window to change the name of the module to **Breaks**.
3. In the Breaks Code window, type the following **WhatDate** procedure:

```
Sub WhatDate()
  Dim curDate As Date
  Dim newDate As Date
  Dim x As Integer

  curDate = Date
  For x = 1 To 365
    newDate = Date + x
  Next x
End Sub
```

The WhatDate procedure uses the `For...Next` loop to calculate the date that is x days in the future. You won't see any result when you run this procedure unless you insert the following instruction in the procedure code just before the `End Sub` keywords:

```
MsgBox "In " & x & " days, it will be " & NewDate
```

However, you don't want to display the individual dates, day after day. Suppose that you want to stop the program when the value of the variable x reaches 211. In other words, you want to know what date will be 211 days from now. To get the answer, you could insert the following statement into your procedure before the `Next x` statement:

```
If x = 211 Then MsgBox "In " & x & " days it will be " & _
 NewDate
```

But this time, you want to get the answer without introducing any new statements into your procedure. If you add watch expressions to the procedure, Visual Basic for Applications will stop the `For...Next` loop when the specified condition is met, and you'll be able to check the values of the desired variables.

4. Choose **Debug | Add Watch**.
5. In the Expression text box, enter the following expression: **x = 211**.
6. In the Context section, choose **WhatDate** from the Procedure combo box and **Breaks** from the Module combo box.
7. In the Watch Type section, select the **Break When Value Is True** option button.
8. Click **OK** to close the Add Watch dialog box. You have now added your first watch expression.
9. In the Code window, position the insertion point anywhere within the name of the **curDate** variable.
10. Choose **Debug | Add Watch** and click **OK** to set up the default watch type with the **Watch Expression** option.
11. In the Code window, position the insertion point anywhere within the name of the **newDate** variable.
12. Choose **Debug | Add Watch** and click **OK** to set up the default watch type with the **Watch Expression** option.

After performing these steps, the WhatDate procedure contains the following three watches:

```
x = 211       Break When Value Is True
curDate       Watch Expression
newDate       Watch Expression
```

13. Position the cursor anywhere inside the code of the WhatDate procedure and press F5.

Visual Basic stops the procedure when x = 211 (see Figure 9.10). Notice that the value of the variable x in the Watches window is the same as the value you specified in the Add Watch dialog box.

In addition, the Watches window shows the value of the variables `curDate` and `newDate`. The procedure is in break mode. You can press F5 to continue, or you can ask another question: What date will be in 277 days? The next step shows how to do this.

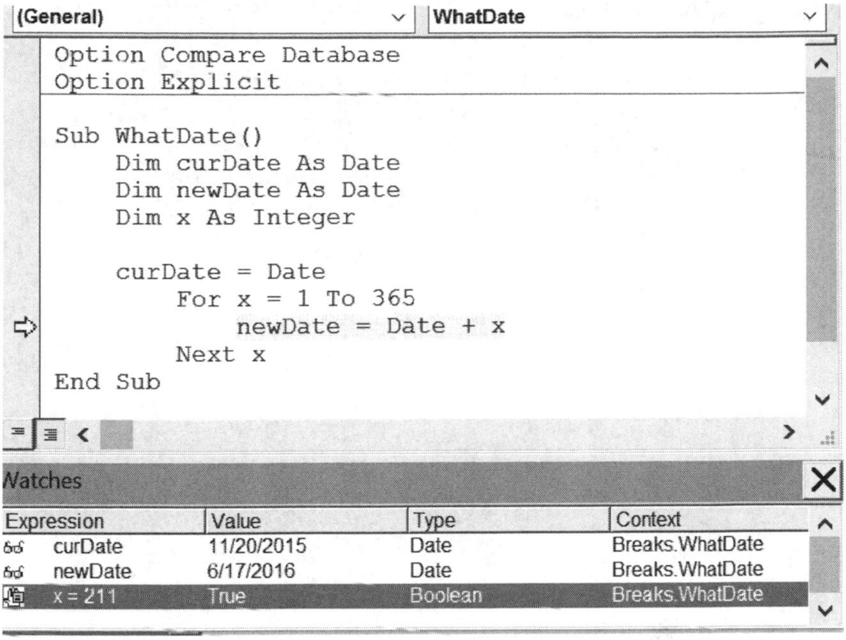

(General)	⌄	WhatDate	⌄

```
    Option Compare Database
    Option Explicit

    Sub WhatDate()
        Dim curDate As Date
        Dim newDate As Date
        Dim x As Integer

        curDate = Date
            For x = 1 To 365
                newDate = Date + x
            Next x
    End Sub
```

Watches ✕

Expression	Value	Type	Context	^
𝟞𝟞 curDate	11/20/2015	Date	Breaks.WhatDate	
𝟞𝟞 newDate	6/17/2016	Date	Breaks.WhatDate	
x = 211	True	Boolean	Breaks.WhatDate	⌄

FIGURE 9.10. Using the Watches window.

14. Choose **Debug | Edit Watch** and enter the following expression: **x = 277**.

You can also display the Edit Watch dialog box by double-clicking the expression in the Watches window.

15. Click **OK** to close the Edit Watch dialog box. Notice that the Watches window now displays a new value of the expression. x is now false.

16. Press **F5**. The procedure stops again when the value of x = 277. The value of curDate is the same; however, the newDate variable now contains a new value—a date that is 277 days from now. You can change the value of the expression again or finish the procedure.

17. Press **F5** to finish the procedure without stopping.

When your procedure is running and a watch expression has a value, the Watches window displays the value of the Watch expression. If you open the Watches window after the procedure has finished, you will see the error "<out of context>" instead of the variable values. In other words, when the watch expression is out of context, it does not have a value.

Removing Watch Expressions

To remove a watch expression, click on the expression you want to remove from the Watches window and press Delete. Remove all the watch expressions you defined in the preceding exercise.

USING QUICK WATCH

To check the value of an expression not defined in the Watches window, you can use Quick Watch (see Figure 9.11).

To access the Quick Watch dialog box while in break mode, position the insertion point anywhere inside a variable name or an expression you want to watch and choose Debug | Quick Watch, or press Shift+F9.

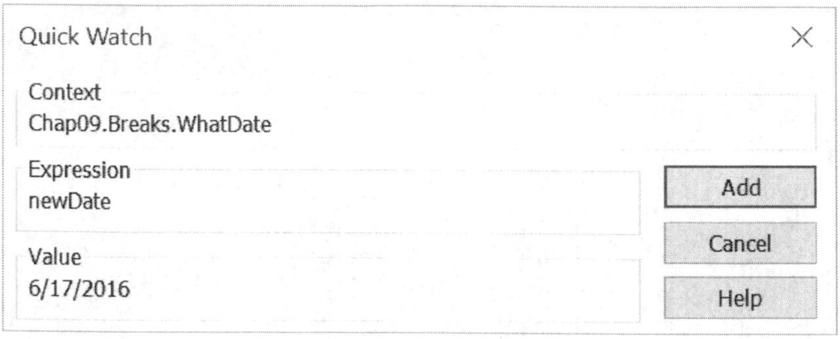

FIGURE 9.11. The Quick Watch dialog box shows the value of the selected expression in a VBA procedure.

The Quick Watch dialog box contains an Add button that allows you to add the expression to the Watches window. Let's see how to take advantage of Quick Watch.

(⊙) Hands-On 9.2. Using the Quick Watch Dialog Box

Note: Remove all the watch expressions you defined in Hands-On 9.1. See the preceding section on how to remove a watch expression from the Watches window.

1. In the **WhatDate** procedure, position the insertion point on the name of the variable **x**.
2. Choose **Debug | Add Watch**.
3. Enter the expression **x = 50**.
4. Choose the **Break When Value Is True** option button, and click **OK**.
5. Run the WhatDate procedure.

   Visual Basic will suspend procedure execution when x = 50. Notice that the Watches window does not contain either the newDate or the curDate variables. To check the values of these variables, you can position the mouse pointer over the appropriate variable name in the Code window, or you can invoke the Quick Watch dialog box.
6. In the Code window, position the mouse inside the **newDate** variable and press **Shift+F9**, or choose **Debug | Quick Watch**.

   The Quick Watch dialog box shows the name of the expression and its current value.
7. Click **Cancel** to return to the Code window.

8. In the Code window, position the mouse inside the **curDate** variable and press **Shift+F9**, or choose **Debug | Quick Watch**.
9. The Quick Watch dialog box now shows the value of the variable `curDate`.
10. Click **Cancel** to return to the Code window.
11. Press **F5** to continue running the procedure.

USING THE LOCALS WINDOW

If you need to keep an eye on all the declared variables and their current values during the execution of a VBA procedure, choose View | Locals Window before you run your procedure. While in break mode, VBA will display a list of variables and their corresponding values in the Locals window (see Figure 9.12).

The Locals window contains three columns: Expression, Value, and Type.

The Expression column displays the names of variables that are declared in the current procedure. The first row displays the name of the module preceded by the plus sign. When you click the plus sign, you can check if any variables have been declared at the module level. Here the class module will show the system variable Me. In the Locals window, global variables and variables used by other projects aren't displayed.

The second column, Value, shows the current variable values. In this column, you can change the value of a variable by clicking on it and typing the new value. After changing the value, press Enter to register the change. You can also press Tab, Shift+Tab, or the up or down arrows, or click anywhere within the Locals window after you've changed the variable value.

Type, the third column, displays the type of each declared variable.

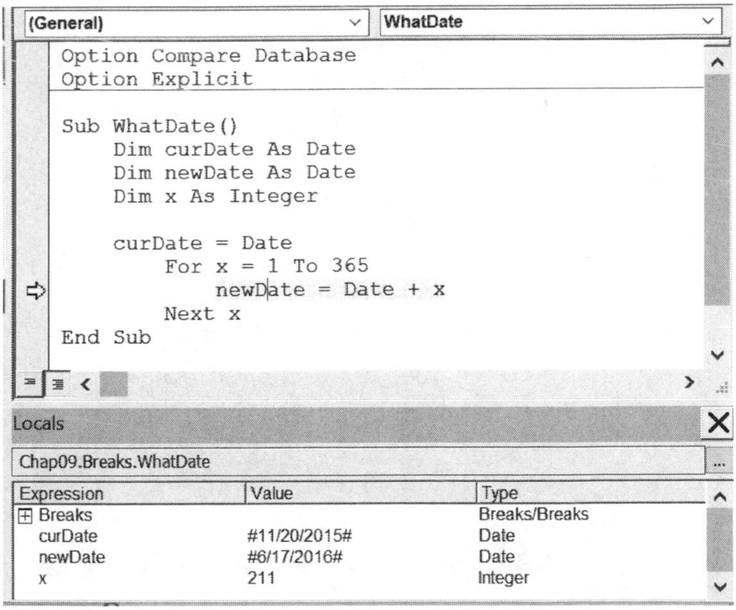

```
(General)                              WhatDate

    Option Compare Database
    Option Explicit

    Sub WhatDate()
        Dim curDate As Date
        Dim newDate As Date
        Dim x As Integer

        curDate = Date
            For x = 1 To 365
                newDate = Date + x
            Next x
    End Sub
```

Expression	Value	Type
⊞ Breaks		Breaks/Breaks
curDate	#11/20/2015#	Date
newDate	#6/17/2016#	Date
x	211	Integer

Chap09.Breaks.WhatDate

FIGURE 9.12. The Locals window displays the current values of all the declared variables in the current VBA procedure.

To observe the variable values in the Locals window, let's proceed to the following hands-on exercise.

Hands-On 9.3. Using the Locals Window

1. Choose **View | Locals Window**.
2. Click anywhere inside the **WhatDate** procedure and press **F8**.

   Pressing F8 places the procedure in break mode. The Locals window displays the name of the current module, the local variables, and their beginning values.
3. Press **F8** a few more times while keeping an eye on the Locals window.
4. Press **F5** to continue running the procedure.

USING THE CALL STACK DIALOG BOX

The Locals window (see Figure 9.12) contains a button with an ellipsis (...). This button opens the Call Stack dialog box (see Figure 9.13), which displays a list of all active procedure calls. An *active procedure call* is a procedure that is started but not completed. You can also activate the Call Stack dialog box by choosing View | Call Stack. This option is available only in break mode.

The Call Stack dialog box is especially helpful for tracing nested procedures. Recall that a nested procedure is a procedure that is being called from within another procedure (see Hands-On 9.5). If a procedure calls another, the name of the called procedure is automatically added to the Calls list in the Call Stack dialog box. When VBA has finished executing the statements of the called procedure, the procedure name is automatically removed from the Call Stack dialog box. You can use the Show button in the Call Stack dialog box to display the statement that calls the next procedure listed in the Call Stack dialog box.

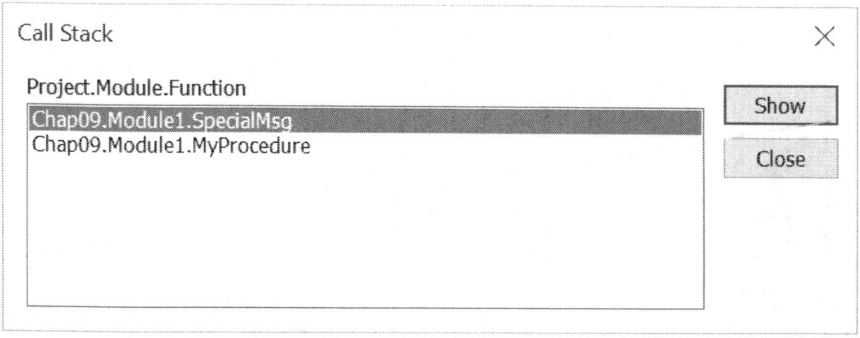

FIGURE 9.13. The Call Stack dialog box displays a list of procedures that are started but not completed.

STEPPING THROUGH VBA PROCEDURES

Stepping through the code means running one statement at a time. This allows you to check every line in every procedure that is encountered. To start stepping through the procedure from the beginning, place the cursor anywhere inside the code of your procedure and choose Debug | Step Into, or press F8. The Debug menu contains several options that allow you to execute a procedure in step mode (see Figure 9.14).

Debug	Run	Tools	Add-Ins	Window	He

	Compile Chap09	
⬛	Step Into	F8
⬛	Step Over	Shift+F8
⬛	Step Out	Ctrl+Shift+F8
⬛	Run To Cursor	Ctrl+F8
	Add Watch...	
	Edit Watch...	Ctrl+W
👓	Quick Watch...	Shift+F9
✋	Toggle Breakpoint	F9
	Clear All Breakpoints	Ctrl+Shift+F9
⇨	Set Next Statement	Ctrl+F9
🔄	Show Next Statement	

FIGURE 9.14. The Debug menu offers many commands for stepping through VBA procedures. Certain commands on this menu are available only in break mode.

When you run a procedure one statement at a time, VBA executes each statement until it encounters the End Sub keywords. If you don't want to step through every statement, you can press F5 at any time to run the remaining code of the procedure without stepping through it.

⊙ Hands-On 9.4. Stepping Through a Procedure

1. Place the cursor anywhere inside the procedure you want to trace.
2. Press **F8** or choose **Debug | Step Into**.
   Visual Basic for Applications executes the current statement, then automatically advances to the next statement and suspends execution. While in break mode, you can activate the Immediate window, the Watches window, or the Locals window to see the effect of a particular statement on the values of variables and expressions. And if the procedure you are stepping through

calls other procedures, you can activate the Call Stack dialog box to see which procedures are currently active.

3. Press **F8** again to execute the selected statement. After executing this statement, VBA will select the next statement, and again the procedure execution will be halted.

4. Continue stepping through the procedure by pressing **F8**, or press **F5** to continue running the code without stopping.

5. You can also choose **Run | Reset** to stop the procedure at the current statement without executing the remaining statements.

When you step over procedures (**Shift+F8**), VBA executes each procedure as if it were a single statement. This option is quite handy if a procedure contains calls to other procedures you don't want to step into because they have already been tested and debugged, or because you want to concentrate only on the new code that has not been debugged yet.

Stepping Over a Procedure

Suppose that the current statement in MyProcedure calls the SpecialMsg procedure. If you choose Debug | Step Over (Shift+F8) instead of Debug | Step Into (F8), VBA will quickly execute all the statements inside the SpecialMsg procedure and select the next statement in the calling procedure, MyProcedure. While the SpecialMsg procedure is being executed, VBA continues to display the current procedure in the Code window.

(•) Hands-On 9.5. Stepping Over a Procedure

This hands-on exercise refers to the Access form named frmTimeSheet that you created in Custom Project 9.1 at the beginning of this chapter.

1. In the Visual Basic Editor window, choose **Insert | Module** to add a new standard module.

2. In the module's Code window, enter the **MyProcedure** and **SpecialMsg** procedures as shown here:

```
Sub MyProcedure()
  Dim myName As String

  myName = Forms!frmTimeSheet.Controls(1).Name

  ' choose Step Over to avoid stepping through the
  ' lines of code in the called procedure - SpecialMsg
  SpecialMsg myName
End Sub

Sub SpecialMsg(n As String)
  If n = "Label1" Then
    MsgBox "You must change the name."
  End If
End Sub
```

3. Add a breakpoint within MyProcedure at the following statement:

```
SpecialMsg myName
```

4. Place the insertion point anywhere within the code of **MyProcedure** and press **F5** to run it.

   Visual Basic halts execution when it reaches the breakpoint.

5. Press **Shift+F8** or choose **Debug | Step Over**.

   Visual Basic runs the SpecialMsg procedure, and then execution advances to the statement immediately after the call to the SpecialMsg procedure.

6. Press **F5** to finish running the procedure without stepping through its code.

   Now suppose you want to execute MyProcedure to the line that calls the SpecialMsg procedure.

7. Click anywhere inside the statement **SpecialMsg myName**.

8. Choose **Debug | Run to Cursor**.

   Visual Basic will stop the procedure when it reaches the specified line.

9. Press **Shift+F8** to step over the SpecialMsg procedure.

10. Press **F5** to execute the rest of the procedure without single stepping.

    Stepping over a procedure is useful when you don't want to analyze individual statements inside the called procedure (SpecialMsg).

Stepping Out of a Procedure

Another command on the Debug menu, Step Out (Ctrl+Shift+F8), is used when you step into a procedure and then decide that you don't want to step all the way through it. When you choose this option, Visual Basic will execute the remaining statements in this procedure in one step and proceed to activate the next statement in the calling procedure.

In the process of stepping through a procedure, you can switch between the Step Into, Step Over, and Step Out options. The option you select depends on which code fragment you wish to analyze at a given moment.

Running a Procedure to Cursor

The Debug menu Run To Cursor command (Ctrl+F8) lets you run your procedure until the line you have selected is encountered. This command is really useful if you want to stop the execution before a large loop or you intend to step over a called procedure.

Setting the Next Statement

At times, you may want to rerun previous lines of code in the procedure or skip over a section of code that is causing trouble. In each of these situations, you can use the Set Next Statement option on the Debug menu. When you halt execution of a procedure, you can resume the procedure from any statement you want. VBA will skip execution of the statements between the selected statement and the statement where execution was suspended.

SIDEBAR   *Skipping Lines of Code*

Although skipping lines of code can be very useful in the process of debugging your VBA procedures, it should be done with care. When you use the Next Statement option, you tell Visual Basic for Applications that this is the line you want to execute next. All lines in between are ignored. This means that certain things you may have expected to occur don't happen, which can lead to unexpected errors.

Showing the Next Statement

If you are not sure where procedure execution will resume, you can choose Debug | Show Next Statement, and VBA will place the cursor on the line that will run next. This is particularly useful when you have been looking at other procedures and are not sure where execution will resume. The Show Next Statement option is available only in break mode.

NAVIGATING WITH BOOKMARKS

In the process of analyzing or reviewing your VBA procedures, you will often find yourself jumping to certain areas of code. Using the built-in bookmark feature, you can easily mark the spots you want to navigate between.

To set up a bookmark:

1. Click anywhere in the statement you want to define as a bookmark.
2. Choose **Edit | Bookmarks | Toggle Bookmark** (or click the **Toggle Bookmark** button on the Edit toolbar).

Visual Basic will place a blue, rounded rectangle in the left margin beside the statement, as shown in Figure 9.15.

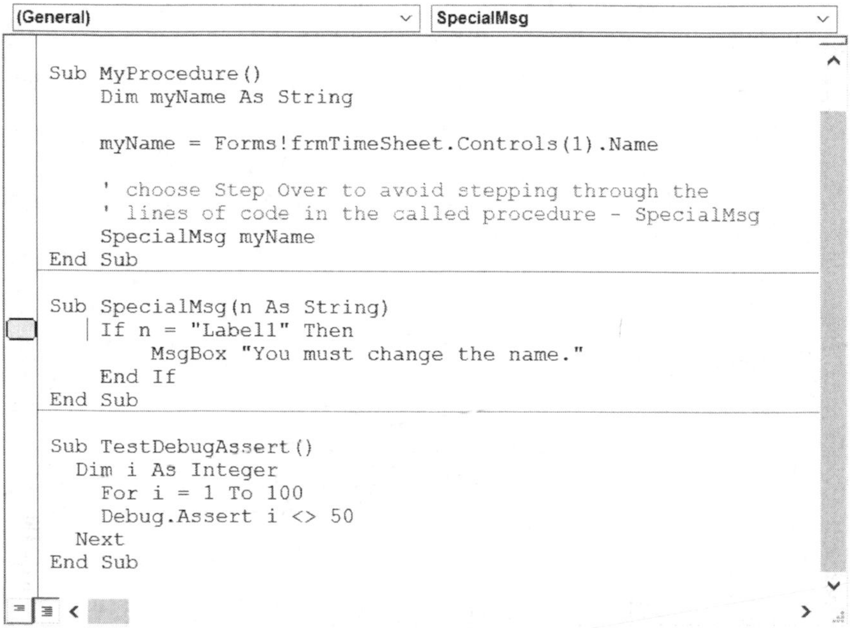

```
(General)                                        SpecialMsg

    Sub MyProcedure()
        Dim myName As String

        myName = Forms!frmTimeSheet.Controls(1).Name

        ' choose Step Over to avoid stepping through the
        ' lines of code in the called procedure - SpecialMsg
        SpecialMsg myName
    End Sub

    Sub SpecialMsg(n As String)
        If n = "Label1" Then
            MsgBox "You must change the name."
        End If
    End Sub

    Sub TestDebugAssert()
        Dim i As Integer
        For i = 1 To 100
        Debug.Assert i <> 50
        Next
    End Sub
```

FIGURE 9.15. Using bookmarks, you can quickly jump between often-used sections of your procedures.

Once you've set up two or more bookmarks, you can jump between the marked locations of your code by choosing Edit | Bookmarks | Next Bookmark or simply clicking the Next Bookmark button on the Edit toolbar. You may also right-click anywhere in the Code window and select Next Bookmark from the shortcut menu. To go to the previous bookmark, select Previous Bookmark. You can remove bookmarks at any time by choosing Edit | Bookmarks | Clear All or by clicking the Clear All Bookmarks button on the Edit toolbar. To remove a single bookmark, click anywhere in the bookmarked statement and choose Edit | Bookmarks | Toggle Bookmark, or click the Toggle Bookmark button on the Edit toolbar.

STOPPING AND RESETTING VBA PROCEDURES

At any time while stepping through the code of a procedure in the Code window, you can press F5 to execute the remaining instructions without stepping through them, or choose Run | Reset to finish the procedure without executing the remaining statements. When you reset your procedure, all the variables lose their current values. Numeric variables assume the initial value of zero (0), variable-length strings are initialized to a zero-length string (""), and fixed-length strings are filled with the character represented by the ASCII character code 0, or Chr(0). Variant variables are initialized to Empty, and the value of Object variables is set to Nothing.

TRAPPING ERRORS

No one writes bug-free programs the first time. For this reason, when you create VBA procedures you have to determine how your program will respond to errors. Many unexpected errors happen at runtime. For example, your procedure may try to give a new file the same name as an open file.

Runtime errors are often discovered not by a programmer but by the user who attempts to do something that the programmer has not anticipated. If an error occurs when the procedure is running, Visual Basic displays an error message and the procedure is stopped. The error message that VBA displays to the user is often quite cryptic.

You can keep users from seeing many runtime errors by including error-handling code in your VBA procedures. This way, when Visual Basic encounters an error, instead of displaying a default error message, it will show a much friendlier, more comprehensive error message, perhaps advising the user how to correct the error.

How do you implement error handling in your VBA procedure? The first step is to place the On Error statement in your procedure. This statement tells VBA what to do if an error happens while your program is running. In other words, VBA uses the On Error statement to activate an error-handling procedure that will trap runtime errors. Depending on the type of procedure, you can exit the error trap by using one of the following statements: `Exit Sub`, `Exit Function`, `Exit Property`, `End Sub`, `End Function`, or `End Property`.

You should write an error-handling routine for each procedure. Table 9.3 shows how the `On Error` statement can be used.

TABLE 9.3. `On Error` statement options.

On Error Statement	Description
On Error GoTo Label	Specifies a label to jump to when an error occurs. This label marks the beginning of the error-handling routine. An *error handler* is a routine for trapping and responding to errors in your application. The label must appear in the same procedure as the `On Error GoTo` statement.
On Error Resume Next	When a runtime error occurs, Visual Basic ignores the line that caused the error and continues the procedure with the next line. An error message is not displayed.
On Error GoTo 0	Turns off error trapping in a procedure. When VBA runs this statement, errors are detected but not trapped within the procedure.

SIDEBAR   *Is This an Error or a Mistake?*

In programming, mistakes and errors are not the same thing. A mistake—such as a misspelled or missing statement, a misplaced quotation mark or comma, or an assignment of a value of one type to a variable of a different (and incompatible) type—can be removed from your program through proper testing and debugging. But even though your code may be free of mistakes, errors can still occur. An error is a result of an event or operation that doesn't work as expected. For example, if your VBA procedure accesses a certain file on disk and someone deleted this file or moved it to another location, you'll get an error no matter what. An error prevents the procedure from carrying out a specific task.

Using the Err Object

Your error-handling code can utilize various properties and methods of the Err object. For example, to check which error occurred, check the value of `Err.Number`. The Number property of the Err object will tell you the value of the last error that occurred, and the Description property will return a description of the error. You can also find the name of the application that caused the error by using the Source property of the Err object (this is very helpful when your procedure launches other applications). After handling the error, use the `Err.Clear` statement to reset the error number. This will set `Err.Number` back to zero.

To test your error-handling code you can use the `Raise` method of the Err object. For example, to raise the "Disk not ready" error, use the following statement:

```
Err.Raise 71
```

The following OpenToRead procedure demonstrates the use of the `On Error` statement and the Err object.

⊙ Hands-On 9.6. Error-Trapping Techniques

1. Copy the **Vacation.txt** file from the companion CD to your VBAPrimerAccess_ByExample folder.
2. In the Visual Basic Editor window, insert a new module and rename it **Error-Traps**.
3. In the Code window, enter the following **OpenToRead** procedure:

```
Sub OpenToRead()
  Dim strFile As String
  Dim strChar As String
  Dim strText As String
  Dim FileExists As Boolean

  FileExists = True

  On Error GoTo ErrorHandler

  strFile = InputBox("Enter the name of file to open:")
  Open strFile For Input As #1

  If FileExists Then
    Do While Not EOF(1) ' loop until the end of file
      strChar = Input(1, #1) ' get one character
      strText = strText + strChar
    Loop
    Debug.Print strText
    ' Close the file
    Close #1
  End If
  Exit Sub

ErrorHandler:
  FileExists = False
  Select Case Err.Number
    Case 71
      MsgBox "The CD/DVD drive is empty."
    Case 53
      MsgBox "This file can't be found on the specified drive."
    Case 76
      MsgBox "File Path was not found."
    Case Else
      MsgBox "Error " & Err.Number & " :" & Err.Description
```

```
        Exit Sub
    End Select
    Resume Next
End Sub
```

Before continuing with this hands-on, let's examine the code of the Open-ToRead procedure. The purpose of the OpenToRead procedure is to read the contents of the user-supplied text file character by character. When the user enters a filename, various errors can occur. For example, the filename may be wrong, the user may attempt to open a file from a CD-ROM or DVD disc without actually placing the disc in the drive, or he may try to open a file that is already open. To trap these errors, the error-handling routine at the end of the OpenToRead procedure uses the Number property of the Err object. The Err object contains information about runtime errors. If an error occurs while the procedure is running, the statement `Err.Number` will return the error number.

If errors 71, 53, or 76 occur, Visual Basic will display the user-friendly messages given inside the `Select Case` block and then proceed to the `Resume Next` statement, which will send it to the line of code following the one that had caused the error. If another (unexpected) error occurs, Visual Basic will return its error code (`Err.Number`) and error description (`Err.Description`).

At the beginning of the procedure, the variable `FileExists` is set to True. If the program doesn't encounter an error, all the instructions inside the `If FileExists Then` block will be executed. However, if VBA encounters an error, the value of the `FileExists` variable will be set to False (see the first statement in the error-handling routine just below the `ErrorHandler` label).

If you comment the `Close #1` instruction, Visual Basic will encounter the error on the next attempt to open the same file. Notice the `Exit Sub` statement before the `ErrorHandler` block. Put the `Exit Sub` statement just above the error-handling routine. You don't want Visual Basic to carry out the error handling if there are no errors.

How does this procedure accomplish the read operation? The `Input` function allows you to return any character from a sequential file. *Sequential access files* are files where data is retrieved in the same order as it is stored, such as files stored in the CSV format (comma-delimited text), TXT format (text separated by tabs), or PRN format (text separated by spaces). Configuration files, error logs, HTML files, and all sorts of plain text files are all sequential files. These files are stored on disk as a sequence of characters. The beginning of a new text line is indicated by two special characters: the carriage return and the linefeed. When you work with sequential files, start at the beginning of the file and move forward character by character, line by line, until you encounter the end of the file. Sequential access files can be easily opened and manipulated by just about any text editor.

If you use the VBA function named LOF (length of file) as the first argument of the Input function, you can quickly read the contents of the sequential file without having to loop through the entire file.

For example, instead of the following Do...While loop statement block:

```
Do While Not EOF(1) ' loop until the end of file
  strChar = Input(1, #1) ' get one character
  strText = strText + strChar
Loop
```

you can simply write the following statement to get the contents of the file at once:

```
strText = Input(LOF(1), #1)
```

The LOF function returns the number of bytes in a file. Each byte corresponds to one character in a text file.

To read data from a file, you must first open the file with the Open statement using the following syntax:

```
Open pathname For mode[Access access] [lock] As [#]filenumber _
[Len=reclength]
```

The Open statement has three required arguments: pathname, mode, and filenumber. Pathname is the name of the file you want to open. The filename may include the name of a drive and folder.

Mode is a keyword that determines how the file was opened. Sequential files can be opened in one of the following modes: Input, Output, or Append. Use Input to read the file, Output to write to a file and overwrite any existing file, and Append to write to a file by adding to any existing information.

Filenumber is a number from 1 to 511. This number is used to refer to the file in subsequent operations. You can obtain a unique file number using the VBA built-in FreeFile function.

The optional Access clause can be used to specify permissions for the file (Read, Write, or Read Write). The optional lock argument determines which file operations are allowed for other processes. For example, if a file is open in a network environment, lock determines how other people can access it. The following lock keywords can be used: Shared, Lock Read, Lock Write, or Lock Read Write. The last element of the Open statement, reclength, specifies the buffer size (total number of characters) for sequential files.

Therefore, to open a sequential file in order to read its data, the example procedure uses the following instruction:

```
Open strFile For Input As #1
```

And to close the sequential file, the following statement is used:

```
Close #1
```

4. Click anywhere within the **OpenToRead** procedure and press **F5** to run it. When prompted for the file to open, type **C:\VBAPrimerAccess_ByExample\Vacation.txt** in the input dialog box and click **OK**. The procedure reads the contents of the **Vacation.txt** file into the Immediate window.

5. Run the **OpenToRead** procedure again. When prompted for the file to open, type **P:\VBAPrimerAccess_ByExample\Vacation.txt** in the input dialog box and click **OK**. This time Visual Basic cannot find the specified file, so it displays the message "File Path was not found."

6. Run the **OpenToRead** procedure again. This time, when prompted for the filename, enter the name of any file that references your CD/DVD drive (when the drive slot is empty). This should trigger error 71 and result in the message "The CD/DVD drive is empty."

7. Comment the **Close #1** statement and run **OpenToRead**. When prompted for the file, enter **C:\VBAPrimerAccess_ByExample\Vacation.txt** as the filename. Run the same procedure again, supplying the same filename. The second run will cause the statements within the `Case Else` block to run. You should get an error 55 "File already open" message because the text file will still be open in memory. To remove the file from memory, type **Close #1** in the Immediate window and press **Enter**. Next, uncomment the **Close # 1** statement in the OpenToRead procedure to return it to the original state.

Procedure Testing

You are responsible for the code you write. Before you give your procedure to others to test, you should test it yourself. After all, you understand best how it is supposed to work. Some programmers think testing their own code is some sort of degrading activity, especially when they work in an organization that has a team devoted to testing. *Don't make this mistake.* The testing process at the programmer level is as important as the code development itself. After you've tested the procedure yourself, you should give it to the users to test. Users will provide you with answers to questions such as: Does the procedure produce the expected results? Is it easy and fun to use? Does it follow the standard conventions? Also, it is a good idea to give the entire application to someone who knows the least about using this type of application, and ask them to play around with it and try to break it.

You can test the ways your program responds to runtime errors by causing them on purpose:

■ Generate any built-in error by entering the following syntax:

```
Error error_number
```

For example, to display the error that occurs on an attempt to divide by zero (0), type the following statement in the Immediate window:

```
Error 11
```

When you press Enter, Visual Basic will display the error message saying, "Run-time error 11. Division by zero."

■ To check the meaning of the generated error, use the following syntax:

```
Error(error_number)
```

For example, to find out what error number 7 means, type the following in the Immediate window:

```
?Error(7)
```

When you press Enter, Visual Basic returns the error description:

```
"Out of memory"
```

To generate the same error at runtime in the form of a message box like the one in Figure 9.16, enter the following in the Immediate window or in your procedure code:

```
Err.Raise 7
```

When you finish debugging your VBA procedures, make sure you remove all statements that raise errors.

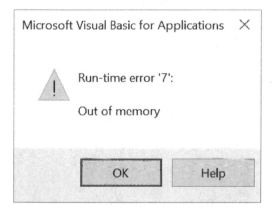

FIGURE 9.16. To test your error-handling code, use the Raise method of the Err object. This will generate a runtime error during the execution of your procedure.

When testing your VBA procedure, use the following guidelines:

■ If you want to analyze your procedure, step through your code one line at a time by pressing F8 or by choosing Debug | Step Into.
■ If you suspect that an error may occur in a specific place in your procedure, use a breakpoint.
■ If you want to monitor the value of a variable or expression used by your procedure, add a watch expression.
■ If you are tired of scrolling through a long procedure to get to sections of code that interest you, set up a bookmark to quickly jump to the desired location.

Setting Error-Trapping Options

You can specify the error-handling settings for your current Visual Basic project by choosing Tools | Options and selecting the General tab (shown in Figure 9.17). The Error Trapping area located on the General tab determines how errors are handled in the Visual Basic environment. The following options are available:

- Break on All Errors
- This setting will cause Visual Basic to enter the break mode on any error, no matter whether an error handler is active or whether the code is in a class module (class modules were covered in Chapter 8).
- Break in Class Module
- This setting will trap any unhandled error in a class module. Visual Basic will activate the break mode when an error occurs and will highlight the line of code in the class module that produced this error.
- Break on Unhandled Errors

This setting will trap errors for which you have not written an error handler. The error will cause Visual Basic to activate the break mode. If the error occurs in a class module, the error will cause Visual Basic to enter break mode on the line of code that called the offending procedure of the class.

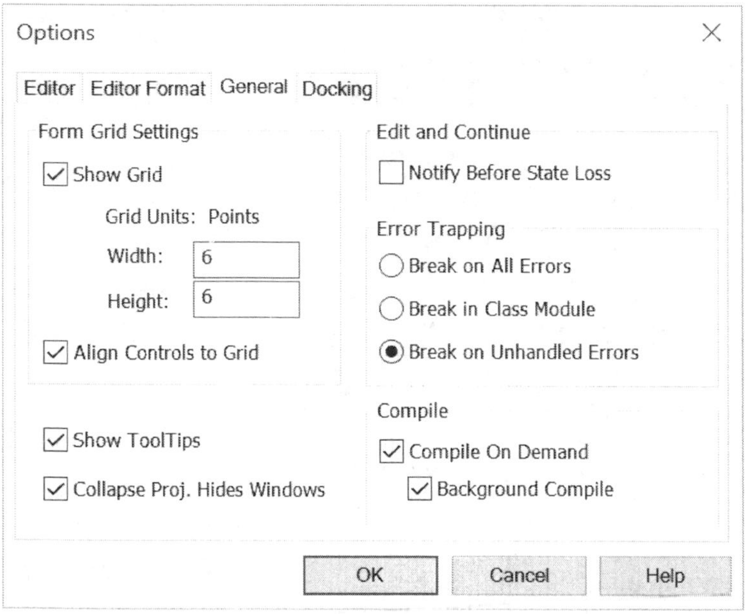

FIGURE 9.17. Setting the error-trapping options in the Options dialog box will affect all instances of Visual Basic started after you change the setting.

SUMMARY

In this chapter, you learned how to test your VBA procedures to make sure they perform as planned. You debugged your code by stepping through it using breakpoints and watches. You learned how to work with the Immediate window in break mode; you found out how the Locals window can help you monitor the values of variables; and you learned how the Call Stack dialog box can be helpful in keeping track of where you are in a complex program. You also learned how to mark your code with bookmarks so you can easily navigate between sections of your procedure. Additionally, this chapter showed you how to trap errors by including an error-handling routine inside your VBA procedure and how to use the VBA Err object.

By using the built-in debugging tools, you can quickly pinpoint the problem spots in your Access VBA procedures. Try to spend more time getting acquainted with the Debug menu options and debugging tools discussed in this chapter. Mastering the art of debugging can save you hours of trial and error.

INDEX